CLIMATE POLITICS IN OCEANIA

CLIMATE POLITICS IN OCEANIA

Renewing Australia-Pacific Relations in a Warming World

Edited by
Susan Harris Rimmer
Wesley Morgan
Caitlin Byrne

MELBOURNE
UNIVERSITY
PRESS

MELBOURNE UNIVERSITY PRESS
An imprint of Melbourne University Publishing Limited
Level 1, 715 Swanston Street, Carlton, Victoria 3053, Australia
mup-contact@unimelb.edu.au
www.mup.com.au

Cover design by Pilar Aguilera
Typeset by Sonya Murphy, Adala Studio
Cover image courtesy Department of Foreign Affairs and Trade
Printed in Australia by McPherson's Printing Group

 A catalogue record for this
book is available from the
NATIONAL LIBRARY OF AUSTRALIA / National Library of Australia

9780522879506 (paperback)
9780522879513 (ebook)

MIX
Paper | Supporting
responsible forestry
FSC
www.fsc.org   FSC® C001695

*Dedicated to Tony de Brum (1945–2017) and all those who seek
to take climate action.
Dedicated to our colleague Brendan Sargeant (1960–2022).*

The authors wish to thank the Griffith University Climate Action Beacon for their support of this project, especially Brendan Mackey and Natasha Hennessey. Thank you also to Matt McDonald, Kate McGuire and Kirstie Petrou.

CONTENTS

CONTRIBUTORS

Professor Mark Beeson is an Adjunct Professor at the University of Technology Sydney and Griffith University. He was previously Professor of International Politics at the University of Western Australia.

Dr Simon Bradshaw is Research Director at the Climate Council of Australia and was formerly the Climate Change Advocacy Lead at Oxfam Australia.

Professor Caitlin Byrne is Pro Vice Chancellor (Business), Griffith University. She is a former Australian diplomat and was most recently Director of the Griffith Asia Institute.

Salā Dr George Carter is a Research Fellow in Geopolitics and Regionalism, at the Department of Pacific Affairs at the Australian National University. He is also the Director for the ANU Pacific Institute.

Ms Melissa Conley Tyler is the Executive Director of the Asia-Pacific Development, Diplomacy & Defence Dialogue. For 13 years she served as National Executive Director of the Australian Institute of International Affairs.

Dr Andrea Haefner is a Senior Lecturer at the Griffith Asia Institute, a Fellow of the Higher Education Academy, and has over 15 years of experience working across Australia, Germany and Southeast Asia.

Professor Susan Harris Rimmer is the Director of the Griffith University's Policy Innovation Hub and is a human rights lawyer and policy expert.

Mr Romitesh Kant is a PhD candidate with the ANU's Department of Pacific Affairs. His research examines the symbiotic relationship of politics and masculinity in the Fijian national context.

Ms Fulori Manoa is a Teaching Assistant and scholar at the University of the South Pacific. She is primarily interested in Pacific diplomacy and online/mobile learning in the Pacific island countries.

Dr Wesley Morgan is a research fellow at the Griffith Asia Institute, Griffith University, and a senior researcher at the Climate Council of Australia.

Dr Johanna Nalau is an adaptation scientist with a PhD in climate change adaptation at Griffith University based on the Gold Coast, Australia.

Dr Tess Newton Cain is an Associate Professor and the project lead of the Pacific Hub at the Griffith Asia Institute.

Dr Mélodie Ruwet is a Lecturer at Queensland University of Technology. Her broader area of research falls into ocean governance, sovereignty issues, small states and the politics of conservation.

Mr Brendan Sargeant was the Professor of Practice in Defence and Strategic Studies and Head of the Strategic and Defence Studies Centre at the Coral Bell School of Asia Pacific Affairs at the Australian National University. He passed away in 2022.

Dr Bec Strating is the Director of La Trobe Asia and an Associate Professor of Politics and International Relations at La Trobe University, Melbourne.

Dr Sandra Tarte is Associate Professor and acting Head of the School of Law and Social Sciences at the University of the South Pacific. She specialises in the international politics of the Pacific islands region.

Dame Meg Taylor DBE is a Papua New Guinean politician who served as Secretary General to the Pacific Islands Forum from 2014 to 2021.

Professor Joanne Wallis is Professor of International Security in the Department of Politics and International Relations at the University of Adelaide.

CLIMATE POLITICS IN OCEANIA
An introduction

Caitlin Byrne, Wesley Morgan and
Susan Harris Rimmer

C LIMATE CHANGE IS a civilisational and ecological threat, the
scale of which we have never seen before. Faced with an unprecedented global crisis, countries are revisiting their interests and their
approach to both domestic and foreign policy. Perhaps nowhere is
this more so than in Oceania—encompassing Australia, New Zealand
and 14 independent Pacific island countries—where climate policy is
especially important for international relations. Over recent decades,
countries in this part of the world have approached climate policy from
different perspectives. Uniquely exposed to the impacts of a warming
planet, Pacific island countries have tried to shape ambitious global
efforts to tackle the problem.

In July 2022, newly elected Australian Prime Minister Anthony
Albanese joined Pacific island leaders in Suva to declare that 'the
Pacific is facing a climate emergency that threatens the livelihoods, the
security and wellbeing of its people and ecosystems ...'.[1] It was the first
time Australia has officially associated itself with climate emergency
warnings, and more importantly, the first time to have done so in alignment with Pacific island leaders. But, as Andrew Tillett reported, the
move was viewed as 'largely symbolic with the Albanese government

standing firm against calls from the region and climate activists to shut down coal mining and gas extraction'.[2] Concerned about potential economic consequences of tackling climate change, Australia has consistently tried to avoid 'costly' commitments, while continuing to promote coal exports to growing economies in Asia. Since winning the national election in May 2022, the Albanese government has put climate leadership back on the agenda, with a particular emphasis on its role in Pacific relations. The notable shift in the nature and tone of climate policy rhetoric has been accompanied by more ambitious policy action, including on greenhouse gas emissions reduction targets. However, the science suggests that more is required. After nearly a decade of policy lag, and in the face of opposing domestic corporate interests, it is not yet entirely clear if the Albanese government is prepared to fully sign up to the policy agenda required to minimise and mitigate the harmful impacts of a fast-changing climate.

Today, the global politics of climate change faces a pivotal moment. Australia now joins governments around the world in treating the climate crisis seriously. Almost all countries have committed to a multilateral framework to tackle greenhouse gas emissions—the 2015 Paris Agreement—and major powers are integrating climate goals into traditional statecraft and foreign policy, including several of the perennial members of the United Nations Security Council and also several members of the G20, such as the United States, China, the United Kingdom and Japan. More than 120 countries have already promised to achieve net-zero emissions by mid-century. In the coming decades, the global economy will be transformed as countries embrace the 'new energy economy'. The context in which states conceive their national interests is shifting. Countries that embrace climate action and prepare for the inevitable economic transition away from carbon-based energy, are well placed to thrive.

In our view, the climate crisis and the global response to it, call for a new approach to regional cooperation in Oceania, and a fundamental re-ordering of strategic priorities. It may also call for a new set of diplomatic skills and tradecraft. Neighbouring states in the region are looking for Australia to join them in what they see as a struggle for survival. If Australia takes a more ambitious approach to climate policy, it will have a chance to reset its relationship with Pacific island countries. Working with Pacific island countries to promote climate action on the global stage would strengthen Australia's credentials as a regional power and do much to enhance Australian soft power.

These contemporary issues of climate politics in Oceania provide the focus of this book. The discussions brought forward here were prompted by a 2020 issue of *Foreign Affairs* titled 'A Foreign Policy for the Climate' in which authors John Podesta and Todd Stern contemplate a return to American leadership on global climate matters and called for the US to 'devise a climate-centred foreign policy.'[3] Ironically, the article begins with a description of the bushfires which ripped through a swathe of eastern Australia in late 2019. The vast destruction captured global attention and ire, providing a harsh reminder of the effects of climate change while shining yet another light on Australia's poor standing on matters of global climate policy.

Reading the article provoked us to similarly contemplate Australia's engagement with climate change through the lens of foreign policy and diplomacy, which inevitably drew in wider themes of national interest and security alongside interlinked narratives about Australia and the Pacific region. Indeed, Australia's approach to climate change over the past decade has been largely characterised by political inertia, policy blind spots and diplomatic isolation. By contrast, the nations of the Pacific offer alternative experiences, narratives and models of climate leadership, including in their leveraging of political opportunity, policy consensus and collective diplomacy.

The book brings together analyses from academics and practitioners from Australia and the Pacific islands to delve further into the issues, challenges and opportunities that now face Australia and the wider Oceania region. Each author offers a unique perspective to critically interrogate the international politics of climate change in Oceania across a range of disciplines—from the scientific to the sociological—and policy perspectives, including defence and strategy, national security, foreign policy, diplomacy and statecraft, soft power and international law. In doing so, the collection seeks to unpack the complex and multidimensional tensions that underpin climate debates in Australia and the region. While recognising the existential nature of the climate threat, particularly for Pacific island nations, this collection challenges the dominant narrative that Pacific island nations are themselves vulnerable actors when it comes to driving climate policy and action, including on the global stage. Bringing a range of voices, including from the Pacific into this conversation, we highlight the need for Australia to rethink its approach to addressing climate change—no longer as a side issue to be managed through political manoeuvres and drafting solutions—but rather as a central concern for the nation's integrated domestic and global policy outlook. Further, we seek to cast light on the potential that a climate-centred approach might hold in bringing Australia closer to the Pacific, while cultivating collective aspirations and facilitating concrete action to tackle the ongoing impacts of a dramatically changing climate.

To provide context for considering climate politics in Oceania, this introductory chapter considers the nexus between domestic climate policy and foreign policy in the Pacific. It explains that Australia's approach to climate policy at home undermines the pursuit of strategic interests in the region. More broadly, Australian policy-makers have struggled to incorporate multiple threats posed by climate change into their conceptualisation of national security. While Australian strategic culture tends to focus on threats of a certain kind—hard power conflict, wars between states, threats at the border—Pacific island countries have come to understand climate change as a first-order security threat and, increasingly, some of Australia's closest allies view climate change in the same way, such as the US. Incorporating climate risks into Australian national security planning remains a key challenge. Finally, this chapter considers what climate policy means for regional diplomacy in the Pacific. We argue that a reset of Australian climate policy would help to cement Australia's place as a member of the Pacific family, but Canberra must embrace the opportunity while it still can.

Out of step? Climate policy and Australia's Pacific strategy

Former Prime Minister Scott Morrison liked to say that Australia is part of the Pacific 'family', and in many respects he was right. Australia is formally a part of many processes of Pacific regionalism and is the most powerful and wealthy member state in the Pacific Islands Forum. Officials in Canberra see themselves as having a special responsibility to promote development and provide security in the Pacific, and there is no doubt Australia is a valued development partner. Australia is also an indispensable Pacific nation in times of major disasters. When island communities are devastated by monster cyclones—increasingly a feature of life in the region—they are glad to see Australian naval vessels on the horizon delivering supplies, and military personnel helping to rebuild villages. Many Pacific islanders have family who live, work and study in Australia, and thousands of Pacific people support Australian regional communities by picking fruit at harvest time, although the treatment of those workers is also a site of tension.[4]

Relations between Australia and Pacific island states are close and broad-ranging. Yet Australian foreign policy in the Pacific has been largely driven by narrow strategic imperatives.[5] The Pacific is seen as a series of small states in Australia's 'backyard', beset with challenges, occasionally serious ones that might impact Australian interests and require direct intervention.[6] At the same time, Pacific island concerns about climate impacts have been sidestepped and neglected. Some might argue that Australia's worldview has continued to be held captive by elements of an outdated colonial mindset that casts the Pacific islands as vulnerable and their interests as insignificant compared to Australia's.[7] Indeed, the ultimate goal of Australia's Pacific policy is still a utilitarian one: to maintain political influence, and to deny influence over the islands to other powers. This has been a key priority of Australia's overall foreign policy since the 19th century.[8] In recent years, strategic concerns have again sharpened the mind of policymakers in Canberra, especially the prospect that China might leverage infrastructure loans to island governments in order to secure a military base in the Pacific. Then Prime Minister Malcolm Turnbull raised the

alarm in 2018, explaining 'we would view with great concern the establishment of any foreign military bases in those Pacific island countries
and neighbours of ours'.[9] Concern about a growing Chinese presence
in the region underpins the 'Pacific Step-Up', a foreign policy initiative
which seeks to integrate Pacific states into Australia's economic and
security institutions.[10]

But the landscape is changing. As the shared priorities of Pacific
island nations have gained traction globally, their leaders have also
come to recognise the heft and influence of their regional voice and
collective action. Pacific island leaders have been more direct about
questioning Australia's climate interests and the credibility of Australia's
place in the Pacific family. The message conveyed to Australia could
not be clearer: until Canberra demonstrates that it is serious about
tackling the climate crisis, it will struggle to pursue strategic interests
in the Pacific.

While this message may have been resisted by former Australian
governments, it appears to have found fertile ground with Australia's
Albanese government. Labor's plans to 'build a stronger Pacific family'
prioritise effective climate leadership and make a commitment to 'listen
and act on Pacific Island warnings of the existential threat of climate
change'[11] as a central platform of a wider promise that encapsulates economic, defence and security cooperation. Notable shifts in Australia's
regional defence and diplomatic policy and engagement underscore
Australia's intent to reset its Pacific relationships. However, Canberra's
resolve to reconcile domestic economic and security interests with
regional and global climate policy is yet to be fully demonstrated.

Differing threat perceptions: Climate change and national security

Fundamentally, climate change has presented a problem for Australia's
relationships in the Pacific because of differences in threat perception.
While Pacific countries understand the climate crisis as a first-order
threat to their security, Australia does not yet see it in the same way.
This has led to a mismatch in strategic priorities. Australia's Pacific

Step-Up is driven by Canberra's security concerns, particularly that China could leverage infrastructure lending to establish a military base. But island leaders remain adamant that climate change is their key security challenge. At the 2018 Pacific Islands Forum, they issued a regional security declaration which reaffirmed climate change as the 'single greatest threat to the livelihoods, security and wellbeing of the peoples of the Pacific'.[12] Compared with dangers posed by a more powerful and coercive China, island leaders see the impacts of climate change—stronger cyclones, devastating floods, rising seas, dying reefs and ocean acidification—as more tangible and immediate threats. As Fiji's military commander Rear Admiral Viliame Naupoto told the 2019 Shangri-La Security Dialogue in Singapore,

> I believe there are three major powers in competition in our region. There is the US, there is China [and] the third competitor is climate change. Of the three, climate change is winning, and climate change exerts the most influence on countries in our part of the world. If there is any competition, it is with climate change.[13]

Increasingly, the rest of the world shares the Pacific's perception of climate change as a first-order security threat. Former UK Prime Minister Boris Johnson told the UN Security Council in early 2021 that, 'it is absolutely clear that climate change is a threat to our collective security and the security of our nations'.[14] United States President Joe Biden understands climate change as an existential threat, noting with some urgency, 'if we don't get this right, nothing else will matter'.[15] US special envoy for climate John Kerry said failing to address the climate crisis was like 'marching forward to what is almost tantamount to a mutual suicide pact'.[16] The US, like Pacific island countries, wants Canberra to do more to reduce emissions, and to move away from coal-fired power.

There is no doubt the climate crisis is a critical security threat to Australia as well. The bushfires of 2019–20—which killed dozens of people, incinerated millions of animals, turned the sky blood-red, and rendered the air in Australian cities a health hazard—were a warning.[17] They were a window to the catastrophic future Australia faces if the world fails to take urgent action to reduce emissions.[18] Australia's interests are now tied to working with allies to promote climate action, especially with key alliance partner the US. The US is now leveraging American power to galvanise global climate action and wants Australia to join the effort. Within days of coming to power, President Biden issued an executive order formally putting the climate crisis at the centre of US foreign policy and national security. Then, in April 2021, Washington hosted a summit of leaders from the world's largest economies, together representing more than 80 per cent of the world's emissions. At that summit, the US doubled its domestic climate ambition by pledging to reduce emissions to 50–52 per cent below 2005 levels by 2030. Other nations followed suit, with the EU, the UK, Japan, Canada and South Korea all announcing new targets to reduce emissions by 2030. In 2022, the US passed the *Inflation Reduction Act*, which contains US$369 billion worth of programs and funding to accelerate the US transition to net zero.[19] The legislation will have global impacts, including in relation to global preferential industrial and trading policy, while also delivering a cut in US greenhouse gas emissions by roughly 2.5 per cent per year, or 42 per cent by 2030.[20] Furthermore, the US has also put climate firmly on the agenda for the Quadrilateral Security Dialogue, an important regional security dialogue between Australia, the US, Japan and India, which has established a 'Climate Working Group' focused on working together 'to strengthen the Paris Agreement and enhance the climate action of all nations'.[21]

Australian conceptions of national security are shaped by particular assumptions about the way the world works. As Brendan Sargeant and Mark Beeson explain in their respective chapters in this book, Australian strategic and defence policy tends to be driven by an essentially realist worldview in which states achieve national security, in a world where hard-power conflict is a feature of life, by pursuing superior weapons systems (such as the AUKUS submarines) and/or alliances with major powers that possess such systems. The AUKUS trilateral security pact between Australia, the United Kingdom and the US was announced in high secrecy in September 2021, and concerns the future acquisition of eight nuclear-powered submarines for the Royal Australia Navy for $368 billion to be delivered in the 2040s. The agreement also signified an enhanced trilateral relationship to share and develop 'cyber capabilities, artificial intelligence, quantum technologies, and additional undersea capabilities'.[22]

These assumptions are of limited utility when responding to the catastrophic security threats posed by climate change. Indeed, the AUKUS pact has been decried as a climate change disaster, a blatant misunderstanding of what is the most predictable and harmful risk that faces Australians.[23] Nevertheless, Australian strategic analysts are beginning to incorporate climate change into their understanding of the country's national security objectives. In April 2021, for example, the Australian Security Leaders Climate Group, made up of current and former defence personnel and security sector staff, called on government to undertake a whole-of-nation climate and security risk assessment, arguing 'there is a poor understanding of the reality of near-future systemic security risks posed by climate change, which constitutes a major strategic gap'.[24] It would appear that the calls of these security leaders have found a sympathetic ear, with the Australian government's 2023 *National Defence Strategic Review* (DSR) firmly identifying climate change as a core national security issue.[25] It is an encouraging step that further cements the place of climate change within Australia's national security policy and analysis discourse, but as critics suggest, the DSR still offers too little in terms of clarity on the climate challenge or the steps to be taken to prepare for and deal adequately with the crises that climate change is likely to bring.[26]

Incrementally, Australian national security scholars are coming to understand climate change in a similar way to policy-makers in Pacific island states. That is to say, climate change presents a major threat to infrastructure, lives and livelihoods, which requires investment in capacity to respond to climate-related disasters (including floods and cyclones, droughts and bushfires) and collaboration across all levels of government to build resilience to climate impacts. Importantly, some Australian security analysts are also aware that multilateral cooperation to reduce emissions, and ultimately to decarbonise the global economy, is the only way to achieve national security in face of a warming planet. As Robert Glasser, head of the Climate and Security Policy Centre at the Australia Strategic Policy Institute, explains:

> the only effective 'forward defence' is to reduce greenhouse gases globally, including in Australia, as quickly as possible. Without far greater ambition on this front, even the most concerted efforts to strengthen the resilience of Australian communities will be overwhelmed by the scale of disasters that lie ahead.[27]

No one country has control of the Earth's fragile atmosphere, and working with other states to reduce emissions is a matter of global climate diplomacy. In this area, Pacific diplomats have much to teach their Australian counterparts.

Climate change and regional diplomacy in Oceania

Pacific island states have developed a unique form of collective diplomacy, guided by pan-Pacific norms and cultural connections, to pursue their shared interests in international affairs. Working through the auspices of the Pacific Islands Forum, island governments have had significant successes. They took a lead role in global negotiations to secure recognition of their exclusive economic zones under the UN Law of the Sea. They banned driftnet fishing in the South Pacific and successfully lobbied to have New Caledonia and French Polynesia added to the UN list of non-self-governing territories. Working with Australia and New Zealand, island states established a South Pacific Nuclear Free Zone, and pressured France to end nuclear testing in the region. Pacific island countries have also pursued collective diplomacy on climate change, since a scientific consensus first emerged on the issue in the late 1980s.

During the 1980s, Australia was a constructive player in nascent global negotiations to protect the environment. Australia signed up to the 1985 Vienna Convention for the Protection of the Ozone Layer and was active in subsequent negotiations for a binding Montreal Protocol (1987) under that convention. Subsequent global diplomacy to tackle greenhouse gas emissions also followed a 'convention-protocol' model at the UN, and Australia was initially a leader in international attempts to address global warming. As Caitlin Byrne writes in this volume, Australia led the way in recognising the significant task of global environmental diplomacy, appointing Sir Ninian Stephen as the world's first Environment Ambassador in 1989. In the same year, Foreign Minister Gareth Evans described climate change as 'the biggest problem, the biggest challenge, faced by mankind [sic] in this or any other age'.[28] At the 1990 World Climate Conference, Australia announced one of the strongest emissions targets of any country in the world, committing to cutting greenhouse gas emissions by 20 per cent by 2005.

Australia was also initially supportive of Pacific climate diplomacy. At the 1991 Pacific Islands Forum, for example, Canberra backed a declaration that global warming and sea level rise presented a 'great risk to the cultural, economic and physical survival' of Pacific nations. Forum leaders called for a 'strong and substantive' global convention that would see immediate reductions in greenhouse gas emissions. From the mid-1990s, however, Australia reassessed its approach. Concerned about potential economic costs, Australia began to drag its feet in the UN climate talks and to minimise its obligations to reduce emissions. Over time, this 'go-slow' approach saw Pacific island countries go *around* Australia, and work outside the Pacific Islands Forum, to pursue climate diplomacy. Pacific diplomats worked with counterparts from island countries in the Caribbean and Indian Ocean as part of the Alliance of Small Island States (AOSIS), an important negotiating coalition in the UN climate talks.[29] Pacific countries aggregated common positions through the Pacific Small Island Developing States (PSIDS) grouping at the UN, and meetings of Pacific ambassadors to

New York became important for the development of negotiating positions.[30] Pacific leaders issued their own regional declarations through the Pacific Islands Development Forum (PIDF), an island-only body, of which neither Australia nor New Zealand are members. Through these forms of independent diplomacy, Pacific island countries helped shape global cooperation on climate change.[31] Furthermore, as Wesley Morgan, George Carter and Fulori Manoa highlight in their contribution to this collection which foregrounds Pacific perspectives, Pacific states working together have played a critical role in driving the global climate agenda. Nowhere is this more evident than in the negotiation of the Paris Agreement, and in the skilful diplomacy of the Marshall Islands, which proved critical to securing the first global, legally binding, climate agreement.

The 2015 Paris Agreement was a major diplomatic achievement, but it was not a 'set-and-forget' agreement. Instead, it provided a framework for states to work together to reduce emissions. Under the agreement, countries are required to set more ambitious climate targets every five years, and it is by this means they will move towards a shared goal of decarbonising the global economy by the middle of this century. So far, the signs are positive (with qualifications). Five years on from Paris (with a one-year delay due to the COVID-19 pandemic), major economies, including all the G7 member countries, have set more ambitious Paris targets to reduce emissions. More than 120 countries have also pledged to achieve net-zero emissions by 2050. China, the world's largest emitter, has set a 2060 target. Collectively these pledges send a powerful signal that the world is starting to take climate change seriously, and the markets are listening. Major finance houses are divesting from fossil fuels. Hundreds of corporations have put net-zero emissions targets in place. There is hope yet we might stabilise the Earth's climate system and avoid the worst impacts of runaway climate change. A remarkable, but little understood, aspect of the global shift towards post-carbon economies is that it might not have come about were it not for the creative and determined diplomacy of Pacific island states. Island states collaborated with major powers, especially the EU and the US, to bring a multilateral deal to fruition. Pacific states will again work with major powers to press countries to meet their Paris Agreement obligations. Susan Harris Rimmer's contribution to this collection further underscores the contribution of Pacific island states to creating a rules-based order to manage the transition and their contribution to new human rights norms under international law.

Global success in tackling the climate crisis will depend on major economies making good on their commitments to reduce emissions, and the extent to which powerful nations prioritise climate action in their foreign policy. The role of the US remains critically important. The very design of the Paris Agreement reflects US domestic political circumstances insofar as it represents the extent of commitments former President Barack Obama could sign up to, using his executive powers, without requiring ratification by Congress (which was in 2015 dominated by Republicans). The 2016 election of President Donald Trump proved a significant challenge to the Paris Agreement, especially when he announced the US would quit the global climate pact. This decision was met with dismay by Pacific leaders (not least because in 2017 Fiji was incoming president of the COP23 UN climate talks). At the 2018 Pacific Islands Forum, island leaders called on the US to return to the Paris Agreement, though Australia pointedly refused to join their regional appeal to Washington.[32] As it was, Trump provided some succour to the conservative government in Australia, which backed away from meaningful climate policy while stopping short of exiting the Paris Agreement altogether.

The election of Joe Biden as US president proved important for climate politics in Oceania. Not only did Biden return the US to the Paris Agreement, but he also positioned the US to resume a mantle of global leadership within the UN climate regime. In April 2021, he convened a summit of major economies, intended to reset global collaboration to reduce emissions as noted above. He committed the US to cutting emissions by half (from 2005 levels) by 2030, and other nations—including the EU, UK, Japan, Canada and South Korea—also pledged to set new, more ambitious, emissions reduction targets.

In December 2021, the UK hosted the UN Climate Conference of Parties, COP26, the most important UN climate talks since the Paris Agreement. Pacific island leaders realised that they now had a friend in the White House and invited President Biden to attend the 2021 Pacific Islands Forum. Fiji's prime minister at the time, Frank Bainimarama, was the first national leader to congratulate Biden on his election victory, 'Together, we have a planet to save from a climate emergency,' he tweeted.

Australia tends to assume it is the regional leader in the Pacific. Policy-makers in Canberra view their island neighbours as small, isolated and uniquely vulnerable, and feel a special responsibility to support them. On the issue of climate change, however, the tables are turned. Pacific island countries are understood to be global leaders, while Australia is increasingly isolated from the international consensus. Only in mid-2022 did Australia finally set a zero emissions target. This reluctance to embrace meaningful climate action has had significant costs for relations with Pacific governments and beyond.

In our view, both the climate crisis itself, and the emerging global response to it, call for a fundamental shift in the way Australia considers climate policy. National interests are not tied to prolonging fossil fuel exports and delaying climate action. Instead, security and prosperity are linked with the opportunities presented by a global shift away from carbon. A new, more ambitious approach to climate policy would allow a reset of Australia's Pacific strategy.

Good relationships with Pacific island countries *are* vitally important for Australia. If Australia begins to shift its approach to climate change, it will have a chance to work with Pacific countries as climate partners. A more ambitious climate policy would help cement Australia's place as a security partner of choice for Pacific countries. As former Fiji Prime Minister Bainimarama has said, 'strong commitments will make strong friendships',[33] and Australia still needs to be a critical friend to Pacific countries. Working through the Pacific Islands Forum to pursue climate diplomacy would strengthen Australia's credentials as a regional power and do much to enhance its image on the global stage.

Canberra must embrace the opportunity while it still can. After decades of divergence from Pacific regional diplomacy on climate change, Australia can only hope it will be welcomed back into the Pacific family. Prime Minister Albanese's early visit to the Pacific Islands Forum to join the declaration of a climate emergency, alongside the relentlessly active Pacific agenda set by Foreign Minister Penny Wong and Minister for International Development and the Pacific Pat Conroy played positively into Australia's Pacific positioning. The Albanese government's *Climate Change Act*, passed in August 2022, enshrines in law an emissions reduction target of 43 per cent from 2005 levels by 2030 and net zero emissions by 2050. Though welcomed by most Pacific leaders it was still seen as inadequate by others. Speaking with his then New Zealand counterpart, Jacinda Ardern, Albanese stated that the two nations would establish annual meetings of Oceania climate change ministers to progress cooperation on climate action, that climate change is the 'single greatest threat to the livelihoods, security and wellbeing of the peoples of the Pacific', and that they recognised an 'urgent need' for countries to keep global warming to 'just 1.5 degrees'.[34] In a further move, Australia has jointly bid with Pacific island partners to host the Conference of the Parties (COP) in 2026. Confirming the proposal, Australia's Climate and Energy Minister, Chris Bowen, announced that this is 'an opportunity to work closely with our Pacific family, and ... to help elevate the case of the Pacific for more climate action'.[35]

Pacific island states have pursued collective diplomacy on climate change for more than 30 years and are likely to continue to pursue their interests as a bloc. Yet Pacific regionalism can also be a fragile thing. Solidarity between island governments is often tested. In early 2021, we saw a dramatic expression of this when five Micronesian member states of the Pacific Islands Forum—nearly a third of its membership— threatened to leave the organisation after their nomination for Secretary-General of the Forum failed to secure the top job.[36] More than just a stoush about leadership of the region's premier political body, this split was the culmination of long-running grievances held by island states in the northern Pacific, who have felt that regional organisations are dominated by countries in the south, from Melanesia and Polynesia. Regional solidarity was also tested in 2009 when Fiji was suspended from the Forum (following the 2006 coup in that country), and the Fiji government established its own alternative regional body, the Pacific Islands Development Forum. Regional divisions are a semi-regular fact of political life in the Pacific. As Greg Fry explains:

> In the 50-year history of attempts to build a Pacific political community among the diverse island societies across Oceania there have been numerous splits and divisions—between leaders, between sub-regions, between large and small states, and between resource-rich and resource-poor states.[37]

Ultimately, however, international action on climate change represents a core interest for Pacific countries. Island governments will continue to pursue collective diplomacy on the issue—whether through the Pacific Islands Forum or through alternative groupings, like the PSIDS at the UN, or through the AOSIS in the UN climate talks. Again, Fry explains, 'climate change has become the Pacific's nuclear testing issue of the 21st Century ... it has brought an urgency and emotional commitment to regional collaboration'.[38] There is no doubt that climate diplomacy will continue to be a defining issue for Pacific regionalism. For Australia, understanding this dynamic will be central to advancing any ambitions for future climate leadership.

Introducing this collection

The first section of the book sets the scene for considering the politics of climate change in Oceania. It begins with a special introduction by Dame Meg Taylor, former Secretary-General of the Pacific Islands Forum, who suggests that all too often there has been a 'disconnect' between policy ambition on climate change and what climate negotiations and diplomacy are delivering. She argues that 'accounting for the politics of climate change within and beyond the region is crucial if we are to not only understand this discord, but also to effectively bridge the policy and practice of climate diplomacy and secure the future of our Blue Pacific continent'. The possible future that faces both Australia and Pacific island states is then considered by Simon Bradshaw. His chapter takes stock of the latest scientific understanding of what may lie ahead, and considers climate impacts under three different scenarios, depending on whether or not countries take the steps needed to drive rapid global decarbonisation and limit global warming to well below 2°C. He explains that the science is clear; inaction presents a profound risk to communities across the region.

The second section of the book considers the ways that climate policy has shaped foreign policy and international relations in Oceania. Australian climate diplomacy is also considered by Caitlin Byrne, Andrea Haefner and Johanna Nalau, who unpack the role played by Australia's Ambassador for the Environment in navigating the challenging domestic and international politics of climate change. They argue that in the 'two-level game' of contemporary climate diplomacy, engaging with and mediating across domestic rather than international constituencies is the primary challenge facing Australia's Environment Ambassador, and it's an unenviable position. In their chapter, Wesley Morgan, George Carter and Fulori Manoa detail the leadership role that Pacific island countries have played in global climate diplomacy. They also consider the way in which the politics of climate change has impacted regional cooperation in the Pacific and ask what prospect there might be for Australia-Pacific climate diplomacy. Recognising that climate diplomacy is a dynamic global project, Tess Newton Cain, Romitesh Kant, Melodie Ruwet and Caitlin Byrne further explore how Pacific island nations have received and responded to the climate diplomacy of others, in this case, China, and ask whether China is perceived as a climate ally. While there are many complexities when it comes to understanding China's role in the Pacific, the clear finding to emerge from their recent study is that there is 'plenty of opportunity for China to *become* a "climate ally" for the Pacific'.

The third section of the book focuses on the security dimensions of climate change. The late Brendan Sargeant argues that Australia's strategic and defence policy structures are not equipped to respond to the security challenge that climate change presents. Having spent decades working within those structures, he suggests that defence policy must be reconceptualised to incorporate a deeper understanding of the risks that climate change embodies, and that doing so would improve perceptions of Australia as a security provider in the Pacific. Melissa Conley Tyler discusses how the election of the Albanese Labor government is affecting the climate agenda for Australia's Pacific development, diplomacy and defence engagement. She explains that coordinated climate action is an opportunity for Australia's development, diplomacy and defence engagement to work together in an integrated way, in order to build a shared future with the Pacific. Mark Beeson goes on to explain that Australia has a unique 'strategic culture' that struggles to incorporate climate risks, and 'the most immediate and tangible threat to Australia's overall security remains something of an afterthought in the calculation of national interests'. Sandra Tarte then considers contending security narratives in Oceania. She explains that increased engagement with island states—prompted by the rise of China—is driven by a 'traditional geo-strategic view of security'. However, this engagement is also an opportunity for Pacific states to advance a different regional security narrative focused on addressing climate change. Tarte considers areas of convergence and divergence in these contending security narratives.

The final section of the book considers climate change and international law. Rebecca Strating and Joanne Wallis consider the implications of global warming and sea level rise for 'maritime sovereignty' in Pacific island states. They explain that Pacific island countries are pursuing options in international law to secure the ongoing legal status of their maritime Exclusive Economic Zones even as islands and coastal features become inundated by rising seas. In the final chapter, Susan

Harris Rimmer considers the intersection between climate change and international human rights law, with a focus on addressing the loss and damage incurred by climate change and the need for mobility and asylum due to displacement. She suggests that diplomacy in the region should pay more attention to advancing a climate justice agenda and demonstrate what this might mean in practice.

The chapters in this book provide unique insight into the complex and multidimensional nature of climate diplomacy in Oceania. Together, they suggest that while there are deep divisions, competing interests and difficult agendas at play, there is also room to move beyond the politics and deliver coherent policy approaches that will make progress in tackling the climate challenge. With a track record for collective diplomacy, Pacific island nations are likely to continue in their leadership role, a proposition made all the more viable by the unwavering commitment to climate action by the US under the Biden administration.

For Australia, no longer able to hide behind a recalcitrant US, the choice has also shifted: to engage actively and constructively in support of a regional position that recognises and reinforces Oceania's interests now and for the benefit of future generations; or to simply fall into the slipstream of global diplomatic action. In a world where engagement signals agency, the former would be the preferred position. The challenge will be to move beyond short-term politics to pursue long-term national and regional interests. Australia, and Pacific island states, have much to gain from working together to tackle the climate crisis.

Notes

1   Pacific Islands Forum, *51st Pacific Islands Forum, Suva, Fiji, 11–14 July 2022: Forum Communiqué*, 2022.
2   A Tillett, 'Albanese Joins Pacific Leaders to Declare Climate Emergency', *Australian Financial Review*, 15 July 2022.
3   J Podesta and T Stern, 'A Foreign Policy for the Climate', *Foreign Affairs*, May/June 2020, pp. 39–46.
4   See further K Petrou and J Connell, *Pacific Island Guestworkers in Australia: The New Blackbirds?* Palgrave Macmillan, Singapore, 2022.

5 H White, 'In Denial: Defending Australia as China looks South', *Australian Foreign Affairs*, vol. 6, July 2019, p. 5.

6 J Schultz, 'Theorising Australia-Pacific Islands Relations', *Australian Journal of International Affairs*, vol. 68, no. 5, 2014, pp. 548–68.

7 See, for example, the discourses of vulnerability that have pervaded thinking about and approaches to small island developing states in J Barnett and E Waters, 'Rethinking Vulnerability of Small Island States: Climate Change and Development in the Pacific Islands', in J Grugel and D Hammett (eds), *The Palgrave Handbook of International Development*, Palgrave Macmillan, London, 2016, pp. 731–47.

8 W Morgan, 'Oceans Apart? Considering the Indo-Pacific and the Blue Pacific', *Security Challenges*, vol. 16, no. 1, 2020, pp. 44–64.

9 D Crowe, 'Great Concern: Malcolm Turnbull Draws a Line in the Sand on Military Bases Near Australia', *Sydney Morning Herald*, 10 April 2018.

10 Australian Government, *Opportunity, Security Strength: 2017 Foreign Policy White Paper*, Commonwealth of Australia, Canberra, 2017.

11 Anthony Albanese, 'Labor's Plan for a Stronger Pacific Family'.

12 Pacific Islands Forum, Boe Declaration on Regional Security, 5 September 2018.

13 V Naupoto, cited in P Hartcher, 'Cool Rationality Replaced by US-China Fight Club', *Sydney Morning Herald*, 4 June 2019.

14 L Goering, 'Small Island States, Britain Warn UN of Climate Threats to Security', *Reuters*, 24 February 2021.

15 J Biden, 'Why America Must Lead Again: Rescuing US Foreign Policy after Trump', *Foreign Affairs*, March/April 2020, pp. 64–76.

16 United States Department of State, 'Secretary Kerry Participates in the UN Security Council Open Debate on Climate and Security', 23 February 2021.

17 Podesta and Stern, 'A Foreign Policy for the Climate'.

18 See, for example, M McDonald, 'After the Fires? Climate Change and Security in Australia', *Australian Journal of Political Science*, vol. 56, no.1, 2021, pp. 1–18.

19 Deloitte, *Overview of the Inflationary Reduction Act and its Impacts on Australia's Green Production Aspirations*, March 2023.

20 S Marcacci, 'The Inflationary Reduction Act is the Most Important Climate Action in US History', *Forbes*, 2 August 2022.

21 J Biden, N Modi, S Morrison and Y Suga, 'Our Four Nations Are Committed to a Free, Open, Secure and Prosperous Indo-Pacific', *Washington Post*, 14 March 2021.

22 S Morrison, B Johnson and J Biden, 'Joint Leaders Statement on AUKUS', Prime Minister of Australia (Press release), 16 September 2021.

23 J Sparrow, 'Opinion: The AUKUS Deal is a Crime Against the world's Climate Future. It Didn't Have to Be Like This', *The Guardian*, 20 March 2023.

24 Australian Security Leaders Climate Group, 'Open Letter to Australia's Political Leaders', 2021.

25 Australian Government, *2023 National Defence Strategic Review*, Commonwealth of Australia, Canberra, 2023, p. 17.

26 R Glasser, 'The ADF Will Have to Deal with the Consequences of Climate Change', *The Strategist*, 28 April 2023.

27 R Glasser, 'Preparing for the Era of Disasters', *The Strategist*, 6 March 2019.

28 G Evans cited in M McDonald, 'Fair Weather Friend? Ethics and Australia's Approach to Global Climate Change', *Australian Journal of Politics and History*, vol. 51, no. 2, pp. 216–34.

29 G Carter, 'Pacific Island States and 30 Years of Global Climate Change Negotiations', in C Klock, P Castro, F Weiler and L Blaxekjar (eds), *Coalitions in the Climate Change Negotiations*, Routledge, London, 2020, pp. 73–90.

30 F Manoa, 'The New Pacific Diplomacy at the United Nations: The Rise of the PSIDS', in G Fry and S Tarte (eds), *The New Pacific Diplomacy*, ANU Press, Canberra, 2015, pp. 89–98.

31 Morgan, 'Oceans Apart?'.

32 K Lyons and B Doherty, 'Australia Tried to Water Down Climate Change Resolution at Pacific Islands Forum: Leader', *The Guardian*, 6 September 2018.

33 N O'Malley, 'Strong Climate Targets Make Strong Friendships, Fiji Tells Australia', *Sydney Morning Herald*, 28 February 2021.

34 Australian Government, 'Albanese Government Passes Climate Change Bill through House of Representatives', Press Release, 4 August 2022.

35 A Thompson, 'Australia Bows Out of Running for COP in 2024, Launches Bid to Cohost in 2026', *Sydney Morning Herald*, 6 November 2022.

36 S Dziedzic, 'What Does the Splitting of the Pacific Islands Forum Mean for Australia?', *ABC News*, 10 February 2021.

37 G Fry, 'The Pacific Islands Forum Split: Possibilities for Pacific Diplomacy', *Devpolicy Blog*, 23 February 2021.

38 G Fry, *Framing the Islands: Power and Diplomatic Agency in Pacific Regionalism*, ANU Press, Canberra, 2019.

STEPPING UP THE BLUE PACIFIC'S CLIMATE DIPLOMACY AND PRACTICE TOWARDS 2050

Dame Meg Taylor

I ASSUMED THE ROLE of Secretary-General of the Pacific Islands Forum in 2014, at a time when key transitions were underway in the region, with the conclusion of the 2013 Review of the Pacific Plan and the birth of the Framework for Pacific Regionalism. Indeed, these pieces of work framed and focused the first two years of my tenure as Secretary-General, as the Secretariat sought to institutionalise an inclusive dimension to regional policy development, streamline the regional agenda and reignite the politics in regionalism. In the years that followed, Forum leaders began to see the emerging fruit of these efforts. Moreso, with the reorientation of Pacific regionalism, particularly the introduction of the Blue Pacific narrative and identity.*

Introduced by the Prime Minister of Samoa in 2017, the Blue Pacific concept and narrative has continuously evolved, and has been

---

* These remarks were made at the initial workshop for the *2050 Strategy for the Blue Pacific Continent*, a key strategy developed by the Pacific island nations. The strategy recognises the economic and cultural role of the ocean for Pacific island nations and uses this importance as a symbol for the need for political cooperation and action.

refined and crystallised further in the last three years around a place of identity—the Blue Pacific Continent—secured through the formal demarcation of the maritime zones of the Forum membership as set out under the United Nations Convention on the Law of the Sea. Indeed, the principles of the Blue Pacific peoples, place and prospects have been embedded across the regional priorities of the Pacific Islands Forum.

Centred and built on the recognition of our collective custodianship of the Pacific Ocean, the Blue Pacific identity has become a catalyst for collective action, engagement and diplomacy for the Pacific Islands Forum to harness our shared ocean identity, geography and resources to drive positive change in the region's sociocultural, political and economic development. Also, the ongoing fluidity of the geopolitical context in the region and globally has added impetus for a reinvigorated approach to collective action.

As we are all aware, the intensification of geostrategic competition in recent years has resulted in a growing interest in the Pacific region and consequently, the emergence and/or strengthening of a range of sub-regional groupings. These sub-regional groupings pursue varied priorities and areas of interest to their respective memberships.

While increased external interest can be beneficial to Forum members, it can also serve to destabilise and disintegrate Forum solidarity, impacting upon the region's collective ability to address the impacts of climate and protect shared oceanic resources. This, perhaps, positions very aptly the value and importance of the *2050 Strategy for the Blue Pacific Continent* through clearly articulating the ambition for regionalism and its identified priorities.

I would offer that the most defining challenge faced by the region at this time can be framed within these two interconnected dimensions of risk—climate change and geopolitics. The impacts of climate change and the implications of heightened geopolitical activity and competition in the region are a threat to Pacific regionalism, but they are also issues that must be addressed through regionalism.

China continues to use climate action as a tool in the ongoing geostrategic tussle with the United States. Indeed, President Xi has repeatedly committed to incremental climate action on the international stage in recent years. The recent pledge by China that it would strive to be carbon neutral by 2060 reflects its position to take international responsibility for addressing climate change.

In our own region, climate change and collective climate action and advocacy has proven to be a highly contested and political discussion in recent years. Testament to this is the settlement of the 2019 Kainaki II Declaration for Urgent Climate Change Action Now.

Relatedly, and perhaps equally concerning for regionalism, the Kainaki Declaration and the subsequent focus of climate diplomacy by the Forum membership, are clear examples of the seeming disconnect in the policy, politics and practice of climate diplomacy in the Pacific region.

While Forum communiqués and declarations are not legally binding, there is an expectation that the commitments made by Forum leaders through these means will be observed and upheld in good faith.

Therefore, it was somewhat disconcerting to read a brief exchange in an Australian Senate Estimates hearing in October 2019, a mere month after the adoption of the Kainaki Declaration, on the implications of the declaration for Australian domestic policy on climate change.

Two months later at COP25, we saw this disconnect yet again in the climate negotiations in Madrid. We saw the preference for, and alliance with, like-minded partners over political commitments taken at the regional level on key priority positions in technical negotiations.

To some extent, it is no wonder that the Pacific region has reverted to sub-regional groupings such as the Pacific Small Island Developing States to clarify and advocate their priorities in the climate negotiations at the multilateral level. Indeed, extensive lobbying continues to be progressed in parallel at the bilateral level by island states to build alliances through the AOSIS and the High Ambition Coalition, as required.

These disconnected nuances between the policy, politics and practice of climate diplomacy were my intended focus. I will say, though, that these emerging disconnects raise the question: Do we really value regionalism as a means to advance the interest of our collective? Or is it just an extension of our foreign policy? Do we have the appropriate regional architecture in place to support, uphold and advance our collective interests?

We will answer these questions in very different ways, but I would offer that the region has a valuable opportunity to explore and elaborate these issues further in the context of the ongoing work on the development of the 2050 Strategy for the Blue Pacific Continent.

POSSIBLE FUTURES

Understanding the science and its implications for Australia and the Pacific

Simon Bradshaw

PACIFIC ISLAND COUNTRIES and communities have long understood the grave threats posed by climate change and the urgent need for stronger global action to bring down global greenhouse gas emissions.

For decades, Pacific island leaders have called for Australia and the world at large to immediately step up their efforts and to move beyond coal, oil and gas. The latest science, coupled with the lived experience of communities throughout the region, has added even more weight and urgency to these calls.

In this chapter we take stock of the latest science of climate change and its implications for Australia and the Pacific. We look at the impacts already being experienced, how these will escalate over the coming decades and, most importantly, how stronger action now and through the 2020s can dramatically limit future harms. In the concluding section, we consider briefly how Australia, under its new government, can work in true partnership with the Pacific in tackling the climate crisis. Moreover, how rising to the challenge can open up many opportunities for a more secure, harmonious, just and prosperous future.

The fierce urgency of now

We are at a precipice. The latest science, collated meticulously in the Sixth Assessment Report of the Intergovernmental Panel on Climate Change (IPCC), is a deeply unsettling read. Read alongside its previous iteration (the Fifth Assessment Report from 2013–14) the heightened sense of urgency is palpable. As summarised in a haunting final paragraph of the Summary for Policy-makers of the Working Group II contribution to the Sixth Assessment Report, covering climate impacts and opportunities for adaptation:

> The cumulative scientific evidence is unequivocal: Climate change is a threat to human well-being and planetary health. Any further delay in concerted anticipatory global action on adaptation and mitigation will miss a brief and rapidly closing window of opportunity to secure a liveable and sustainable future for all. (Very high confidence.)[1]

In the seven years since the last Assessment Report, global emissions have continued to rise, temperature records have been obliterated, and the world, including our region, has witnessed a terrifying run of unprecedented extreme weather disasters, from Tropical Cyclones Pam and Winston to Australia's devastating 2019–20 fire season and record-breaking 2020 floods. Those seven years have also seen major advances in our understanding of links between climate change and these extreme events, as well as a clearer picture of what to expect over the coming decades. The need for deep and rapid cuts to emissions is even clearer than before. Moreover, a failure to achieve steep global emissions reductions *this decade* would likely prove catastrophic.

IPCC author and leading Australian climate change communicator Joëlle Gergis concluded that 'this [latest] IPCC assessment is probably the scientific community's last chance to really make a difference', and that failure to heed its warnings 'will lock in an irreversibly apocalyptic future.'[2] Without far stronger action now, by the time of the next

Assessment Report, in around 2030, the fate of the Pacific, and much of humanity, will have been sealed.

Put another way, our decisions and actions now, this year, and through the make-or-break decade of the 2020s will impact massively upon the lives and prospects of today's young people, let alone future generations.

Achieving the goals of the Paris Agreement demands that global emissions be roughly halved by 2030.[3] Based on the science, and considering Australia's very high emissions, economic strength, and untapped opportunities for renewable energy and other climate solutions, the Climate Council of Australia has argued that Australia should aim to reduce its greenhouse emissions by 75 per cent below 2005 levels by 2030.[4]

An age of consequences

Decades of inadequate action on climate change in the face of mounting scientific warnings mean we are now faced with severe and worsening impacts.

In its Sixth Assessment Report, the IPCC revealed that many of the well-established consequences of climate change—including rising temperatures, rising sea levels, shifting rainfall patterns, and an increase in the intensity and destructive power of extreme weather events—are unfolding at an accelerating rate. In other words, our climate is not merely changing, but the rate of change is increasing. While stronger action now will substantially limit future harms, it is inevitable that we will continue to face worsening impacts over the coming decades.[5]

Remarkably, each of the seven years since the previous assessment report in 2013–14 has been warmer than any year prior to 2014.[6] The rate of ice sheet loss increased by a factor of four between 1992–9 and 2010–19.[7] Between 2006 and 2018, the rate of sea level rise was around twice as fast as between 1971 and 2006.[8] Global average temperatures have now risen by around 1.2°C, and by almost a quarter of a degree over the last five years alone. Temperatures over the last decade were higher than any reconstructed centennial-scale temperature ranges for the current interglacial period, which began around 11 700 years ago.[9] While there have been periods during the current and previous interglacial eras that have come close to today's temperature, the warming in those cases occurred over a much longer period: it took around 5000 years for the planet to warm by 5°C—a rate of around 0.1°C per century—following the peak of the last ice age. Since 1970, the planet has been warming at around 17 times that rate, or the equivalent of around 1.7°C per century.[10]

The rate and magnitude of the impacts we are now seeing come as little surprise when we consider the extent and rate of human interference in the climate system. Owing to the burning of coal, oil and gas, along with the plundering of terrestrial and marine ecosystems, atmospheric concentrations of carbon dioxide (CO_2) are now higher than at any time in at least the last two million years.[11] The rate by which the atmospheric concentration of CO_2 has increased since 1900 is at least ten times faster than at any other point in the last 800 000 years. By one account, and with the exception of the period following the meteorite strike 66 million years ago that saw the extinction of dinosaurs, our climate is now changing more rapidly than at any known point in Earth's history.[12]

Through human interferences in the climate system, we have altered the conditions under which all weather forms, raised global average temperatures, and triggered the melting of land and sea ice. Our atmosphere is now warmer, wetter and packing more energy, leading to an increase in the incidence and destructive power of extreme weather events. In the remainder of this chapter, I look at some of the specific ways in which climate change is already impacting upon Pacific island countries and communities.

More destructive tropical cyclones

Tropical cyclones are a part of life in many Pacific island countries, including Fiji, Vanuatu, Solomon Islands and Tonga. However, climate change is changing the conditions in which tropical cyclones form and develop, and increasing the likelihood of them becoming highly destructive.

Globally, it is likely that the proportion of tropical cyclones that reach Category 3–5 strength has already increased, and that climate change has driven an increase in the amount of rainfall associated with tropical cyclones.[13] Looking more specifically at the South Pacific region, recent research also indicates an increase in the number of intense tropical cyclones.[14] Furthermore, rising seas mean that storm surges are higher and more destructive than in the past, regardless of changes in tropical cyclone intensity.

In addition to stronger wind speeds, heavier rainfall, and storm surges riding on higher seas, there are a number of other ways in which climate change could be affecting tropical cyclone behaviour, all of which make them more dangerous. On average, tropical cyclones may be intensifying more rapidly,[15] providing communities with less warning and time to prepare. They may also be staying stronger after making landfall,[16] and moving more slowly[17]—exposing a given area to damaging winds and rainfall for longer.

Recent record-breaking tropical cyclones in the Pacific have been consistent with longstanding warnings from climate scientists and have taken a massive toll on local economies. In 2015, Category 5 Tropical Cyclone Pam, then the strongest South Pacific cyclone on record, caused damages equivalent to 64 per cent of Vanuatu's Gross Domestic Product (GDP), including heavy damages to food production.[18] Monster swells caused severe impacts as far away as the atoll nations Tuvalu and Kiribati—more than 1000 kilometres from Tropical Cyclone Pam's track.[19] In Tuvalu, the loss and damage, including damage to infrastructure, water resources and food production, was equivalent to more than 25 per cent of the country's GDP.

A year later, Tropical Cyclone Winston, an even stronger cyclone, devastated Fiji with damage amounting to 31 per cent of GDP.[20] In 2018, Tropical Cyclone Gita—the strongest to hit Tonga since the start of modern records—affected around 80 per cent of the nation's population, destroying houses and infrastructure including the more than 100-year-old Tongan Parliament building, and resulting in losses and damage equivalent to around 38 per cent of GDP.[21] In 2020, Tropical Cyclone Harold, the second strongest cyclone to hit Vanuatu after Cyclone Pam, caused major damage in Vanuatu, Solomon Islands, Fiji and Tonga, adding to the economic impact of COVID-19.[22]

Looking to the future, projections broadly indicate that while the total number of tropical cyclones will remain largely unchanged or even slightly decline, the intensity and destructive power of tropical cyclones will continue to increase.

Rising seas

Sea level rise is a profound threat to many communities in the Pacific. For the atoll countries—Kiribati, Tuvalu and the Marshall Islands— as well as individual low-lying islands in many other Pacific island countries, sea level rise is a truly existential challenge. Sea level rise and coastal inundation are also major challenges for low-lying coastal areas of larger and more elevated islands, especially given the difficulties of relocation. Around half the population of the Pacific region live within 10 kilometres of the coast, and around half the infrastructure is located within 500 metres of the coast.[23]

Rising sea levels are a particular threat to freshwater availability for communities living on atolls and other low-lying islands. Groundwater, the main source of freshwater, is threatened by sea level rise due to both intrusion from below and inundation from above. Salinisation of groundwater and increasing soil salinity are also a threat to food production.[24]

Global mean sea level rose by around 20 centimetres between 1901 and 2018, with the rate of sea level rise increasing since the 1990s.[25] Sea levels are expected to rise by a further 10–25 centimetres by 2050, regardless of how quickly we manage to reduce global greenhouse gas emissions. However, how far and how quickly the sea rises beyond 2050 depends on how quickly we manage to move beyond fossil fuels and reduce global greenhouse gas emissions. Under a low emissions scenario, the IPCC estimates that by 2300 sea level could rise by 0.3– 3.1 metres. Under a very high emissions scenario, the likely increase is estimated at 1.7–6.8 metres, with a rise of up to 16 metres if there is major ice loss around Antarctica.[26]

Continued warming of the deep ocean and melting ice sheets mean that seas will continue to rise long after we have managed to stabilise the global average temperature. However, while we cannot avoid a certain amount of further sea level rise, for many communities in the Pacific and beyond, determined global action to reduce emissions this decade may be the difference between a rate of sea level rise to which it is possible—albeit with great difficulty—to adapt, and one that sees communities overwhelmed and forcibly displaced.

Our changing ocean

Climate change and the burning of fossil fuels are altering the temperature, pH, dissolved oxygen, circulation and overall health of our oceans. Pacific island countries and communities are highly sensitive and vulnerable to these changes, owing to their close proximity to and deep connection with the ocean, and heavy reliance on its resources.

The past decade has witnessed several episodes of severe coral bleaching in many Pacific island countries causing loss of fish habitats.[27] Coral bleaching during the 2015–16 El Niño was the most damaging on record worldwide. This event also saw mass fish deaths on the Coral Coast of Fiji and in Vanuatu, likely due to high water temperatures and reduced oxygen levels.[28]

Climate change is also projected to alter the distribution of some fish populations in the Pacific, including multiple species of tuna, with potentially serious consequences for food security, as well as economic consequences for Pacific island countries that rely on revenue from selling fishing licences to foreign fleets. Reducing emissions in line with the Paris Agreement would help to sustain tuna populations within Pacific island countries' waters.[29]

Droughts and flooding rains

Rainfall in the Pacific region is already highly variable from year to year—in particular through the influence of the El Niño Southern Oscillation. During an El Niño event, countries in the central Pacific experience above average rainfall, increasing the risk of floods, while those in the southwest Pacific experience below average rainfall, increasing the risk of drought. During La Niña, the opposite occurs.

Droughts during the 2016–17 El Niño event caused widespread loss of crops in countries including Vanuatu and Papua New Guinea.[30]

Evidence suggests there has been greater variability in the El Niño Southern Oscillation since the 1950s than in past centuries, and both El Niño and La Niña events are expected to increase in frequency and intensity due to climate change.[31] Climate change will therefore likely further exacerbate the rainfall variations already experienced in the Pacific. Droughts pose a particularly severe threat to atoll communities that rely on groundwater in the form of fragile freshwater lenses.

Compounding impacts

Not all Pacific communities face the same threats from climate change, with local impacts reflecting a geographically diverse region spanning many degrees of latitude and consisting variously of low-lying atolls, mountainous volcanic islands and other types of islands. All face a par-ticular combination of risks that impact variously upon food and water supplies, livelihoods, health and other factors in human security. These risks typically compound and exacerbate one another. For example, the risk from increasing intensity of tropical cyclones is compounded by rising sea levels, leading to more dangerous storm surges. Similarly, the combined impact of shifting rainfall patterns, more extreme weather events, loss of land and salinisation of freshwater supplies will com-bine to reduce crop yields and food production.[32] More frequent and intense extreme weather events mean the recovery time between events becomes shorter, with the increasing likelihood of communities facing another disaster before they have had time to recover from the last.

Behind the numbers: The human face of climate change

The impacts of climate change are often quantified in terms of eco-nomic losses and other metrics. While these measures matter, they are inevitably unable to give a full picture of the impacts upon individual and community wellbeing. Beyond the impacts on physical security and livelihoods, climate change can have a profound impact upon a community's culture and traditions. If a community is permanently displaced due to rising seas, it may lose a connection to its land and sea that has been built over many centuries, and which is an indelible part of its identity, as well as its source of security and sustenance.[33] No assessment of the impacts of climate change and planning for action can be complete without consideration of these non-economic losses.

Our common challenge

The Pacific is home to some of the most 'climate vulnerable' countries on Earth. The situation facing Pacific island countries and communities epitomises the injustice and inequity at the heart of the climate crisis: the impacts of climate change continue to be felt first and hardest by countries and communities that have contributed the least to its causes and have fewer economic resources with which to adapt. However, recent years have shown beyond doubt that no country or community is immune to the impacts of climate change.

The Australian summer of 2019–20 was characterised by successive deadly heatwaves and the most destructive fire season on record. All told, 21 per cent of eastern Australia's temperate broadleaf and mixed forest burned during the Black Summer fires,[34] and an estimated three billion animals were killed or displaced.[35] Even areas previously considered too wet to burn, including large parts of the Gondwana rainforest—a living link to the ancient Gondwana supercontinent—were heavily damaged. Sydney, Melbourne and Canberra—together home to nearly half the country's population—were repeatedly blanketed by thick smoke as millions of hectares of surrounding bushland burned. One study showed that nearly 80 per cent of Australians were either directly or indirectly affected by the fires.[36]

The years since Australia's horror 2019–20 fire season have been characterised by above average rainfall and extreme flooding for much of the country, influenced by back-to-back La Niña events and exacerbated by climate change. Devastating floods that affected southeast Queensland and northern New South Wales in late February and early March 2022 became one of Australia's most severe and costly extreme weather disasters on record.[37]

Every fraction of a degree matters

In her book, *Humanity's Moment*, published in 2022, Joëlle Gergis writes:

> While there is no going back from some changes, what we do right now will reduce the scale and the magnitude of the disaster. We have reached a fateful fork in the road ... How we choose to respond to rising greenhouse gas emissions over the next five to ten years will determine our future climate conditions and the fate of human societies for thousands of years to come.[38]

Past inaction and the inertia in the climate system mean we must prepare for worse impacts from climate change over the coming decades, but collectively we still have the power to avoid a truly nightmare scenario, and to give vulnerable communities in Australia and the Pacific the chance of a better, more secure and more dignified future. The science is unequivocal: every choice, every year, every fraction of avoided warming matters, and will be measured in lives, livelihoods, communities, species and ecosystems saved.

In Paris in 2015, in addition to agreeing to 'pursuing efforts to limit the temperature increase to 1.5°C above pre-industrial levels', governments requested the IPCC to produce a special report on the impacts associated with warming of 1.5°C and the emissions reductions required to keep within this limit. Published in 2018, the IPCC's Special Report on Global Warming of 1.5°C (SR1.5) strongly validated the successful push by Pacific island countries for a stronger temperature goal in the Paris Agreement, revealing in compelling terms why we must continually strive to limit warming to 1.5°C, and why every fraction of a degree matters.[39] This is no clearer than when it comes to the health of our oceans. Healthy oceans are critical to the sustenance, livelihoods and security of the peoples of the Pacific and for communities worldwide. Coral reefs are at the centre of the ocean's health and biodiversity. In addition to providing food and livelihoods, coral reefs help protect coastlines from storms.

Today's level of warming has already proved perilous for coral reefs worldwide, including the Great Barrier Reef. Since 2016, the Great Barrier Reef has suffered four mass bleaching events (2016, 2017, 2020 and 2021),[40] resulting in devastating loss of corals and the species they support. The most recent event occurred during a La Niña event, which would normally be expected to provide corals with some reprieve due to increased cloud cover. At a temperature rise of 1.5°C coral reefs 'are projected to decline by a further 70–90%'. At 2°C, tropical reef-building corals are projected to 'mostly disappear'.[41] In other words, limiting warming to 1.5°C compared to 2°C may be the difference between giving coral reefs and the communities who depend on them a chance of survival, versus the near complete destruction of the world's remaining coral reefs, with knock-on effects for food security, coastal erosion and ocean life at large that are barely conceivable.

Further illustration of why every fraction of a degree of avoided warming matters comes from growing evidence that the climate system contains thresholds—or tipping points. If crossed, these tipping points may result in abrupt, uncontrollable and irreversible changes that prove catastrophic for human societies. Examples include sudden changes in ocean circulation, causing dramatic shifts in rainfall patterns; the rapid collapse of ice sheets, triggering far greater rises in sea level than currently anticipated; and large-scale die-off in one or more of the world's major terrestrial carbon sinks such as the Amazon rainforest.

In its Sixth Assessment Report, the IPCC recognises that truly catastrophic turns of events, including far greater near-term temperature increases than suggested by current models, can't be ruled out, and should be part of our risk assessments.[42] The risk of transgressing one or more tipping points increases with every fraction of a degree of warming. In other words, the magnitude of climate impacts will not simply increase in more-or-less linear fashion as the world warms, but may jump quickly from the tolerable into the territory of truly existential risks.

The IPCC first introduced the idea of tipping points, which it referred to as 'large-scale discontinuities', over 20 years ago. At that stage it was assessed that we would likely only cross such thresholds if we reached around 5°C of warming. More recent studies suggest that many such thresholds lie at far lower temperature levels. Indeed, at today's level of warming—around 1.2°C—we have already entered a region of moderate risk of some abrupt and irreversible changes. The closer we get to 1.5°C, the greater that risk becomes. Evidence today suggests that warming beyond 2°C, which was once considered an appropriate upper limit, would be very dangerous for humanity indeed.[43]

The positive impacts of today's efforts to limit warming will not be felt immediately, though they may nonetheless be realised sooner than is often appreciated. When it comes to extreme heat, the impact of strong action today will begin to show in about 20 years. Beyond 2040, we would start to see fewer deadly heatwaves than we would expect under a high greenhouse gas emissions scenario. By the end of the century, well within the lifespan of many young people alive today, ambitious action through the 2020s will have strongly limited many other impacts that would otherwise occur.[44]

Rising to the challenge

The threat of catastrophic climate change cannot be overstated, but neither can the opportunities to strengthen our communities, reduce inequalities, reinvigorate international relationships, and deliver a brighter future for all, should we truly rise to the challenge.

The Australian Labor government of Anthony Albanese has placed action on climate change at the centre of its foreign policy, in particular its diplomacy with Pacific island countries. It has strengthened Australia's Nationally Determined Contribution to the Paris Agreement (NDC)—committing to reduce Australia's emissions by at least 43 per cent by 2030—and put in place a range of policies and investments to accelerate Australia's energy transformation. However, the science compels Australia to further step up in multiple ways, including:

- Further strengthening Australia's 2030 emissions reduction target.
- A full reckoning with Australia's status as one of the largest producers and exporters of coal and gas.

- Increasing Australia's contribution of international climate finance. That is, support to less developed countries with reducing emissions and transforming their energy systems (climate change mitigation), and building resilience to the impacts of climate change that can no longer be avoided (climate change adaptation).
- Supporting efforts to address loss and damage from climate change, including providing funding beyond that committed to mitigation and adaptation, and helping ensure those communities who may be forced or choose to move are able to do so safely, with dignity and on their own terms.
- Deepening partnerships at all levels, from working with traditional allies including the United States to develop the secure and adequate supply chains needed for the rapid transformation of energy systems, to supporting the region's most vulnerable communities to adapt to climate impacts in ways that build upon their local knowledge and strengths.

Australia: From fossil fuel giant to renewable energy superpower

While Australia—already a land of extremes—has perhaps the most to lose among all developed countries should the world fail to radically curb its emissions over the coming years, it is also in a position to play a positive and disproportionately large role in driving solutions globally. Furthermore, this route may provide Australia with the key to its future security and prosperity.

Australia is one of the sunniest and windiest countries on Earth, with almost unrivalled potential to generate renewable electricity. Unleashing this potential will enable Australia not only to meet its domestic electricity needs, but to lead the world in low-carbon manufacturing, and to set itself up as a major exporter of renewable energy and associated technologies.[45] Australia also has substantial reserves of minerals that will be required to support the decarbonisation of the world's energy systems.[46] Independent research institute Beyond Zero Emissions has estimated that Australia could build a clean export industry worth A$333 billion a year by 2050, more than triple the current value of Australia's fossil fuel exports.[47]

In helping drive the uptake of renewable energy beyond its shores, Australia can also help to reduce poverty and inequality, support local economic development, and support the stability and resilience of its region and beyond. Today, renewable energy offers the cheapest, healthiest, fastest and most reliable means of enabling access to electricity for the many people worldwide who still live without it.[48] Household and community-owned schemes offer particular advantages when it comes to reducing inequality and supporting local economies. Once the initial investment has been recouped through saving on energy bills, the family or community is then owner of a productive asset. It no longer faces ongoing fuel costs and a hefty portion of its wealth being handed over to big energy producers and retailers.[49]

Addressing the unavoidable impacts

While we must make every possible effort to limit future warming, it is also necessary to adapt to the impacts that, owing to past inaction, can no longer be avoided.

Typically it is those countries and communities that have contributed the least to the causes of climate change—including Pacific island countries—that are being hit first and hardest by its impacts, and in many cases have fewer resources with which to adapt.

Wealthy developed countries including Australia have a clear responsibility under the United Nations Framework Convention on Climate Change (UNFCCC) and Paris Agreement to support vulnerable countries with their response to the climate crisis—both their commitments to emissions reduction and, as importantly, their efforts to adapt to the greater threats from extreme weather and other impacts of climate change they now face. Australia has ensured that a significant share of its overall contribution of international climate finance is spent on supporting climate change adaptation in the Pacific, though it has fallen far short of providing what can be reasonably considered a fair share towards the longstanding global goal of mobilising

US$100 billion a year to support climate action in developing countries.[50] In addition, Australia withdrew from the Green Climate Fund in 2020—the world's largest climate fund and a critical element of cooperation under the Paris Agreement. Despite repeated requests from Pacific island countries, Australia refused to re-engage with the Green Climate Fund and resume its contributions until October 2023, after Minister Wong announced Australia would make a modest contribution.

In the Pacific, as in almost every part of the world, there remains a considerable gap between adaptation funding needs and available support. Much more can and should be done to support communities with building resilience to the impacts they face, from better climate information services to supporting small-scale farmers and fishers with adapting to the new climate realities, to building more resilient infrastructure. Importantly, support must be aligned with the needs and priorities of affected communities themselves, rather than the agendas of development partners.

Pacific island countries are already experiencing loss and damage from climate change, including losses related to sea level rise. This includes the growing risk of displacement. While at present almost all those who are displaced in the context of climate change remain within their country's borders, future sea level rise and other climate impacts present a truly existential challenge for some states, notably the atoll countries, and may ultimately force more people to move across borders. Forced displacement epitomises the injustice of the climate crisis and carries impacts beyond the loss of livelihoods and security, affecting a community's connection to its ancestral land and seas, and undermining its culture and identity. The reality of this threat demands that the world's major emitters, including Australia, do everything possible to minimise the risk of forced displacement through deep and sustained cuts to emissions and supporting communities to adapt to the impacts they face. In the event that a community is ultimately left with no choice but to relocate, it should be able to do so safely, with dignity, and on its own terms.

Addressing loss and damage in the Pacific, including forced displacement, will require both financial and non-financial support from Australia and other wealthy countries. In addition to far stronger efforts to reduce emissions and greater funding for adaptation, Australia should support the establishment of a dedicated new loss and damage finance facility under the UNFCCC and commit to making a contribution to this proposed new facility.

If a community ultimately is forced to relocate and relocation within its country is not an option, then Australia and other countries with the capacity to do so must provide avenues for communities to migrate, to build strong diasporas that enable continuity of culture, and to become valued citizens of their adopted country.[51]

A brighter future for all

Determined action on climate change, informed by the best science coupled with local traditional knowledge, and developed and implemented in true partnership and collaboration, holds the promise of a better future.

The benefits of renewable energy are no clearer than in the Pacific. In the past, those with access to electricity have relied largely on expensive imported fuels. Renewable energy is freeing communities from expensive diesel imports, increasing rates of electricity access in remote communities, and enabling countries to be more energy-independent and thereby less exposed to volatile fossil fuel markets.[52]

Responding to climate change demands elevating the voices of Indigenous peoples, women, young people, and others who have too often been marginalised, excluded from decision-making, or otherwise disadvantaged.

In many societies, women still hold greater responsibility for tasks that are made more difficult by climate change, including sourcing food and water, and caring for the sick or elderly. In other words, as climate-fuelled extreme weather increases the health burden on a community, or when water scarcity means it is necessary to travel further to gather water, the extra work typically falls to women. Extreme weather disasters are also often followed by an increase in gender-based violence.[53]

Young people also face a disproportionate burden on their health as a result of climate change. Moreover, young people have more skin in the game than today's older generations. As already acknowledged, stronger action on climate change today will have an enormous impact on the life prospects of young people.

Building effective responses to the climate crisis begins with listening to those on the front line, including First Nations, women and young people, and ensuring they have greater control over the decisions that affect their lives. Throughout the Pacific, traditional knowledge is considered fundamental to coping with the new challenges of climate change. Similarly, climate change adaptation is most effective when it is led by local communities and builds on their strengths. Such measures, combined with the aforementioned ability of renewable energy and other climate solutions to redistribute power and wealth, can deliver benefits to society beyond reducing emissions and tackling climate change. The climate crisis is also an opportunity to address entrenched disadvantage and the legacies of colonisation, reduce inequality within and between nations, and build stronger communities.

Conclusion

If climate change is the defining challenge of our times, the future will belong to those countries and communities that rise to the challenge.

Recognising the existential threat they face, the 'large ocean states' of the Pacific have worked for many years to shape the world's response to the climate crisis and to catalyse stronger action.[54] It is long past time for Australia to follow their lead.

Australia's lost decade of climate inaction came at a considerable cost to its international reputation and to the safety of communities in Australia and the Pacific. The Australian government's recent return to the fold, including strengthening Australia's 2030 emissions reduction target, is already bringing benefits in terms of renewed international relationships and economic opportunities.[55] Aligning with the true scale and pace of action that the science demands will require it to go much further, including ending coal and gas production and stepping up support to vulnerable communities in the Pacific.

Our actions this decade will profoundly affect the security and wellbeing of communities throughout the Pacific, Australia and the wider world for generations to come—and reverberate beyond human timescales. There is no more time to lose.

Notes

1 IPCC (Intergovernmental Panel on Climate Change), *Climate Change 2022: Impacts, Adaptation and Vulnerability (The Working Group II contribution to the Sixth Assessment Report)*, 2022.

2 J Gergis, *Humanity's Moment: A Climate Scientist's Case for Hope,* Black Inc., Melbourne, 2022.

3 IPCC (Intergovernmental Panel on Climate Change), *Special Report on Global Warming of 1.5°C.* (Report, 2018).

4 T Baxter et al., *Primed for Action: A Resilient Recovery for Australia,* Climate Council, 2022.

5 IPCC (Intergovernmental Panel on Climate Change), *Climate Change 2021: The Physical Science Basis (The Working Group I contribution to the Sixth Assessment Report),* 2021.

6 NOAA (National Oceanic and Atmospheric Administration), *Annual Global Climate Report—2020,* 2021.

7 IPCC, *Climate Change 2021.*

8 Ibid.

9 Ibid.

10 IPCC, *Climate Change 2021,* cited in J Gergis, *Humanity's Moment.*

11 IPCC, *Climate Change 2021.*

12 CH Lear et al., 'Geological Society of London Scientific Statement: What the Geological Record Tells Us about Our Present and Future Climate', *Journal of the Geological Society,* vol. 178, no. 1, 2021, p. 178.

13 IPCC, *Climate Change 2021.*

14 W Morgan, A Dean and S Bradshaw, *A Fight for Survival: Tackling the Climate Crisis Is Key to Security in the Blue Pacific,* Climate Council, 2022.

15 KT Bhatia et al., 'Recent Increases in Tropical Cyclone Intensification Rates', *Nature Communications,* vol. 10, no. 1, 2019.

16 L Li and P Chakraborty, 'Slower Decay of Landfalling Hurricanes in a Warming World', *Nature,* vol. 587, 2020.

17 JP Kossin, 'A Global Slowdown of Tropical-Cyclone Translation Speed', *Nature,* vol. 558, 2018.

18 IPCC, *Climate Change 2022*.
19 RK Hoeke, H Damlamian, J Aucan and M Wandres, 'Severe Flooding in the Atoll Nations of Tuvalu and Kiribati Triggered by a Distant Tropical Cyclone Pam', *Frontiers in Marine Science*, 2021.
20 IPCC, *Climate Change*, 2022.
21 ADB (Asian Development Bank), *Cyclone Gita Recovery Project: Report and Recommendation of the President. Summary Assessment of Damages and Needs: Energy Sector*, 2018; Government of Tonga, *Post Disaster Rapid Assessment. Tropical Cyclone Gita*, 12 February 2018.
22 M Taylor, 'Christiana Figueres Oration at the 7th Australian Emissions Reduction Summit', 3 December 2020.
23 IPCC, *Climate Change 2022*.
24 Morgan, Dean and Bradshaw, *A Fight for Survival*.
25 IPCC, *Climate Change 2021*.
26 IPCC, *Climate Change 2021*, cited in Gergis, *Humanity's Moment*.
27 LXC Dutra et al., 'Impacts of Climate Change on Corals Relevant to the Pacific Islands', Commonwealth Marine Economies Program, 2018; JE Johnson et al., 'Impacts of Climate Change on Fish and Shellfish Relevant to the Pacific Islands, and the Coastal Fisheries they Support', Commonwealth Marine Economies Program, 2018.
28 Johnson et al., 'Impacts of Climate Change on Fish and Shellfish Relevant to the Pacific Islands'.
29 JD Bell et al., 'Pathways to Sustaining Tuna-Dependent Pacific Island Economies During Climate Change', *Nature Sustainability*, vol. 4, 2021.
30 V Iese et al., 'Agriculture Under a Changing Climate', in L. Kumar (ed.), *Climate Change and Impacts in the Pacific*, Springer Nature, Switzerland, 2020.
31 W Cai et al., 'Changing El Niño-Southern Oscillation in a Warming Climate', *Nature Reviews Earth and Environment*, vol. 2, 2021.
32 Iese, 'Agriculture Under a Changing Climate'.
33 Morgan, *A Fight for Survival*.
34 MM Boer, V Resco de Dios and RA Bradstock, 'Unprecedented Burn Area of Australian Mega Forest Fires, *Nature Climate Change*, vol. 10, 2020.
35 WWF, *Australia's 2019–2020 Bushfires: The Wildlife Toll*, 2020.
36 N Biddle, B Edwards, D Herz and T Makkai, *Exposure and the Impact on Attitudes of the 2019–20 Australian Bushfires*, ANU Centre for Social Research and Methods, Canberra, 2020.
37 M Rice et al., *A Supercharged Climate: Rain Bombs, Flash Flooding and Destruction*, Climate Council, 2022.
38 Gergis, *Humanity's Moment*.
39 IPCC (Intergovernmental Panel on Climate Change), *Special Report on Global Warming of 1.5°C*, 2018.

40 AIMS (Australian Institute of Marine Sciences), Annual Summary Report of Coral Reef Condition 2021/22, 2022.

41 IPCC, *Special Report on Global Warming of 1.5°C*.

42 IPCC, *Climate Change 2021*.

43 W Steffen et al., *Aim High, Go Fast: Why Emissions Need to Plummet This Decade*, Climate Council, 2021.

44 IPCC, *Climate Change 2021*.

45 Baxter et al., *Primed for Action*.

46 E Weisbrot, L Brailsford, A Stock and G Bourne, *Leaders and Legends: Thousands of Clean Jobs for Queenslanders*, Climate Council, 2020.

47 BZE (Beyond Zero Emissions), *Export Powerhouse: Australia's $333 Billion Opportunity*, 2021.

48 Oxfam, *More Coal Equals More Poverty: Transforming Our World through Renewable Energy*, 2017.

49 Oxfam, *Australia's Energy Future and the Recovery from Covid-19: How We Can Help End Poverty and Fight the Climate Crisis*, 2020.

50 S Hardefeldt et al., *Falling Short: Australia's Role in Funding Fairer Climate Action in a Warming World*, Oxfam, Action Aid, The Australia Institute, Jubilee Australia, Caritas Australia, Edmund Rice Centre, 2022.

51 J-A Richards and S Bradshaw, *Uprooted by Climate Change: Responding to the Growing Risk of Displacement*, Oxfam, 2017.

52 Oxfam, *Powering Up Against Poverty: Why Renewable Energy Is the Future*, 2015; Oxfam, *More Coal Equals More Poverty*.

53 UN Women Fiji, *Climate Change Disasters and Gender-Based Violence in the Pacific*, 2014.

54 W Morgan and T Newton-Cain, *Strengthening Australia's Relationships with Countries in the Pacific Region*, Policy Brief, Griffith Asia Institute, 2020.

55 P Hartcher, 'What's Our Globetrotting PM Learnt about Australia's Place in the World?', *Sydney Morning Herald*, 24 September 2022.

AN UNENVIABLE APPOINTMENT

Australia's environment ambassador

Caitlin Byrne, Andrea Haefner and Johanna Nalau

AUSTRALIA APPOINTED ITS first-ever Ambassador for the Environment just over 30 years ago, in 1989. Taken up by former High Court judge and Governor-General, Sir Ninian Stephen, the appointment was a surprise to many, including Stephen himself.[1] It also represented an important juncture in Australian diplomacy with international cooperation on environmental issues taking on a new emphasis in the nation's foreign policy. Importantly, it was a world first, and pioneering step for recognition of environmental diplomacy within the global community.[2]

When he announced the role, the Prime Minister at the time, Bob Hawke, flagged his vision: for Australia to lead faster international action to preserve the environment and 'address forces including global warming induced by the greenhouse effect, the loss of biodiversity, trans-national pollution and waste disposal, and the exploitation of the world's oceans and fisheries'.[3] He noted the dual purpose of this ambassadorial role, to 'give Australia a stronger, clearer voice on global environmental issues ... and to have strong consistent capacity to be represented in the increasing rounds of international negotiations and forums that would characterise the nation's involvement in these issues'.[4]

More than three decades on, and there is no doubt the position of Australian environment ambassador faces particular challenges. Charged with representing the nation's distinctive national interests—recognising the deep economic reliance on commodities—in global arenas, they work with and across myriad stakeholders at home and abroad. At the same time, they bear the weighty expectations of a global constituency to deliver moral consensus on climate action, including for future generations. They are confronted—more than their traditional counterparts—by competing political interests, influential industry stakeholders and fluid public opinion—all interacting within the nation's short-term electoral cycles. Together, these complex dynamics have fostered a diplomatic approach that moves carefully, with a tendency towards pragmatism and an eye for outcomes based on 'radical incrementalism' rather than transformational leaps forward.[5]

This chapter reviews the evolving role of Australia's environment ambassador drawing on the practice and experiences of those who have been charged to execute it. It begins with a brief overview of special ambassadorial appointments, which in Australia's case starts with the appointment of an Ambassador for the Environment. It examines the circumstances and rationale which led to the inaugural appointment of Sir Ninian Stephen who, from 1989 to 1992 shaped expectations of what Australia's environment ambassador might achieve. Using a range of primary sources, including policy statements and speeches, the chapter then draws on the experiences of others who have held the role to identify priority themes and tensions that underpin the conduct of duties for this special role. The view is complemented by media reports, interviews and conversations with former environment ambassadors and officials working with them—which provide a broader understanding of the nature and conduct of this role across the past three decades, and its significance into the future.

A special appointment
The Ambassador for the Environment is a unique role in the international system. It falls into the category of a 'special interest ambassador';

that is, one who is 'specially appointed' to represent the nation on an important international issue. While appointed in much the same way as the traditional ambassadors and taking on a representational role, these special interest ambassadors differ from their 'extraordinary and plenipotentiary' counterparts in three key ways.

Firstly, they are not accredited to another state and so are usually based at home with 'roaming' responsibilities, rather than being accredited to a permanent mission based within the boundaries of another nation-state. Secondly, by virtue of the policy focus of their remit, they must respond to a range of domestic stakeholders across industry, academia, media and community. Moreover, they are accountable to a variety of political masters, some of whom have competing interests. Thirdly, they are not invested with the full power to transact business on behalf of the head of state—that is, with treaty-making powers, in the same way as traditional ambassadors. They do, however, adhere to the core functions of the diplomatic practice—representation, communication and negotiation—as articulated in article 3 of the *Vienna Convention on Diplomatic Relations 1961*.

In Australia's case, the Ambassador for the Environment was the first special-interest ambassadorial appointment and the only such appointment made in the first hundred years of Federation. Since 2003, other special-interest policy areas have received similar attention with ambassadorial appointments made relating to:

- i) arms control and counter-proliferation
- ii) countering modern slavery, people smuggling and human trafficking
- iii) counter-terrorism
- iv) cyber affairs and critical technology
- v) First Nations people
- vi) gender equality
- vii) human rights
- viii) regional health security.

These appointments are not necessarily replicated across other nations, but they speak to the policy significance for Australia's national interests, reflecting the potentially competing demands of the global multilateral and domestic political agendas. Each of these special appointments varies in scope, bureaucratic and budgetary resourcing and political engagement and accountability.

Why appoint an Ambassador for the Environment?

The challenging and contested nature of climate policy and politics in Australia has been the subject of much scholarly attention, especially over the last decade. However, the specialised role and contribution made by its special ambassador gets little attention, particularly in the public mind. Most Australians are unlikely to know there is such a position, let alone who holds it.

When Stephen was appointed as Australia's Ambassador for the Environment, the world was going through significant tumult. The fall of the Berlin Wall in late 1989 signalled the beginning of the end of the Cold War and a new era in global politics. For many, particularly in the West, there was a sense of optimism squarely attached to the ascendancy of US global leadership and the primacy of liberal democracy. Some suggested the era marked 'the end of history'. But others were more cautious. Writing in the 1989 issue of *Foreign Affairs* under the title 'A New World and its Troubles', Stanley Hoffman noted that the world had not moved into the anticipated new phase of peace and quiet. He identified the emergence of environmental issues as a source of potential conflict—particularly between advanced and developing economies—and pleaded the case for renewed emphasis on liberal institutionalism over American exceptionalism to address shared concerns regarding the environment. Hoffman further noted that:

> the most dangerous remaining tension, and the most difficult to overcome, is that between the global dimension of the issues that foreign policy will have to deal with and the fact that political life remains, at best, limited to the horizons of the state and is, often, even challenging the unity, the borders and the effectiveness of the state.[6]

Issues associated with environmental degradation had gained ground as issues of shared global concern.[7] The 1972 United Nations Stockholm Conference on the Human Environment put the environment on the global agenda, leading to the creation of the UN Environment Programme (UNEP). A little over a decade later, in 1983 the World Commission on the Environment and Development (Brundtland Commission) was formed to focus on environmental and development problems and solutions. The Brundtland Report, titled 'A Common Future' issued in 1987 brought the idea of sustainable development into sharp relief for the international community. It identified environmental protection as critical to global sustainable development and pointed to disparities between poverty and development needs in the global South on the one hand, and the insatiable consumption patterns of the global North on the other, as underlying the emerging global environmental crisis.[8] The Brundtland Report, unanimously accepted by the UN General Assembly, paved the way for the UN Conference on Environment and Development (UNCED) scheduled for Rio de Janeiro in June 1992 (also known as the 'Earth Summit'). As the Brundtland Commission was delivering its key findings, the World Conference on the Changing Atmosphere meeting in Toronto in 1988 agreed to cut global carbon dioxide emission levels by 20 per cent by 2005, taking 1988 as the base level (the Australian government adopted this target in 1990). The Intergovernmental Panel on Climate Change (the IPCC) was jointly established by the World Meteorological Organisation and the UN Environment Programme, and in 1989, the Declaration of the Hague called for a Convention on Climate Change. Australia, along with 23 other countries, signed that Declaration.

Australian diplomacy was actively engaged in these foundational international environmental discussions. As Australia's Permanent Representative to UNESCO (1983–6), former Prime Minister Gough Whitlam led the charge. Whitlam was no stranger to the global environmental agenda, having signed Australia up to a range of international environmental treaties, including *The Convention on Wetlands of International Importance Especially as Waterfowl Habitat*

('Ramsar Convention') and the *Convention for the Protection of the World Cultural and Natural Heritage* during his earlier term as Prime Minister (1972–5). Recognising the expanding global environmental agenda, he advocated for a special ambassadorial appointment that would enable Australia to more visibly represent its position and engage on critical issues across key arenas.[9] Tactically, Stephen's appointment was timed to ensure Australia was equipped to take part in the schedule of preparatory meetings leading into the Rio Earth Summit.[10] More broadly, it reflected a 'pioneering step' to ensure, as then Foreign Minister Gareth Evans observed, Australia was 'at the forefront of international cooperation on the environment'.[11]

The global environmental agenda was finding its place within Australia's foreign policy thinking at the time. It reflected, as Evans flagged, the multidimensional nature of Australia's interests, which included an imperative to be 'a good international citizen' or put another way, to pursue 'purposes beyond ourselves'.[12] To this end, Evans (1988) suggested that Australia had to look more closely at 'non-military threats to security' which required global solutions; towards which Australia had a role to play. Global environment problems such as the damage done to the ozone layer—Australia had signed the *Montreal Protocol on Substances that Deplete the Ozone Layer* in June that year—and the preservation of the Antarctic were at the top of his list. Fittingly Evans later grouped these issues under what he termed 'the New Internationalist Agenda'.[13]

Environmental issues also loomed large in Australia's domestic landscape, with political debates of the time providing an important backdrop to the creation of the environment ambassador role. For example, Prime Minister Hawke came into power in 1983 on the back of an election campaign that was resolved to block the construction of Tasmania's Franklin Dam. In taking up this case, Hawke lent on Australia's obligations under the 1972 *Convention for the Protection of the World Cultural and Natural Heritage*. Defending the Franklin River (which had been identified on the World Heritage List since late 1982) was a defining aspect of Hawke's prime ministership and a move that relied on and reinforced the Commonwealth's responsibility for the environment within section 51 (xxix) of the Australian Constitution under its 'external affairs' power, a power later upheld by the High Court in *The Commonwealth v Tasmania* (1983).

The Franklin Dam case drove home the international significance of Australia's environmental priorities (which also included the Antarctic Treaty system). While the Department of Foreign Affairs and Trade had specific policy officers focused on these issues both in Canberra and overseas, the global policy domain related to the environment required greater attention, increasing expertise and—as one official later described—'needed to be put up in lights'.[14] All this was combined with Hawke's political realisation at the time that winning votes demanded a greener turn in politics.

When he announced Stephen's appointment, Hawke also unveiled a range of domestic landcare initiatives including among others a $320 million commitment to address soil degradation over three years, the promise to plant one billion trees, and a sales tax reduction on recycled goods. While these initiatives gained the endorsement of key domestic stakeholders including the National Farmers Federation and the Australian Conservation Foundation (ACF), it was still seen as falling short of the mark. For many, the emphasis on landcare rather than the emerging global issue of greenhouse gas emissions appeared to be a missed opportunity. It represented the 'struggle between those Cabinet Ministers keen to capitalise on the conservationist vote and others more eager to promote Australian industry in the face of continuing trade-figure blow-outs'.[15] Philip Toyne, the CEO of ACF, remarked, 'Instead of setting targets for reduction of greenhouse gases, the Commonwealth has adopted an expedient and self-interested approach which advocates that Australia may even need to increase greenhouse gases to accommodate growth of internationally competitive exports'.[16] For others, it reflected the 'right idea, but the wrong level of financial support.'[17]

It was against this backdrop that Sir Ninian Stephen took up his role. The terms appeared straightforward: 'to represent Australia at international forums concerned with environmental matters and advise the government on international environmental policy'.[18] But it was no small task. Despite enthusiastic engagement with environmental issues, it was clear that 'Australia's national circumstances—especially its high dependence on industries that emit large quantities of greenhouse gases ... [would mean it] must work harder than others' to represent and advance its interests.[19] This tension continues to define the role today.

Building consensus behind the scenes

It was important that Australia's inaugural environment ambassador was an eminent person—someone who brought status and gravitas to the role at home and abroad. Stephen knew heads of state from his previous roles, not least as the nation's 20th Governor-General, and could speak directly with them in various global arenas.[20] As one insider later noted, 'access and influence were the currencies Stephen brought to the role'.[21] Importantly, too, Stephen's earlier work as one of Australia's leading constitutional lawyers saw him in possession of a deep knowledge of the Australian Constitution, and it was expected that Stephen would navigate the difficult and contested terrain between the Commonwealth and the states in matters of the environment.[22] Indeed, this was an area of preoccupation, and Stephen spoke on various occasions about 'the ways in which the external affairs power in the Australian Constitution—Section 51 (xxix)—had been used by Canberra, by way of the High Court, to weaken the federal compact'.[23]

Even though Stephen was consumed by an evolving global warming agenda, a more significant issue—preservation of the Antarctic— demanded his immediate attention. A US–UK bid for regulated mining in the Antarctic as represented by a proposed *Convention on the Regulation of Antarctic Mineral Resource Activity* (CRAMRA) was in play. For Hawke, it represented a political opportunity for building further support within the Australian constituency.[24] At Hawke's direction, and to the irritation of some in his Cabinet, Stephen was charged with opposing the proposed CRAMRA and building the necessary diplomatic momentum to secure the pristine Antarctic as a wildlife reserve. From the outset it seemed a pessimistic endeavour, given the support already secured for CRAMRA. And it entailed some risk, 'if the bid for a wilderness reserve failed, Antarctica might be left with no protection at all against mining'.[25] Working in tandem with his French counterparts—who, with the advocacy of famous ocean-ographer Jacques Cousteau, were like-minded on the issue—Stephen embarked on a major campaign targeting, among others, Chile, Sweden, Germany, Belgium, the European Community, Italy, India and the USSR. Hawke provided the political heft to ultimately sway American support. In 1991, the parties to the Antarctic Treaty signed up to the *Protocol on Environmental Protection* (the Madrid Protocol). A milestone for the inaugural Ambassador for the Environment, it represented a high point for Australian environmental diplomacy and 'a pivotal moment' in global environmental conservation.[26]

While Stephen was focused on Antarctica, debates around the environment intensified at home and Australians were at odds on the issues at play. Disagreements emerged between the Commonwealth, states and territories, between and within political parties, and between farming and mining sectors, environmentalists and Indigenous communities. Although, despite striking differences in perspective, advocates and activists across industry and community sectors appeared united in their distrust of the government. Most disagreements centred on the tensions between environmental, economic and traditional Indigenous interests—like proposed mining at Coronation Hill, Northern Territory, which was set to compromise sacred Indigenous land in Kakadu National Park—exposing domestic political fault-lines[27] replicated in the international sphere. Stephen's positioning on Coronation Hill, which ultimately saw him propose the establishment of a new statutory decision-making authority on environmental issues, was construed to reflect his lack of confidence in, and putting him at odds with, the government he served.

Stephen's three-year appointment concluded slightly ahead of schedule in 1992 following his engagement by the British government to chair the second strand of peace talks in Northern Ireland. From that point the position of Australian environment ambassador transitioned from a political to a public service appointment, attracting career diplomats and seasoned policy-makers into the role. In many ways, the shift made sense. By the early 1990s, the all-consuming nature of the role alongside the need for policy and technical expertise, and networks across the proliferating system of international conferences, had become increasingly evident. With other high-profile roles to his name, it had become clear that Stephen was simply not able to devote the attention or provide the expertise that environment ambassador demanded.[28] The ability to navigate the complex legal frameworks and bureaucracies, while managing an array of drafting solutions, called for intellectual grunt over political gravitas. As one policy official confirmed, 'the appointment of a career diplomat reflects the evolving demands of the role and the status of global dialogue'.[29] Others suggest that the decision to move away from political appointees reflected the emerging trend for governments to manage the environment agenda, its surrounding narrative, and political consequences more closely.[30]

The evolving role of Australia's environment ambassador

Some 13 individuals have held the special ambassadorial appointment in the years since Ninian Stephen, including Penny Wensley, Stephen's immediate successor and one of Australia's most distinguished diplomats. Others have included seasoned climate policy specialist Howard Bamsey, career diplomat and trade specialist Jan Adams, now Secretary of DFAT, and well-known multilateralist Peter Woolcott, who later took on the post of Australian Public Service Commissioner. Kristin Tilley, appointed in 2022, brought expertise in climate change policy through her experience with the Commonwealth Department of Climate Change, Energy, the Environment and Water.

Tilley's appointment also saw the role renamed to Australia's Ambassador for Climate Change, reinforcing Australia's interests in addressing climate change as the driving political and diplomatic focus. In announcing the appointment of Tilley, the Albanese government signalled its desire 'to demonstrate to the world Australia's resolve to urgently step up the pace of action, and work alongside global partners, particularly in the Pacific, to tackle the climate crisis'.[31] The language and associated narrative reflects a return to the framing of the role under the ALP Rudd–Gillard governments between 2007 and 2014. It sits apart from the approach of the intervening Abbott–Turnbull–Morrison LNP governments (2014–22), which sought to downplay the climate change dimensions of the position.

To review three decades of Australia's engagement with global environmental concerns, including climate change, is to see the nation's longstanding diplomatic commitment to addressing these issues. At the same time, one might rightly ask whether and how Australia's environment ambassadors have delivered on the core purpose of their role. Despite early ambitions for leadership, Australia's environment ambassador has been associated with the nation's lagging global reputation on climate action in recent years.

Critiques of Australia's diplomatic engagement in key global climate diplomacy conferences routinely call Australia out as one of a few nations that appears to regularly undermine rather than advance outcomes on the global stage.[32] Pacific island leaders have been clear in voicing their frustration at Australia's continued failure to prioritise the environment within foreign and defence policy as well as through diplomatic engagements.[33] Australian diplomats themselves have voiced concerns about Australia's approach. In a recent interview on Australia's approach to climate diplomacy, former environment ambassador and global climate policy expert Howard Bamsey noted that others 'had different things in mind when we came to a negotiating room. They wanted to demonstrate that they were meeting the needs of the vulnerable and the poor. Our [Australia's] approach was very cold and analytical ...'.[34] He recalled, 'someone once said to me that Australian interventions in the UN climate convention were scary, because there was no emotion ...'. Essentially, it was an approach that reflected the 'pragmatic and analytical approach that we brought' to the role.[35]

Table 1: Environment ambassadors and their terms of office

Position	Name	Term	Prime Minister*
Ambassador for the Environment	Sir Ninian Stephen	1989–92	Hawke (ALP)
Ambassador for the Environment	Penelope Wensley	1992–Jan 1996	Keating (ALP)
Ambassador for the Environment	Howard Bamsey	Jan 1996–Sept 1997	Howard (LNP)
Ambassador for the Environment	Meg McDonald	Sept 1997–Nov 1998	Howard (LNP)
Ambassador for the Environment	Ralph Hillman	Nov 1998–Mar 2002	Howard (LNP)
Ambassador for the Environment	Christopher Langman	Mar 2002–Feb 2004	Howard (LNP)
Ambassador for the Environment	Justin Brown	Oct 2004–Jan 2005	Howard (LNP)
Ambassador for the Environment	Jan Adams	Jan 2005–2007	Howard (LNP)
Ambassador for Climate Change	Jan Adams	2007–Feb 2009	Rudd (ALP)
Ambassador for Climate Change	Louise Hand	Feb 2009–May 2012	Rudd (ALP)
Ambassador for Climate Change	Justin Lee	May 2012–Nov 2014	Gillard (ALP)
Ambassador for the Environment	Peter Woollcott	2014–16	Abbott (LNP)
Ambassador for the Environment	Patrick Suckling	2016–19	Turnbull (LNP)
Ambassador for the Environment	Jamie Isbister	2019–22	Morrison (LNP)
Ambassador for Climate Change	Kristin Tilley	2022–	Albanese (ALP)

Source: Author
* At the time of appointment

The critiques of Australia's approach are not simply about style; they are also about substance. In the lead-up to the 2021 UN Climate Conference in Glasgow (COP26), a group of former diplomats warned that Australia's 'inertia' on climate change commitments 'undermines our credibility as a regional partner' and 'our reliability in the minds of our strategic allies'.[36] In their open letter to the Morrison government, the Diplomats for Climate Action Now pointed to the fact that interests beyond the national interest were at stake, noting that, 'The challenges of climate change are matters of public importance which we believe go beyond politics; and acting on climate change now is our ethical and moral responsibility towards future generations'.[37]

While the tone of Australia's rhetoric on climate action may have taken a more positive turn under the Albanese government, some observers remain sceptical about the rate and pace of practical change. Having observed Australia's participation in the 2022 UN Climate Conference in Cairo (COP27), Pacific advocate Joseph Sikulu made this point: 'What we know at the moment is in our region, Australia still isn't stepping up to where they need to be'.[38]

At home, Australian political debate on climate change remains a notoriously fractious space with deep political, industry and community fault-lines dividing discourse.[39] As David Fickling describes, climate change is the issue that has 'made and broken Australian governments for more than a decade'.[40] In keeping with that sentiment, it proved to be the defining issue for the 2022 federal election, with many ordinary Australians seeking, at that point in time, greater policy ambition from their political leaders. Indeed, 'concern about the climate crisis was the No 1 issue that prompted Australians to switch their vote to an independent candidate at this year's federal election'.[41] In contrast to the early days of Ninian Stephen's appointment, Australia's environment ambassadors have been largely invisible in the intensely divisive public domestic debates of recent years.

The recent push for change mobilised through advocacy and fundraising platforms such as Climate 200 saw a wave of new and independent 'teal' candidates—all with climate action as a core commitment—successfully elected to the 47th federal Parliament.[42] Displacing largely moderate conservatives, the combined success of the new 'teal' and established 'green' candidates essentially represented the 'fracturing [of] the voting blocs that have given Labor and the long-standing Liberal-National coalition a duopoly of power since World War II'.[43] Already, over fifteen months into their term, the influence of the progressive climate-focused candidates has had impact, with the Albanese government agreeing to more ambitious national climate targets, including on emissions reduction. In June 2022, Prime Minister Albanese and Chris Bowen, Minister for Climate Change and Energy, officially updated the UN on Australia's new emissions reduction target to achieve 43 per cent below 2005 levels by 2030; a position that will, among other things, be advocated by the nation's new Ambassador for Climate Change.

Navigating competing interests

Ninian Stephen laid an important foundation for subsequent Australian environment ambassadors, role-modelling active and constructive engagement in the global agenda. Many aspects of the role have remained intact in the decades since. The broad terms of reference—publicly set out with each appointment—have remained relatively unchanged. Official announcements refer to the ambassador's primary focus being the promotion of 'Australia's national interests and policies on global environmental issues overseas and in Australia, representing the government at international conferences and negotiations on the environment and providing policy advice to government on global environment issues'.[44] Nonetheless, the demands of the role have changed significantly over time. For example, the proliferation of substantive issues, the prominent role of scientific evidence and increasingly technical nature of environmental negotiations alongside the involvement of non-traditional nonstate actors, to name a few, have complicated the domestic and international environmental landscapes. Interestingly, as one confidential source noted, the Ambassador for Climate Change under the Albanese government is no longer the head of climate negotiations—but is instead charged with representing and advocating Australia's interests with high-level counterparts on the global stage.[45]

When reviewing the role and performance of Australia's environment ambassadors from Stephen onwards, three core features emerge. The first of these relates to commitment to the pursuit of global cooperation underpinning necessary action on climate change. Multilateral diplomacy is at the centre of this commitment and Australia's environment ambassadors have 'played a major role in multilateral climate negotiations, international forums and leaders' dialogues' for three decades,[46] from the development of the landmark 1994 UN Framework Convention on Climate Change (UNFCCC) through to agreement to the 2018 Katowice Rulebook. But the diplomatic role has been neither easy nor uncomplicated. Peter Woolcott argues that such imperfection is inherent in the international environmental regime. 'Not only is the engineering obsolete, the decision-making machinery is cumbersome.'[47] With some 196 Parties to the Convention taking decisions by consensus any progress tends to be excruciatingly slow, usually resulting in 'lowest common denominator outcomes'.[48]

Additionally, Australia's positioning on key points of global environmental negotiation has been routinely out of step with international consensus. For example, at the 1995 Berlin Conference on Global Warming, Australia was described as 'almost alone' in resisting a binding emissions framework, while at the same time seeking to ensure developing countries took on some of the emissions burden. It was a position that came at a cost. Australia's environment ambassador, Penny Wensley, was heavily criticised at the time for 'blocking effective strategy for limiting greenhouse emissions'.[49] Wensley's arguments ultimately set the scene for differentiated national commitments, which have since become an accepted feature of the climate negotiations framework. While the ethics of Australia's approach may be open to criticism,[50] in narrow terms Australia's diplomacy has achieved desired results in advancing the national interest. As one source observed, 'it was a far better strategy [for Australia] to be inside the tent as an active participant, than outside looking in',[51] a familiar refrain for Australian environmental diplomacy. Bamsey and Rowley suggest this is the value of active diplomacy whereby, 'Australia could defend its position, but only if it is well and truly on the front foot in the climate negotiations, actively engaged in a constructive fashion'.[52]

Not everyone agrees with Bamsey's reflection of constructive diplomacy. Lorraine Elliott argues that Australia's approach indicates a fundamental 'distrust of multilateral institutions and cooperation, reminiscent of a Realist conception of global politics'.[53]

This leads to the second and more recent feature of Australia's performance: the primacy of domestic politics in setting national interests. Australia's early position on global warming and emissions reductions, as pursued by Wensley and others, has been consistently centred on the nation's distinctive economic circumstances, arising in particular from high dependence on farming and extractive industries. There are no surprises here. Representing one of the world's biggest fossil fuel producers and exporters with 'an important stake in both when and how the world pursues emissions reductions',[54] Australian diplomats actively advanced these interests on the global stage. Again, they were at times unpopular. For example, the so-called Kyoto protocol's 'Australia rule', which ensured Australia could incorporate land-clearing activities within its emissions reduction accounting framework, was seen by some as undermining the intent of the protocol. But gained through credible diplomatic engagement, it was nonetheless framed as a win by Australia's political leaders.

Critics suggest that Australia's environmental diplomacy has been cast through a narrow political lens shaped by domestic constituency interests. Marian Wilkinson[55] observes that, 'Ever since the Rio Earth Summit, Australia's climate policy under both Liberal and Labor Governments had followed one rigid rule, crudely called "No Regrets". It meant Australia would only reduce its greenhouse gas emissions if it didn't cost us'. The 'No Regrets' imperative took on greater prominence under the Liberal-National Coalition governments led by Abbott (2013–16), Turnbull (2015–18) and Morrison (2018–22) reflecting, as Wilkinson argues, the influence of powerful lobby groups on the nature, direction and effectiveness of Australia's diplomatic engagement. Suspicion of the international environmental movement resulted in the government's retreat from key global forums. Prime Minister Morrison's statement about 'negative globalism that coercively seeks to impose a mandate from an often ill-defined borderless global community',[56] a tacit reference to global climate conferences, reinforced the sentiment of suspicion.

Amid this change, Australia's environment ambassadors found themselves operating on the margins of the climate negotiations while engaging, albeit quietly, with domestic stakeholders. As one former ambassador confidentially observed: even when Australia's global ambitions appear low, 'it is still important for Australia to be seen to be a credible partner on the international stage; managing the range of issues and concerns at home while also (re)building domestic confidence in the international process'.[57] Some argue that the domestic gaze of recent environment ambassadors was only focused towards and perhaps even captured by certain influential domestic actors and their interests.[58] While that may be so, it is also true that the range and potential impact of influential domestic stakeholders is expanding. It is also clear that targeted engagement of key corporate, industry (agricultural and mining), academic and community stakeholders has been a priority of recent environment ambassadors, and that Australia's engagement in international forums has been accompanied by more regular and reasonably open civil society consultation processes.

Some key stakeholders—notably Australia's Indigenous communities—remain largely absent from the conversations. Ninian Stephen spoke about the significant place that Indigenous knowledge and culture offered to conversations about the environment. Addressing an Engineering Conference in 1991, he called for a change in the psyche of the nation from the heroic—characterised by the desire to conquer nature—to an approach more aligned to that of Australia's Indigenous peoples in being 'wholly sensitive to nature'.[59] Some 30 years later, while he held the ambassadorial appointment, Patrick

Suckling drew on similar themes to suggest that Australia's national psyche was 'deeply anchored by our relationship with our environment ... apparent through the song-lines and dreamtime of our first peoples navigating complex cultural and geographic pathways across our great Southern Land'.[60] Yet, in reality, the continued exclusion of Indigenous communities from key dialogues and sanctioned destruction of sacred Indigenous cultural sites for the benefit of commercial gain[61] suggests that Suckling's rhetoric, though well intentioned, was more rhetorical flourish than substance.

Finally, a third feature of Australia's climate diplomacy relates to the significance of Pacific interests. Environment ambassadors have had to locate Australia's position on the environment vis-à-vis Pacific interests over the decades. The 1995 Berlin Conference brought the vulnerabilities of small island nations 'hit hardest by the forces of climate change' to the fore of global diplomacy. Calling for a global response, one Solomon Islands diplomat called for the UN members 'to save our islands before we drown'.[62] Drawing on the language of the Pacific island counterparts, Australia's Ambassador for the Environment at the time, Penny Wensley, also described Australia at the same meeting as 'vulnerable' based on the economic impacts of climate action. Australia's resort to the language of vulnerability coupled with calls for Pacific island nations to share the burden of climate action drew the ire of her Pacific counterparts. Pene Lefale, South Pacific Coordinator of the Climate Action Network, called Australia out for 'an act of betrayal against the Pacific region and the Pacific Forum' of which it was a member.[63]

While Australia's political leaders have continued to dismiss Pacific island concerns about global warming, even after announcing their Pacific Step Up in 2018, environment ambassadors have engaged more thoughtfully with the concerns of regional counterparts. One former ambassador spoke confidentially about the challenges:

And for [Pacific island nations] climate change is seen as one of their top security priorities, and it's the biggest bugbear in the relationship with Australia. They are frustrated with Australia's position on the issue, and for that reason I'm committed to maintaining strong dialogue. I can't necessarily change Australia's position on the matter, but I can explain the challenges that we face, and I can listen to their concerns. I also work closely with the Small Island Developing States (SIDS)—which of course includes Pacific island nations because we have to continue to build bridges and maintain dialogue.[64]

Conclusion

Stephen's appointment as Ambassador for the Environment was reflective of the nation's slow turn, pushed ahead through the Whitlam years, towards a new internationalist era. The environment, recognised as a new frontier in international relations,[65] was increasingly at the centre of global diplomacy and demanded attention and expertise. At the time, Australia was at the forefront of global diplomatic practice in appointing the first-ever Ambassador for the Environment, with the intent of building influence in the new frontiers of global environmental policy. Ninian Stephen brought gravitas and visibility to Australia's environmental interests on the international stage, while also advocating for their place at home. His success in advancing environmental and national interests, particularly in relation to the Antarctic, were notable. When he concluded his term in 1992, the position was demoted to a more conventional diplomatic appointment held by senior public servants and career diplomats, but it remained caught up in an intensely political and complex web of interests.

Australia's ability to wield influence as a leader of global environmental and climate policy diminished in the years following Stephen. However, this is not a reflection on the skill and ability of those holding the appointment, for they represent rather than define the policy interests of the nation. It is more a reflection of the narrow casting of Australia's national interests, the dominance of a core set of domestic economic concerns, and the politically charged nature of the debates. Working across an imperfect global system to address competing interests and priorities, Australia's global ambassadors have nonetheless persisted to secure Australia's place in global negotiations, to make constructive contributions to the substance of debate and to listen and work cooperatively with regional counterparts where possible.

Drawing on the experiences of those who have held the appointment, it becomes clear that the environment ambassador sometimes has the benefit of forging outcomes in uncharted territory, where the potential for transformational change exists. Such was the experience of Stephen in taking forward Australia's ambitions for the Antarctic. At other times—as was the case for Wensley and Bamsey, the environment ambassador has worked skilfully to reconcile competing domestic and international interests, holding fast to national interest, while keeping a stake in the negotiations and not standing in the way of a larger outcome.

For outside observers, the claim made by the title of this chapter— that to be appointed an Ambassador for the Environment is to be placed in an 'unenviable role'—holds up. But those who have held it might argue otherwise. To be an Ambassador for the Environment and Climate is to be engaged in a unique facet of Australian diplomacy. It is a role that tests the diplomatic skill and capacity of its incumbent simultaneously in multiple arenas: global, regional, domestic; and across policy domains. Notwithstanding Australia's lagging climate policy over recent decades, the role of environment and/or climate change ambassador continues to offer value. In the main, the role has reflected and advanced Australia's overall commitment to participate in global multilateral dialogue while bringing important regional and domestic audiences into the conversation.

There remains significant opportunity for Australia's Ambassador for Climate Change to listen to, learn from and reflect a greater diversity of voice—including Indigenous and Pacific voices—which have been too distant and too often dismissed, and yet remain critical to climate solutions. However, the different experiences of Australia's environment and climate change ambassadors to date—taken individually and together—illuminate at the very least some potential to work as agents of change, set at the pace of radical incrementalism within those slow-moving structures and processes of international climate diplomacy. Drawing on the compass points of diplomacy, their role to navigate the multiplicity of interests and wield influence across diverse stakeholders and deliver better global needs while not compromising on national interests has become ever-more urgent.

Notes

1　B Stannard, 'The Ambassador for Common Sense', *The Bulletin*, 27 February 1990.

2　N Stephen, Interview, C-SPAN, 3 December 1989.

3　R Hawke, 'Regarding the Appointment of Sir Ninian Stephen as Ambassador for the Environment', Press Release, 20 July 1989.

4　Ibid.

5　P Varghese, 'Parting Reflections', Secretary's Speech to the IPAA, Canberra, 9 June 2016.

6　S Hoffman, 'A New World and its Troubles', *Foreign Affairs*, vol. 69, no. 4, 1990, pp. 115–22.

7　A Burnett, 'Defence of the Environment: The New Issue in International Relations', *The Australian Quarterly*, vol. 61, no. 4, 1989, pp. 428–38.

8　Burnett, 'Defence of the Environment'; P Ayres, *Fortunate Voyager: The Worlds of Ninian Stephen*, Melbourne University Press, Melbourne, 2013.

9　Confidential interviews with officials, August 2020–January 2023.

10　Ayres, *Fortunate Voyager*.

11　G Evans, 'Australia's Foreign Policy and the Environment', *The Roundtable*, vol. 79, no. 315, 1990, pp. 297–305.

12　H Bull, *The Anarchical Society: A Study of Order in World Politics*, 4th ed, Bloomsbury, London, 2012.

13　G Evans, 'Australia's Place in the World: The Dynamics of Foreign Policy Decision-Making', Address to ANU Strategic and Defence Studies Centre Bicentennial Conference, *Australia and the World: Prologue and Prospects*, Canberra, 6 December 1988.

14　Confidential interviews with officials, August 2020–January 2023.

15　R Dunn, 'Hawke Environment Statement Leaves Conservationists Fuming', *Australian Financial Review*, 21 July 1989.

16　Ibid.

17　P Bailey, 'All Praise for Our Green Envoy', *Sydney Morning Herald*, 22 July 1989.

18　Ibid.

19　H Bamsey, 'Climate Change and Australia', *Australia in the World* podcast, Episode 63, 16 December 2020.

20 P Flood, *Dancing with Warriors: A Diplomatic Memoir*, Arcadia, North Melbourne, 2011, p. 146.

21 Confidential interview.

22 M Secombe, 'Hawke Backed in Bid to Gain Ecology-Industry Harmony', *Sydney Morning Herald*, 2 December 1989.

23 Ayres, *Fortunate Voyager*.

24 L Goldsworthy, 'Audacious Visions for the Antarctic: The Unexpected Life of an Activist', *Griffith Review*, vol. 77, 2022, p. 77.

25 A Gyngell, *Fear of Abandonment: Australia in the World Since 1942*, 2nd ed., La Trobe University Press, Carlton, 2021, p. 321.

26 Goldsworthy, 'Audacious Visions for the Antarctic', p. 77.

27 C Hamilton, 'Mining in Kakadu: Lessons from Coronation Hill', Discussion Paper No. 9, Australia Institute, July 1996.

28 Ayres, *Fortunate Voyager*.

29 Confidential interviews with officials, August 2020–January 2023.

30 Ibid.

31 Department of Climate Change, Energy, the Environment and Water, 'New Ambassador for Climate Change', Media Release, 9 November 2022.

32 M Robinson, Barbara Ward Lecture, Delivered to the International Institute for Economics and Development, London, 11 December 2006. See also Mary Robinson, *Climate Justice: A Man-Made Problem with a Feminist Solution*, Bloomsbury, London, 2019, p. 8.

33 M McDonald, 'Highly Touted UN Climate Summit Failed to Deliver and Scott Morrison Failed to Show Up', *The Conversation*, 24 September 2019; K Lyons, 'Torres Strait Islanders Ask UN to Hold Australia to Account on Climate Human Rights Abuses', *The Conversation*, 27 May 2019; W Morgan, 'Pacific Pariah: How Australia's Love of Coal has Left it Out in the Diplomatic Cold', *The Conversation*, 7 September 2016.

34 Bamsey, 'Climate Change and Australia'.

35 Ibid.

36 M Hunt, 'Former Diplomats Challenge Australian Government on Climate Change Inaction', *Global Government Forum*, 30 September 2021.

37 R Nath, 'COP27: Australia's Level of Commitment Disappointing Say Pacific NGOs', *RNZ*, 15 November, 2022.

38 Ibid.

39 M Beeson and M McDonald, 'The Politics of Climate Change in Australia', *Australian Journal of Politics and History*, vol. 73, no. 3, 2013.

40 D Fickling, 'How Climate is Splintering Australia's Political Parties', *Washington Post*, 16 May 2022.

41 A Morton and K Murphy, 'Climate Concern the Main Reason Voters Swung to Independents at Federal Election, Study Finds', *The Guardian*, 28 November 2022.

42 A Nethery, 'The Big Teal Steal: Independent Candidates Rock the Liberal Vote', *The Conversation*, 21 May 2022.

43 Ibid.

44 A Downer, 'Diplomatic Appointment: Ambassador for the Environment', Press Release, 22 September 1997; A Downer, 'Diplomatic Appointment: Ambassador for the Environment', Press Release, 18 November 1998; A Downer, 'Diplomatic Appointment: Ambassador for the Environment, Press Release', 6 February 2002; A Downer, 'Diplomatic Appointment: Ambassador for the Environment', Press Release, 6 February 2004; J Bishop, 'Ambassador for the Environment', Media Release 29 February, 2016.

45 Confidential interviews with officials, August 2020–January 2023.

46 H Bamsey and K Rowley, 'Australia and Climate Change Negotiations: At the Table or on the Menu?', Lowy Institute Paper, 25 March 2015.

47 P Woolcott, 'The Multilateral System and the Environment', Speech to the University of Queensland, Brisbane, 2015.

48 Ibid.

49 A McCathie, 'Australia Roasted over Gas Emissions', *Sydney Morning Herald*, 31 March 1995.

50 M McDonald, 'Fair Weather Friend? Ethics and Australia's Approach to Global Climate Change', *Australian Journal of Politics and History*, vol. 51, no. 2, 2005, pp. 216–34.

51 Confidential interview, 2020.

52 Bamsey and Rowley, 'Australia and Climate Change Negotiations'.

53 L Elliott, 'Environmental Politics', in M Hanson and W Tow (eds), *International Relations in the New Century: An Australian Perspective*, Oxford University Press, Melbourne, 2001, p. 248.

54 Bamsey and Rowley, 'Australia and Climate Change Negotiations'.

55 Marian Wilkinson, *The Carbon Club*, Allen & Unwin, Sydney, 2020, p. 12.

56 S Morrison, Lowy Lecture, Sydney, 4 October 2019.

57 Confidential interview, 2022.

58 McDonald, 'Fair Weather Friend?'; Wilkinson, *The Carbon Club*.

59 N Stephen, 'Environment in Crisis—Engineering: From Heroic Conquest to Integrated Solutions', Speech to National Engineering Conference, Hobart, 1991.

60 P Suckling, 'Australia and the Paris Agreement', Speech to the Climate Leadership Conference, Sydney, 2018.

61 Rio Tinto's lawful blasting of the Aboriginal heritage sites at Juukan Gorge, Western Australia, in May 2020 in pursuit of a $135 million iron ore project demonstrated the deep and ongoing disconnect between the interests, influence and voice of Australian Indigenous communities, powerful mining entities and government on matters of environmental protection. See: P Ker, 'The

Inside Story of How Juukan Gorge Was Lost', *Australian Financial Review*, 12 December 2020; L Allan and C Wahlquist, 'A Year on from the Juukan Gorge Destruction Aboriginal Heritage Sites Remain Unprotected', *The Guardian*, 24 May 2021.

62 McCathie, 'Australia Roasted over Gas Emissions'.

63 Ibid.

64 Confidential interviews with officials, August 2020–January 2023.

65 M Kirby and B Huf, 'Enter the Internationalist: Whitlam on the World Stage', *Griffith Review*, vol. 77, August 2022, pp. 188–99; Burnett, 'Defence of the Environment'.

PACIFIC PERSPECTIVES: REGIONAL COOPERATION IN A WARMING WORLD?

Prospects for Australia-Pacific climate diplomacy

Wesley Morgan, George Carter and Fulori Manoa

PACIFIC ISLAND COUNTRIES tend to be framed as small, isolated and uniquely vulnerable developing countries. Furthermore, in Australia at least, Pacific island states are very often described as relatively powerless actors within Australia's sphere of influence. In reality, Pacific island countries are significant players on the international stage in their own right. They form an important bloc at the United Nations and collectively have sovereign rights across a large swathe of the Earth's surface. Island leaders have also successfully pursued their interests in global politics, and nowhere is this more evident than in relation to climate change.

This chapter considers the role that Pacific island states have played in multilateral climate diplomacy. It explains that Pacific states have had a disproportionate influence in United Nations climate negotiations. By working together and with other states in a series of diplomatic blocs, and leveraging their unique moral authority, they have shaped new rules intended to reduce emissions. The diplomatic leadership of Pacific island countries was crucially important for achieving the 2015 Paris Agreement, which remains the central mechanism for countries to work together to avoid cataclysmic changes to our planet's climate system.

In stark contrast to Pacific island nations, Australia has tended to equate national interests with its fossil fuel industry and has sought to avoid obligations to reduce greenhouse gas emissions even while expanding coal and gas exports. Australia has played a limited role in global efforts to tackle climate change, and has at times acted as a brake on progress in the UN climate negotiations. Divergent approaches to climate change have proved a lasting challenge for regional cooperation between Australia and Pacific island states.

Driven by its own security concerns—and particularly strategic anxieties about China's growing presence in the region—Australia launched the Pacific Step-Up strategy in 2018, intended to shore up influence and to integrate Pacific island states into Australian economic and security institutions. However, climate policy has continued to undermine relations. Island leaders have repeatedly declared climate change the 'single greatest threat' to security in the region, and look to Australia to take action to reduce emissions and to help drive global climate ambition.

As this chapter explains, the election of a Labor government in mid-2022 improved prospects for regional collaboration on climate change. The new government strengthened Australia's target to cut emissions by 2030, and Prime Minister Anthony Albanese joined island leaders to declare a Pacific Climate Emergency. Australia also announced plans to co-host a UN climate summit with Pacific nations in 2026, a move welcomed by island leaders. Working with Pacific island countries to press for global climate action could help to cement Australia's place as part of the Pacific family. First, however, Pacific leaders expect the Australian government to show it is taking the climate crisis seriously, and responding accordingly.

Locating the Blue Pacific: Regionalism and collective diplomacy in the Pacific islands

Before exploring the role Pacific island states have played in global efforts to tackle the climate crisis, and prospects for collaboration with Australia on climate diplomacy, it is important to consider the unique forms of collective diplomacy that Pacific island nations have developed to pursue their interests. Regionalism in the Pacific is marked by a distinct form of diplomacy. As island states gained independence and navigated their place in international affairs, they developed a form of collective diplomacy built on the norms and protocols of a 'Pacific way'. Pacific leaders asserted a shared regional identity linked with longstanding cultural connections to the ocean.[1] Dubbed 'indigenous regionalism', this form of cooperation was embraced by island leaders as a means to assert shared interests when faced with common challenges like nuclear testing in the Pacific, management of ocean resources, and climate change.[2]

For its part, Australia has had a somewhat ambiguous relationship with Pacific regionalism. The largest and most powerful country in the region, Australia has tended to be referred to as a 'big brother' to Pacific island countries—part of the family by geography and history, but apart by wealth and national identity. Perennially concerned that a major power with interests inimical to its own might establish a presence in the southwest Pacific, Australia has tended to engage with island states driven by a strategic imperative to maintain influence with island governments, and it is through this prism that Australia has supported regional diplomatic processes.

Despite differences in identity, Australia has worked with New Zealand and 14 Pacific island states to develop shared regional institutions, most notably the Pacific Islands Forum. It is through the auspices of the Forum, established in 1971 as the South Pacific Forum, that Australia has worked with island states to pursue shared positions, with some notable successes, including recognition of exclusive economic zones under the UN Law of the Sea treaty, a ban on driftnet fishing in the South Pacific, shared management of fisheries and maritime areas, negotiation of the South Pacific Nuclear Free Zone Treaty, and a successful campaign to have New Caledonia added to the UN's list of non-self-governing territories.[3]

The Forum is organised around an annual meeting between island leaders and their counterparts from Australia and New Zealand. It is the key decision-making body for regional cooperation and collective diplomacy in the Pacific. The annual meeting brings together Pacific leaders to discuss a wide range of shared challenges, such as security, trade and economic development. The Forum has 18 members, including Australia, New Zealand, 14 independent Pacific island states and two French territories, New Caledonia and French Polynesia. Pacific island leaders engage collectively with nations from outside the region as well, and the annual Forum leaders' meeting is followed by a Post-Forum Dialogue, which involves partner countries, including the United States, China, Japan, the European Union, the United Kingdom and France.

Since 2017, Pacific island leaders have developed a new shared narrative for their maritime region, which they have labelled the 'Blue Pacific'. Subverting the idea that Pacific nations are small, isolated and vulnerable, island governments have asserted a contemporary identity as 'large ocean states', with sovereign rights across a large part of the Earth. Drawing on pre-colonial relationships between island societies, Pacific leaders have committed to working together as a 'maritime continent'. Through the Pacific Islands Forum, island leaders have endorsed 'a long-term foreign policy commitment to act as one Blue Continent'.[4] In 2022, Forum leaders formally endorsed a shared '2050 strategy for the Blue Pacific Continent'.[5] As one of the most culturally and linguistically diverse regions on Earth, the Blue Pacific is home to hundreds of societies, spread across thousands of islands, in a vast expanse of ocean (see Figure 1).

A long fight for survival: Pacific islands in the global climate regime

For decades, Pacific island countries have led global efforts to tackle climate change. Quick to identify the devastating ramifications of global warming for island ecosystems and societies, Pacific leaders responded by developing innovative diplomatic strategies to accelerate global efforts to reduce greenhouse gas emissions. These strategies have been successful in important ways, and have helped secure shared rules for all countries to cut emissions.

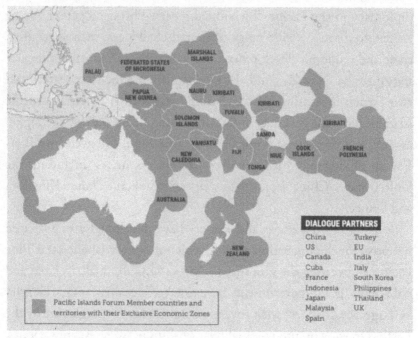

Figure 1: Locating the Blue Pacific[6]

In the late 1980s, a scientific consensus emerged that global warming presented a unique challenge to Pacific island countries. Sea level rise linked with global warming was seen as a particular threat to low-lying atoll states in the region. In 1991, leaders at the South Pacific Forum declared 'the cultural, economic and physical survival of Pacific nations is at great risk', and called for urgent international action through the conclusion of a global convention with commitments to reduce emissions of greenhouse gases.[7] Subsequently, Pacific island states took shared negotiating positions to global climate talks at the UN. The UN Framework Convention on Climate Change (UNFCCC) was established in 1992, and Pacific leaders and diplomats proved to be pivotal players in negotiations held under the convention. Working together, they were able to shape the multilateral response to the existential, planetary-scale, challenge.

Five strategies have proved important for the disproportionate influence that Pacific island states have had in the context of the UN climate negotiations. First, Pacific island states have been able to aggregate their positions to act as a coordinated bloc of countries. In 1990, Pacific island countries formed a diplomatic alliance with island nations in the Caribbean and the Indian Ocean to pursue shared interests in the UN climate talks. This Alliance of Small Island States (AOSIS) became a particularly influential negotiating coalition, but Pacific states also work through other UNFCCC negotiating coalitions as well.[8] Second, Pacific island states have leveraged their moral authority, as countries that are uniquely vulnerable to the impacts of climate change. They have deployed their own vulnerability as a form of ideational power to frame 'appropriate' responses to global warming, and pressure other states to take more ambitious action to reduce emissions. Third, Pacific island states have recruited independent expertise—individuals and non-state organisations that have scientific, legal and diplomatic skills relevant to the unique context of the UN climate regime—to strengthen their climate diplomacy. Fourth, Pacific island states have earned a reputation for 'sticking to the science' by consistently calling for global climate action that is necessary to avoid climate harm, and to ensure the survival of vulnerable islands and ecosystems. Finally, Pacific island states have formed coalitions between and across traditional negotiating blocs at the UN, and have been prepared to collaborate with major powers at key points in the UN climate negotiations.

The first draft of the 1997 Kyoto Protocol—an agreement negotiated under the UNFCCC which required wealthy nations to reduce greenhouse gas emissions—was put forward by Nauru on behalf of the AOSIS.[9] While the final text of the Kyoto Protocol was not what island states had hoped for, their proposal formed a basis for negotiations and made far less ambitious proposals politically unacceptable.

Most significantly, Pacific island nations were crucial in negotiating a successor to the Kyoto Protocol in Paris in 2015. By this time UN climate talks were stalled by arguments between wealthy nations and developing countries about who was responsible for addressing climate change, and how much support should be provided to help poorer nations to deal with its impacts. In the months leading up to the Paris climate summit, the Marshall Islands Foreign Minister at the time, Tony de Brum, quietly coordinated a coalition of countries from across these traditional negotiating divides at the UN. This proved to be genius strategy. De Brum convened a core group of foreign ministers from both developed and developing countries who met at least three times in 2015, including in the side lines of the UN General Assembly in New York, to arrive at shared positions for a new global agreement. Worried their plans would be compromised by others, they met in secret and handwrote their most sensitive communications. During the talks in Paris, this core group of countries was joined by other nations from Africa and the Caribbean, and then by the EU and the US as well. Halfway through two weeks of negotiations in Paris, de Brum formally announced this new 'High Ambition Coalition', and it proved to be vital for securing the first truly global climate agreement.[10]

The diplomacy of Pacific island countries shaped the final design of the Paris Agreement, especially the agreement's ultimate goal of limiting warming to 1.5°C above the long-term average. The slogan that de Brum and other Pacific island negotiators took to the Paris talks was '1.5 to stay alive'. This was no arbitrary figure. Scientific assessments have clarified 1.5°C warming is a key threshold for the survival of vulnerable Pacific island states and the ecosystems they depend on, such as coral reefs.[11] To achieve the goal of limiting warming to 1.5°C, the Paris Agreement requires all countries to set national targets to cut emissions and to strengthen them by setting new, more ambitious, targets every five years. It is by this means that countries intend to work together to shift to a net-zero emissions global economy by the second half of this century.

The Paris Agreement represented a real breakthrough. Three decades after a global scientific consensus had emerged on the issue, countries finally had a truly global agreement to tackle greenhouse gas emissions. And there is no doubt that Pacific island countries were key to securing the agreement. When Tony de Brum walked to the main plenary hall for the final negotiating session in Paris, he was flanked by EU Climate Commissioner Michel Canete and US Special Envoy for Climate Change Todd Stern. All three wore medallions on their lapels that had been fashioned from coconut leaves by women from the Marshall Islands delegation, to signal their membership of the High Ambition Coalition formed by de Brum. The leadership of Pacific island nations was widely recognised. When President Barack Obama met with Pacific island leaders in 2016, he noted 'we could not have gotten a Paris Agreement without the incredible efforts and hard work of island nations'.[12]

While Australia is the largest member of the Pacific Islands Forum, it was not a member of the High Ambition Coalition or part of the group's strategy to secure the Paris Agreement. Australian Foreign Minister Julie Bishop tried to join the High Ambition Coalition in Paris, but Tony de Brum explained membership would require more ambitious commitments to cut emissions. He told media 'we are delighted to learn of Australia's interest, and we look forward to hearing what more they might be able to do to join our coalition'. When Australia announced its first Paris Agreement target—to reduce emissions by 26 to 28 per cent below 2005 levels by 2030—de Brum argued that if the rest of the world followed Australia's lead, vulnerable nations such as his would disappear.[13] In April 2016, when members of the High Ambition Coalition met at a New York signing ceremony for the Paris Agreement, Australia was not invited.[14] As a major fossil fuel producer, Australia has had a much less ambitious approach to climate action than its Pacific island neighbours, and divergent approaches to climate change have proved a lasting challenge for regional cooperation between Australia and Pacific island states.

A persistent challenge: Climate change and regional diplomacy in the Pacific islands

There has been a dynamic nexus between collective diplomacy of Pacific island states at the regional level and collective diplomacy at the global level, including in the UN climate talks. Typically, shared positions have been aggregated at the regional level first, for example at the annual Pacific Islands Forum leaders' meeting, and then taken to the global stage—that is, to the UN General Assembly or the annual UNFCCC Conference of the Parties (COP) summits. Initially, Australia worked together with New Zealand and Pacific island states, as a Pacific regional bloc, to advocate for global climate action. From the late 1990s, however, Australia took a significantly less ambitious approach to climate action. Influenced by a powerful fossil fuel lobby, the Australian government decided that taking serious action to cut emissions was not in the country's best interests. The argument was that Australia was a fossil fuel-dependent economy, thus making it relatively more costly for the country to reduce emissions. In turn, a brutal assessment was made: rather than promote climate action, Australia would do what it could to avoid obligations to reduce emissions and instead focus on expanding its coal and gas exports. This assessment of Australia's perceived national interests—misguided as it was—then shaped Australia's approach to UN climate talks for decades.

Divergent approaches to the UN climate talks proved a persistent challenge for Australia's relations with Pacific island countries. Australia's 'go slow' approach to UN climate talks diluted Pacific regional diplomacy by denying island countries the chance to use the Pacific Islands Forum to press for shared climate goals. Repeatedly, Canberra has sought to exercise a veto over regional declarations put forward by Pacific island countries at key moments in the global climate discussion, including in the lead-up to three major climate summits: the 1997 Kyoto Protocol, the ill-fated 2009 Copenhagen conference and the 2015 Paris climate talks.

At the 1997 Pacific Islands Forum, held in the Cook Islands in the run-up to global negotiations in Kyoto, differences between Australia and Pacific island nations came to a head. Pacific countries were backing a proposal for the Kyoto conference, for a binding treaty to cut emissions, that had been developed by the AOSIS. At the Forum leaders' retreat, island leaders tried to persuade Australian Prime Minister John Howard to support their position. Discussions proved bitter and ran into overtime at the airport's VIP lounge in Rarotonga. Ultimately island leaders compromised. While the Forum communiqué urged parties to the UNFCCC to consider the AOSIS draft protocol, it also 'recognized that participants at the Kyoto Conference can be expected to adopt different approaches'.[15] In the aftermath, Cook Islands Prime Minister

Geoffrey Henry argued Australia's approach was a 'self-serving' attempt to protect 'its coal and energy intensive industries'.[16] Tuvalu Prime Minister Bikenibeu Paeniu told media 'Australia dominates us so much in this region ... For once we would have liked to get some respect'.[17] For his part, Howard dismissed concern that sea level rise could threaten the existence of island states as 'exaggerated' and 'apocalyptic'.[18] At the talks in Kyoto, Australian negotiators secured concessions that allowed Australia to *increase* emissions by 8 per cent by 2012. Moreover, by including land-clearing in the baseline year, Australia was able to meet its Kyoto target without making any significant change in domestic policy, and while expanding coal and gas exports.

When world leaders met in Copenhagen in 2009 to negotiate a successor to the Kyoto Protocol, which was due to expire in 2012, Pacific nations again pressed for an ambitious outcome. In the lead-up to the Copenhagen summit, they put forward a proposal (via the AOSIS) that would limit warming to well below 1.5°C and see countries collectively reduce emissions by 95 per cent by 2050.[19] That year, however, Australia hosted Pacific leaders in Cairns for the annual Pacific Islands Forum. At that meeting Australian Prime Minister Kevin Rudd convinced island leaders to sign up to Australia's preferred negotiating positions, in a Forum statement that called for an outcome in Copenhagen that would limit warming to 2°C and reduce emissions by at least 50 per cent by 2050.[20] As it turned out, when they went to Copenhagen, Pacific officials ignored the Forum statement and backed their own AOSIS targets. As talks broke down in Copenhagen, a frustrated Rudd told Tuvalu's lead climate negotiator he was being 'unhelpful and unproductive', while Tuvalu Prime Minister Apisai Ielemia complained Rudd was lobbying Pacific governments 'to probably water down our position on 1.5°C'.

Ahead of the 2015 Paris summit, Australia again attempted to exercise a veto power over Pacific climate diplomacy. In the months before the Paris talks, island leaders had made their climate positions quite clear, both at UN discussions in New York, and in a string of 'sub-regional' declarations.[21] All of these declarations called for a global climate treaty to limit global warming to 1.5°C above pre-industrial levels. This was a threshold Pacific island states consistently argued should not be crossed, because doing so would threaten the very existence of low-lying states such as Kiribati, Tuvalu and the Marshall Islands. Despite this, Australian Prime Minister Tony Abbott refused to back the position of island states, and the climate declaration issued at the 2015 Pacific Islands Forum failed to reference the 1.5°C temperature goal. In response, Kiribati President Anote Tong suggested Australia should leave the Forum altogether if it wasn't prepared to back the islands' positions in global climate negotiations.[22] Just days after the meeting, Abbott was caught on camera making jokes with his Immigration Minister, Peter Dutton, about the plight of Pacific people facing sea level rise.[23]

Repeated clashes on climate ambition reinforced a perceived rift between Australia and Pacific island states. From 2009, and partly in response to these differences on climate change, Pacific governments pursued collective diplomacy *outside* the auspices of the Pacific Islands Forum, collaborating at the regional level through the Pacific Islands Development Forum (PIDF)—a regional body established by Fiji, of which neither Australia nor New Zealand were members—and at the global level through the Pacific Small Island Developing States (PSIDS) grouping at the UN.[24] Regular meetings of Pacific island ambassadors to New York proved a key site for the development of common PSIDS positions on climate change.[25] For example, working together, the PSIDS grouping put forward a UN General Assembly resolution on 'Climate change and its possible security implications', which was passed unanimously in mid-2009. This was the first time the UN had passed a resolution establishing a direct link between climate change and international peace and security. Pacific island countries also lobbied the UN Security Council to recognise climate change as a key security threat.

By 2018, Australian policy-makers became increasingly interested in Pacific island states in the context of Australia's own security interests, particularly a growing concern about China's intentions in the region. However, differences on climate change threatened to undermine Australia's efforts to maintain influence with island governments.

Climate change and Australia's Pacific Step-Up

Australian engagement with Pacific island countries is driven above all by a strategic imperative to maintain political influence and deny the islands to other powers. Sometimes referred to as Australia's Monroe Doctrine, Canberra has a longstanding, but only periodically prioritised, policy of strategic denial that is aimed at limiting access to islands in the southwest Pacific by other potentially hostile states. In 2018, concerns about geostrategic competition in the region, which had ebbed at the end of the Cold War, were again front-of-mind. Australian policy-makers became especially concerned about the growing influence of a more powerful China. Most pointedly they worried that Beijing might leverage loans for infrastructure projects to establish a military base in the Pacific. Australian Prime Minister Malcolm Turnbull raised the alarm, explaining 'we would view with great concern the establishment of any foreign military bases in those Pacific island countries and neighbours of ours'.[26] These concerns underpinned a new foreign policy initiative— the Pacific Step-Up—which sought to integrate Pacific island countries into Australia's security institutions and reaffirm Australia's place as a security partner of choice for Pacific island countries. Hampered by a lack of action on climate change, however, the Pacific Step-Up quickly threatened to become a Pacific stumble.

When he came to power in mid-2018, Prime Minister Scott Morrison was enthusiastic about the Pacific Step-Up. In his first year as prime minister he visited Fiji (twice), Solomon Islands, Tuvalu and Vanuatu—a personal investment in the relationship with Pacific island countries unheard of from an Australian prime minister. He was, for the most part, warmly embraced by island leaders. But there remained one area where tensions remained high. When Morrison joined the Fijian Prime Minister Frank Bainimarama for a public dinner in Suva, Bainimarama was blunt: 'From where we are sitting,' he told Morrison, 'we cannot imagine how the interests of any single industry can be placed above the welfare of Pacific peoples [and] vulnerable people the world over'.[27] There was no getting beyond it, Australia was the world's largest coal exporter, and Pacific leaders understood climate change as a direct threat to their security. Tuvalu's Prime Minister Enele Sopoaga spelled it out: 'we cannot be regional partners under this step up initiative—genuine and durable partners—unless the government of Australia takes a more progressive response to climate change'.[28]

Pacific island countries remained adamant that climate change was the key threat to the region. At the 2018 Pacific Islands Forum, leaders issued a regional security declaration reaffirming climate change as the 'single greatest threat to the livelihoods, security and well-being of peoples of the Pacific'.[29] Compared with geostrategic competition between the US and China, Pacific leaders regarded the impacts of climate change—stronger cyclones, devastating floods, rising seas, dying reefs and ocean acidification—as more tangible and immediate threats. Fiji's military commander, Rear Admiral Viliame Naupoto, told the 2019 Shangri-La Security Dialogue in Singapore:

> I believe there are three major powers in competition in our region. There is the US ... there is China [and] the third competitor is climate change. Of the three, climate change is winning, and climate change exerts the most influence on countries in our part of the world. If there is any competition, it is with climate change.[30]

At the 2019 Pacific Islands Forum, held in Tuvalu, Morrison met with Pacific leaders in an open-air community hall on the atoll island of Funafuti. As they deliberated, they could see ocean waves pounding the reef out of one window, and calm waters of the lagoon out of the other. The threat posed by rising seas can't have been far from anyone's mind. Pacific leaders implored Morrison to support a regional declaration calling for urgent action on climate change. The ailing Tongan prime minister even shed tears. But Morrison ruled out language in the draft declaration that would be difficult for him at home, especially on emissions reduction and phasing out coal. He repeatedly reminded island leaders of Australia's financial support to Pacific countries and pointed out Australia's carbon emissions were dwarfed by those of China. Island leaders were incensed. The leaders' retreat became a bruising 12-hour-long stand-off which almost broke down altogether. There were again calls for Australia to be ousted from the Pacific Islands Forum. Leaders from Samoa and Fiji suggested China may be a preferable partner. Bainimarama told reporters, 'I thought Morrison was a good friend of mine, apparently not. The Chinese don't insult us. They don't go down and tell the world that we've given this much money to the Pacific islands. They don't do that. They're good people, definitely better than Morrison'.[31]

Frayed relations on climate policy cannot have helped Australian policy in the Pacific. For its part, China continued to seek closer relations, including new security arrangements, with Pacific island nations. Within weeks of the 2019 Forum leaders meeting in Tuvalu, the Solomon Islands government switched diplomatic relations from Taiwan to China. Solomon Islands Prime Minister Manasseh Sogavare argued relations with Beijing were a good opportunity to attract investment and development assistance, especially for infrastructure. However, the new relationship also included a security dimension. In April 2022, Solomon Islands signed a security deal with China. The text of the deal remained confidential, but if it was anything like a draft leaked online it contained ambiguous provisions allowing for a Chinese military and police presence, and for new port facilities for Chinese ship resupply. This rang alarm bells in Canberra, and in Washington. It changed the dynamic of a region that had traditionally aligned with the West. Penny Wong, who became Australian Foreign Minister in May 2022, described it as 'the biggest foreign policy failure in the Pacific since the Second World War'.[32] While Australia's lacklustre position on climate change was not the decisive factor in Solomon Islands' decisions to deepen relations with China, it was increasingly clear that Australia's domestic climate policies were complicating the pursuit of its strategic interests in the Pacific. A change of approach would be needed.

Prospects for Australia-Pacific climate diplomacy

The election of a Labor government in May 2022 saw a significant shift in Australia's approach to the Pacific with regard to climate change. The new government sought to assure Pacific leaders that it would make more ambitious cuts to emissions and explicitly linked climate action with the goal of cementing Australia's place as 'security partner of choice' for Pacific nations. Perhaps most significantly, Australia showed a willingness to work with island states to pursue collective climate diplomacy, announcing plans to co-host the annual UN climate talks with island governments.

Within days of being elected, Australia's new Foreign Minister, Penny Wong, delivered a speech at the Pacific Islands Forum Secretariat in Suva, Fiji, acknowledging Pacific island states had 'led the global debate' on climate change, while 'Australia has neglected its responsibility to act'.[33] She told island governments they had been 'crystal clear and consistent' that climate change was their key security threat, and said Australia would now stand 'shoulder to shoulder with our Pacific family' to address the climate crisis. At the 2022 Pacific Islands Forum, Prime Minister Anthony Albanese joined Pacific leaders to formally declare a Pacific Climate Emergency.

Pacific leaders were broadly welcoming of the Australian government's new approach. As Samoan Prime Minister Fiamē Naomi Mata'afa explained: 'with the new Australian government, the policy shift brings them closer into alignment with the Pacific's advocacy for climate change ... we feel this will strengthen the Pacific's position on climate change'.[34] At the 2022 Pacific Islands Forum, leaders 'welcomed the interest from Australia to host a UN Framework Convention on Climate Change Conference of the Parties in partnership with the Pacific'.[35]

In November 2022, Minister for Climate Change Chris Bowen announced Australia would bid to co-host the COP31 UN climate talks with Pacific island nations in 2026. In response, Germany and Switzerland withdrew tentative bids, leaving Australia and the Pacific in a strong position, vying only with Turkey as potential host. Holding the annual climate summit in the region would be a very big deal. It would be the largest diplomatic event Australia has ever held. A major city like Sydney or Melbourne would most likely host the main conference, as between 20 000 and 40 000 delegates would be expected to attend. Satellite events and pre-conference meetings would likely be held in Pacific nations. It would be an opportunity to send a message to the world that Australia is working with Pacific island countries to drive global climate action.

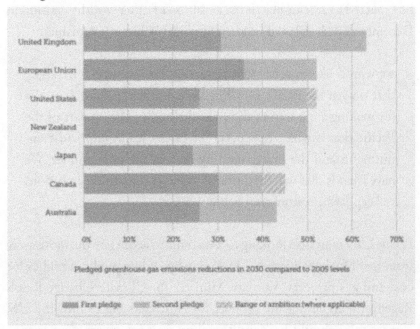

Figure 2: 2030 Emissions reduction targets under the Paris Agreement[36]

To work together successfully, however, Australia would need to show it is finally serious about tackling the climate crisis by making deeper cuts to emissions. While Pacific leaders welcomed Australia's new 2030 emissions target—to cut emissions by 43 per cent from 2005 levels—they clearly expected more. Bainimarama pointedly argued Albanese should 'go further for our family's shared future by aligning Australia's commitment to the 1.5-degree target'.[37] The Intergovernmental Panel on Climate Change (IPCC) is clear that if we are to have any chance of achieving the Paris Agreement goal of limiting warming to 1.5°C, *global* emissions must be halved by 2030.[38] The Climate Council of Australia explains that, to do its share of the global effort, a wealthy nation like Australia—with vast, untapped resources for renewable energy—should be aiming to reduce emissions by 75 per cent by 2030.[39]

Even with its strengthened 2030 target, Australia still has the least ambitious emissions reduction target in the developed world (see Figure 2). If Australia is to co-host the UN climate talks in 2026, it will be expected to at least match the ambition of other wealthy nations. In December 2022, Palau's President Surangel Whipps Jr explained

> we would like to see a 50% reduction [in emissions] by 2030, that is what the Pacific is calling for ... but we applaud Australia for making a big step in the right direction ... being part of the Pacific that is what we expect. We expect leadership and commitment, and the understanding that we are going under. We have islands that will disappear if we don't raise those ambitions to keep [temperature rise] below 1.5°C.[40]

Pacific leaders are also looking for Australia to accelerate the move away from fossil fuel production—including by ending public subsidies for coal and gas projects. Vanuatu Minister for Climate Change Ralph Regenvanu argues Pacific support for Australia's bid to host the UN climate talks should be 'conditional on no new government money being given to fossil fuels'.[41] Today, Australia is the world's third largest fossil fuel exporter, behind only Russia and Saudi Arabia. Australia is the world's largest exporter of coking coal (used to make steel); second largest exporter of thermal coal (used in coal-fired power stations to make electricity); and largest exporter of liquified gas.[42] Since 2005, even while Pacific nations have called for global action to cut emissions, Australia's fossil fuel exports have doubled.[43] Coal and gas exports are now Australia's biggest contribution to the climate crisis, and emissions from coal and gas burned in other countries are more than double Australia's domestic emissions.

Prime Minister Anthony Albanese argues that Australia has a once-in-a-generation opportunity to become a renewable energy super-power.[44] He is right. The global energy transition has fundamentally altered Australia's economic interests. Hundreds of nations, together representing more than 90 per cent of the global economy, have now committed to achieving net-zero emissions by mid-century. Key desti-nation markets for Australian coal and gas—including Japan, Korea, India and China—have set plans to achieve net-zero, effectively calling time on Australia's fossil fuel exports. Australia is, however, well placed to thrive in a world shifting towards net-zero emissions. Australia has world-class renewable energy resources and enviable reserves of miner-als needed for the electric vehicles, batteries and wind turbines of the future. A comparative advantage in renewable energy means Australia can competitively produce zero-carbon commodities including steel, aluminium, hydrogen and fertilisers. Co-hosting the UN climate talks with Pacific island nations would be a prime opportunity to signal Australia's shift from fossil fuel heavyweight to renewables superpower.

Conclusion

This chapter has explained that Pacific island countries are powerful actors on the international stage. In the decades following independ-ence, Pacific nations have developed regional strategies of collective diplomacy that have allowed them to influence global cooperation to tackle issues like climate change and ocean management. They are world leaders in climate diplomacy. Australia, by contrast, has dragged its feet on cutting emissions and has at times played a spoiler role in cli-mate change negotiations at the UN. This has undermined Australia's relations with Pacific island countries, and made it more difficult for Australia to pursue its strategic objectives in the region. For island nations that view climate change as their key security threat, Australia's reluctance to take action to reduce emissions clashes with its claim to be the security partner of choice for the Pacific.

In 2022, a newly elected Australian government committed to working with Pacific island nations to tackle the climate crisis, including by co-hosting a conference of the UN climate negotiations in 2026. Working together to accelerate global efforts to reduce emissions is key to security in the Pacific. The very survival of Pacific island nations is at stake. In the past Australia has refused to back the positions of island nations in the global climate negotiations and has on numerous occasions tried to water down statements on climate by the Pacific Islands Forum. To earn the trust of the rest of the region Australia will need to take meaningful action to cut emissions at home and to accelerate the shift away from fossil fuel production. These changes are inevitable, and moving faster from laggard to leader is in Australia's national interest. By co-hosting the UN climate talks with island nations, Australia could broker a new round of global ambition to cut emissions and cement its place as part of the Pacific family. But first Australia will need to show it is taking this crisis seriously.

Notes

1 For discussion see, W Morgan, 'Large Ocean States: Pacific Regionalism and Climate Security in a New Era of Geostrategic Competition', *East Asia*, vol. 39, no. 2, 2022.

2 For discussion see, G Fry, *Framing the Islands: Power and Diplomatic Agency in Pacific Regionalism*, ANU Press, Canberra, 2019.

3 See W Morgan, 'Oceans Apart? Considering the Indo-Pacific and the Blue Pacific', *Security Challenges*, vol. 16, no. 1, 2020.

4 Pacific Islands Forum, *48th Pacific Islands Forum, Apia, Samoa, 5–8 September 2017: Forum Communiqué*, 2017.

5 Pacific Islands Forum, *51st Pacific Islands Forum, Suva, Fiji, 11–14 July 2022: Forum Communiqué*, 2022.

6 Image source: W Morgan, S Bradshaw and A Dean, *A Fight for Survival: Tackling the Climate Crisis Is Key to Security in the Blue Pacific*, Climate Council, 2022.

7 South Pacific Forum, *22nd South Pacific Forum, Palikir, Pohnpei, Federated States of Micronesia, 29–30 July: Forum Communiqué*, 1991.

8 See G Carter, 'Pacific Island States and 30 years of Global Climate Change Negotiations', in C Klock, P Castro, F Weiler and L Blaxekjar (eds), *Coalitions in the Climate Change Negotiations*, Routledge, Abingdon, 2020.

9 See M Moses, 'The Role and Influence of the Alliance of Small Island States in UN Climate Change Negotiations', Public Lecture, Crawford School of Public Policy, Australian National University, 19 February 2013.

10 W Morgan, 'Ripple Effect: How Climate Inaction Jeopardises Our Pacific Standing', *Australian Foreign Affairs*, no. 12, July 2021.

11 W Steffen, W Rice, L Hughes and A Dean, *The Good, the Bad and the Ugly: Limiting Temperature Rise to 1.5°C*, Climate Council, 2018.

12 White House, 'Remarks by the President to Leaders from the Pacific Island Conference of Leaders and the International Union for the Conservation of Nature World Conservation Congress', 1 September 2016.

13 Pacific Beat, 'Marshall Islands Foreign Minister Tony de Brum Slams Australia's Proposed 2030 Carbon Emissions Targets', ABC Radio, 11 August 2015.

14 T Arup and A Morton, 'Australia Snubbed by "High Ambition" Group at Climate Talks in New York', *Sydney Morning Herald,* 22 April 2016.

15 South Pacific Forum, *28th South Pacific Forum, Rarotonga, Cook Islands, 17–19 September 1997: Forum Communiqué,* 1997.

16 In X Yu and R Taplin, 'The Australian Position at the Kyoto Conference', in A Gillespie and W Burns (eds), *Climate Change in the South Pacific: Impacts and Responses in Australia, New Zealand, and Small Island States*, Dordrecht, Neth., 2000, p. 113.

17 B Hussein, 'The Big Retreat', *Pacific Islands Monthly*, November 1997, p. 11.

18 In M McDonald, 'Fair Weather Friend? Ethics and Australia's Approach to Global Climate Change', *Australian Journal of Politics & History*, vol. 51, no. 2, 2005, p. 227.

19 See N Maclellan, 'The Region in Review: International Issues and Events, 2010', *The Contemporary Pacific*, 2011, pp. 411–12.

20 Pacific Islands Forum, 'Pacific Leaders Call to Action on Climate Change', *Pacific Islands Forum Communiqué,* 2009.

21 Regional declarations issued in the lead-up to the Paris climate negotiations included: The Melanesian Spearhead Group Declaration on the Environment and Climate Change (2015), and the Polynesian Leaders Group Taputapuatea Declaration on Climate Change (2015). Pacific island countries also issued a Lifou Declaration on Climate Change at a regional meeting in Noumea in April 2015. Leaders from the Smaller Island States sub-grouping of the Pacific Islands Forum issued a Smaller Island States Leaders' Port Moresby Declaration on Climate Change, which also called for a global treaty to limit warming to below 1.5°C.

22 See L Cochrane, 'Pacific Islands Forum: Australia May Be Asked to Leave Group Unless Action Is Taken On Climate Change', ABC News, 8 September 2015.

23 F Keany, 'Peter Dutton Overheard Joking about Rising Sea Levels in Pacific Island Nations', ABC News, 11 September 2015.

24 See G Fry and S Tarte (eds), *New Pacific Diplomacy*, ANU Press, Canberra, 2016, p. 7.

25 F Manoa, 'The New Pacific Diplomacy at the United Nations: The Rise of the PSIDS', in G Fry and S Tarte (eds), *New Pacific Diplomacy*, ANU Press, Canberra, 2016, p. 90.

26 A Tillet and M Smith, 'China Military Plan for Vanuatu Sparks Alarm for Australia's National Interests', *Australian Financial Review*, 10 April 2018.

27 Special Broadcasting Service (SBS), 'Australian Coal Is Killing the Pacific, Fiji PM Tells Scott Morrison', 17 January 2019.

28 S Dziedzic, 'Tuvalu Prime Minister Enele Sopoaga Says Australia's Climate Change Inaction Undermines its "Pacific Pivot"', ABC News, 4 December 2018.

29 Pacific Islands Forum, 'Boe Declaration on Regional Security', 2018.

30 Cited in P Hartcher, 'Cool Rationality Replaced by US-China Fight Club', *Sydney Morning Herald*, 4 June 2019.

31 K Lyons, 'Fiji PM Accuses Scott Morrison of "Insulting" and Alienating Pacific Leaders', *The Guardian*, 17 August 2019.

32 D Hurst, 'Australia to Stand with Pacific Islands on Climate Crisis and "Respect: Region"', Penny Wong Says', *The Guardian*, 23 May 2022.

33 P Wong, 'A New Era in Australian Engagement in the Pacific: Speech to the Pacific Islands Forum Secretariat', 26 May 2022.

34 A Tillet, 'China "Overreached" in Pushing for a Pacific Pact', *Australian Financial Review,* 2 June 2022.

35 Pacific Islands Forum, *51st Pacific Islands Forum Communiqué.*

36 Image source: W Morgan et al., *G'Day COP27: Australia's Global Climate Reset,* Climate Council, 2022.

37 Cited in W Morgan, 'Pacific Islands Are Back on the Map, and Climate Action is Not-Negotiable for Would-Be Allies', *The Conversation*, 18 July 2022.

38 IPCC (Intergovernmental Panel on Climate Change), *Special Report on Global Warming of 1.5°C*, 2018. See also, *Climate Change 2021: The Physical Science Basis (The Working Group I Contribution to the Sixth Assessment Report)*, 2021.

39 W Steffen et al., *Aim High, Go Fast: Why Emissions Need to Plummet This Decade*, Climate Council, 2021.

40 ABC Radio National, 'President of Palau to Meet with Australian Delegation', 13 December 2022.

41 A Morton, 'Australia Told to End New Fossil Fuel Subsidies if it Wants Pacific Support to Host Climate Summit', *The Guardian*, 17 November 2022.

42 Morgan, *G'Day COP27.*

43 J Moss, 'Australia's Net-Zero Plan Fails to Tackle Our Biggest Contribution to Climate Change: Fossil Fuels', *The Conversation*, 27 October 2021.

44 A Albanese, 'Address to the Sydney Energy Forum', 12 July 2022.

CLIMATE CONVERSATIONS AND DISCONNECTED DISCOURSES

An examination of how Chinese engagement on climate change aligns with Pacific priorities

Tess Newton Cain, Romitesh Kant, Melodie Ruwet
and Caitlin Byrne

INCREASED GEOSTRATEGIC FOCUS on the Pacific islands region increasingly intersects with the growing urgency in addressing the impacts of climate change.[1] And it is this that Pacific island countries have long identified as their first and foremost concern when it comes to security.

Much has been written about the increasing presence of China in the Pacific islands region. However, the place of climate change in engagement between China and Pacific island nations has been given very little attention to date. This is an area that reflects diversity and complexity. It is also an aspect of China–Pacific engagement that is developing and evolving. During the time in which our pilot research project was conducted, significant changes and developments have emerged. Our findings indicate that engagement with China in relation to climate change is a diverse concept, as is so often the way in the Pacific islands region. The nature of the engagement differs between different countries, and the way the engagement operates at the regional level is often different again. This is influenced by several factors, including the maturity of given diplomatic relationships, the attitudes that Pacific officials adopt, and the nature of initiatives that may be under consideration. At this particular time, the geostrategic focus on the Pacific islands region intersects with longstanding discourses, creating opportunities and challenges.

Across the four countries that we targeted in our research and at the regional level, it is evident that this aspect of engagement is one that has largely been undeveloped to date. However, our Pacific interlocutors note there are multiple opportunities for this aspect of both bilateral and multilateral relationships to evolve further.

Perhaps the most significant finding is that whether or not issues relating to climate change—mitigation, adaptation or disaster readiness/response—feature in engagements between Pacific and Chinese parties largely depends on what those on the Pacific side of the table introduce. It was a common refrain that Chinese officials and contractors were willing and able to discuss relevant issues as a reaction to them being introduced by their Pacific counterparts.

Following on from this, we found that it was not a common occurrence at the national level for Pacific politicians or bureaucrats to bring climate concerns to the table when engaging with China as a development partner and/or Chinese contractors. This indicates a disconnect between how the leaders of Pacific island countries engage at the regional and/or global level and how they negotiate for development assistance and/or investment when working at home. It also indicates a disconnect between civil society actors in the target countries and their political representatives.

Bilateral relationships between Pacific island countries and China are largely seen as being transactional in nature. Civil society and academic observers expressed a concern that at the national level, those who engage with Chinese officials do not prioritise climate change or environmental concerns. Given that China's work in the region has had such a strong focus on infrastructure, it is not surprising that this was an area of interest in discussions around adaptation to climate change in the Pacific.

At the regional level, officials are more likely to see issues of economic development and climate change as being interconnected. For them, climate change is much more central to all of the conversations that they have, with all partners. However, and possibly as a result of this, they see the climate change engagement with China as being limited in nature.

As part of this research which forms the basis of this chapter, we road tested the term 'climate ally' to see how well it resonated as a description of China from a Pacific perspective. We were interested to note that the most common response was that there was plenty of opportunity for China to *become* a 'climate ally' for the Pacific.

Across the board, we heard from our participants that there was room for China to make significant contributions in relation to addressing climate change in the Pacific. A number of the responses we received, particularly from our regional interlocutors, lead us to ask whether there are opportunities for greater collaboration and cooperation with China on the part of Australia, the United States and other development and security partners.

One of the most telling responses to this work that we received from more than one of our research participants was that there was very little discussion with Chinese stakeholders in relation to climate change. It was indicated to us that some felt that this was a gap in the overall engagement, particularly at the national level. We will be interested to see if further to this work, climate change issues become more prevalent or pronounced in interactions between Pacific stakeholders and their Chinese counterparts.

The research we conducted was designed to explore and assess the extent to which China's diplomatic effort, development activity and economic investment towards Pacific island nations supports Pacific interests, with a specific focus on the collective Pacific ambition for global action on climate change.

There is no question that China has stepped up its engagement in the Pacific in a bid to build influence in the region over the past ten to fifteen years. Much of the literature addressing Chinese activity in the Pacific is focused on China's interests, means and motivations, or the response of other powers (such as the US and Australia) to those diplomatic activities. There is a gap when it comes to examining Chinese activity from a Pacific perspective. We have inverted this focus by exploring whether and how China engages with Pacific officials and priorities on climate action.

Our research examines how this issue plays out in Papua New Guinea (PNG), Samoa, Solomon Islands, Vanuatu and at a regional level.

The Pacific context for Chinese engagement in relation to climate change

The research that inspired this chapter was framed around the following research questions, which were designed to ensure that the data we collected was focused on understanding the Pacific context for Chinese engagement in relation to climate change and, more specifically, Pacific perspectives on that engagement.

For our research project we sought to answer several questions: How does China's position about climate change engagement and climate diplomacy in the Pacific islands region align with its positions elsewhere (e.g. domestically, on the global stage)? How does China engage around climate change within bilateral relationships with Pacific island countries? How does China engage around climate change at the regional level in the Pacific (e.g. with Council of Regional Organisations of the Pacific agencies, as a Forum dialogue partner)? How is China's engagement in climate change perceived in the Pacific islands region? To what extent, if at all, does China's engagement about climate change influence how it is seen as a diplomatic/development partner in the Pacific islands region?

This project included a desktop study and a series of semi-structured interviews. It was a key priority for our research project to gain insights from local experts who have knowledge of decision/policy-making, advocacy and research into Pacific diplomacy and climate policy and priorities. We also identified key participants from regional organisations, who were predominantly located in Fiji. A further group from which some of the key informants were selected was the academic community, including in Australia. Our study involved interviews with 14 participants, including policy-makers, media and civil society representatives from target nations.

China: A leader (or future leader) in climate diplomacy?

China is currently the world's largest carbon emitter,[2] responsible for over 25 per cent of total global emissions. In recent years, China has also become a champion in renewable energies, particularly wind and solar power.[3] Domestically, President Xi Jinping has made several commitments regarding climate change mitigation. In April 2021, he announced China would strictly control coal production by 2025 and phase it down by 2030. He had previously announced China would get to net zero carbon emissions by 2060.[4]

China has increasingly become more active in global climate change policy. In 2015, there was a shift in the Chinese rhetoric regarding international cooperation on climate issues.[5] Xi Jinping's words in 2017 at the 19th Party Congress revealed that China considers itself a leader in climate cooperation: 'taking a driving seat in international cooperation to respond to climate change, China has become an important participant, contributor, and torchbearer in the global endeavour for ecological civilisation'.[6] Increasingly, China is considered to be—or to have the potential to become—a leader in climate diplomacy.[7]

However, China considers the lack of development assistance from developed countries to developing countries the biggest obstacle in tackling climate change.[8] China's climate change aid to other countries is coordinated by the China International Development Cooperation Agency (CIDCA), which was created in April 2018, and its climate change aid is closely tied to its humanitarian and development support. In comparison to other significant actors like Australia, the European Union and the Green Climate Fund, China's contribution to humanitarian (disaster response) and climate change help is marginal.[9]

China's climate change policy in the Pacific

In 2014, China established a South–South Cooperation Climate Fund, to which they pledged US$3 billion.[10] In addition, China signed more than 30 Memorandums of Understanding (MoUs) on Climate Change South–South cooperation, along with announcing 28 climate change mitigation and adaptation projects, and various training sessions.[11] All of these mechanisms have included participation by Pacific island countries.

China has been seen by some as having capitalised on the lack of leadership in the Pacific region by Australia and the US[12] when it comes to climate change. In October 2021, China announced it would establish a cooperation centre on climate change with Pacific island countries, in addition to supporting the Blue Pacific initiative and the South Pacific Regional Environment Programme.[13]

Denghua Zhang notes that concerns about climate change have grown more prevalent during high-level China–Pacific diplomatic exchanges in recent years.[14] China's climate change aid to the Pacific is not well documented, but when looking at the concrete climate change–related aid given to Pacific Islands, available through the Lowy Institute Pacific Aid Map[15] we can make a distinction between projects that directly address climate change, and projects that do not explicitly mention it but might have a climate change–related dimension.

Additionally, according to Zhang, there are three main areas in which the nation has helped: donations in the wake of natural catastrophes; the building of climate change mitigation or adaptation infrastructure (e.g. hydropower plants); and capacity building through government scholarships and short-term training programs.[16] Furthermore, there is also funding of expenses related to the United Nations or other forums. For instance, China helped fund the Fiji Conference of Parties presidency (COP23 in 2018).[17]

Pacific responses to China's role as a potential climate leader

The image of China as a global leader in South–South cooperation is a powerful soft power tool for the Chinese government in the Pacific islands region.[18] So far absent from existing understandings, however, is how the Pacific (including civil society) addresses the role(s) of China in relation to climate change issues.

Based on Pacific leaders' discourse, China might be viewed as a potential climate partner. For instance, in 2019, when Kiribati and Solomon Islands switched their diplomatic recognition of Taiwan to China, both mentioned climate leadership. Senior officials from Solomon Islands recognised that, while there were economic reasons for the switch, climate change was also a factor.[19] In that regard, Prime Minister Manasseh Sogavare of Solomon Islands commented:

> We would be simply irresponsible to isolate a global, willing player to assist developing and least-developing countries in the pursuance of the United Nations Sustainable Development Goals, including actions on climate change.[20]

In addition to a review of available literature, we undertook a media scan over an 18-month period,[21] to identify statements and/or speeches by leading Pacific island voices that spoke to what is hoped for or expected when it comes to China's role as a 'climate ally' for the region. We anticipated that these would fall into items that are directed at the global community, which do not particularly reference China (or anyone else) and items that are directed to or particularly reference China (either alone or in conjunction with reference to other countries).

Statements and calls to action of the first type, directed at the global community, occur quite frequently. Indeed, these calls are ones that have been part of the global leadership on climate diplomacy in which Pacific voices have featured for many years. Calls of this type often occur as part of addresses to the UN General Assembly by leaders of Pacific governments. For example, in September 2021, the Prime Minister of Samoa, Afioga Fiamē Naomi Mataʻafa, gave her first address to the General Assembly. During her speech, she made the position of her government very clear:

> There is no greater challenge confronting the global community now than that of climate change. For Pacific communities, the real challenge is not about securing more scientific evidence,

setting new global targets, and more talk shops. It is about action for survival and we all need to shoulder our responsibilities and play our part. The big polluters and emitters need to demonstrate more commitment and leadership.[22]

Elsewhere, Prime Minister Mata'afa has noted that even where increased emissions reductions have been announced, and welcomed, that 'the emissions gap is worrisome and still puts us on a catastrophic pathway of 2°C of global heating'.[23]

Also, in 2021, Prime Minister James Marape of Papua New Guinea made a call on large emitters to take action in the context of his expressed desire to save the rainforest of his country and use it to leverage sustainable financing: 'We want to see major carbon emitters in the industrialized nations be genuine and committed in their actions to fund climate change mitigation and adaptations'.[24]

While it is very common for the phrase 'big polluters and emitters' or something similar to be used as an umbrella term for countries such as the US, China and Australia, there are also instances where Pacific leaders have identified China as a particular focus for concern. In remarks made in October 2020, Prime Minister Sogavare of Solomon Islands identified both the US and China as 'major global emitters'.[25] In the lead-up to COP26 in 2021, the Secretary-General of the Pacific Islands Forum, Henry Puna, singled out China as an emitter of whom more was expected: 'In our view, as a major emitter, there is much work for China to do'.[26]

Similar sentiments were expressed by then President David Panuelo of the Federated States of Micronesia, at the 2021 (inaugural) meeting of the Chinese and Pacific foreign ministers, President Panuelo called on the US and China as 'our two allies' to work together in relation to climate change, including by way of persuading other countries such as Brazil and Australia to improve their positions.[27] If we fast forward to May 2022, we see that the importance of action on climate change was a strong theme during the meetings that Chinese State Councillor and Foreign Minister Wang Yi held with his counterparts during a ten-day tour of eight countries, including all of those that are the focus of this study.

Also included in the minister's itinerary was a meeting with Secretary-General Puna of the Pacific Islands Forum, who put this issue front and centre as a point of engagement:

> Firstly, urgent and ambitious climate change action. Our Forum Leaders have identified climate change as the single greatest threat facing our Blue Pacific region. Action to keep our world below 1.5 degrees is vital for the future prosperity and wellbeing of our region. We welcome China's climate change commitments and as we look to COP 27 in Egypt and call on all our international partners to submit enhanced Nationally Determined Contributions in line with the 1.5 degrees pathway and net zero by 2050.[28]

Similarly, then Prime Minister Bainimarama of Fiji also stated that in the second joint China–Pacific Foreign Ministers' meeting (held on 30 May 2022) he had urged China to make stronger climate commitments when it comes to cutting emissions—noting that he urges all countries to do this.[29]

Prime Minister Sogavare of Solomon Islands is something of a standout as a Pacific leader who has spoken positively of China when it comes to action on climate change. In October 2020, he remarked that China was among the first countries to sign the Paris Agreement and that the Chinese government sets aside 'trillions of dollars' to address climate change.[30] He also made reference to steps taken by China in decommissioning coal-fired power plants, reducing pollution, introducing improved regulation and establishing three sustainable development zones in Shenzen, Gulin and Taiyuan. He commented:

> These are positive moves which bring comfort to small and vulnerable states like Solomon Islands—that a powerful country and a sizable emitter in the world not only listens to the concern of small vulnerable countries in the world, but commits resources

and is taking positive steps to address pollution ... In this regard, we are comforted and indeed note with great admiration the positive steps taken by China in the war against pollution.[31]

We have also seen examples of statements from Chinese officials that have identified addressing climate change as a focus for increased cooperation with Pacific island countries. For example, in 2021 during a call between President Xi Jinping and Prime Minister Marape of Papua New Guinea, this was an area that Xi noted as one where there should be more coordination and cooperation between the two countries.[32] During a call between President Xi and then Prime Minister Bainimarama of Fiji, the issue of climate change was not specifically referenced. However, Prime Minister Bainimarama did express his hope that the two countries could 'strengthen communication and coordination in international affairs'.[33]

Spotlight: BRI and Green BRI in the Pacific

The 'One Belt, One Road' (Belt and Road, BRI) initiative was launched by China in 2013. It is China's main international cooperation and economic strategy,[34] and includes a land component—the Silk Road Economic Belt—and a maritime component—the 'maritime silk route'.[35] While initially the BRI's two corridors (land and maritime) were not going through the Pacific, as of January 2022 ten Pacific island countries have signed MoUs: Cook Islands, Federated States of Micronesia, Fiji, Kiribati, Niue, PNG, Samoa, Solomon Islands, Tonga and Vanuatu. The majority of these agreements were signed during 2018.

The BRI initially attracted some negative commentary with regard to environmental impacts.[36] Subsequently, in 2015, China launched a 'Green Silk Road', later often referred to as Green BRI.[37] In 2017, President Xi announced a BRI International Green Development Coalition (BIGDC), an:

open, inclusive and voluntary international network which brings together the environmental expertise of all partners to

ensure that the Belt and Road brings long-term green and sustainable development to all concerned countries in support of
the 2030 Agenda for Sustainable Development.[38]

It was officially established at the second Belt and Road forum, in April
2019. No Pacific ministry, non-governmental organisation (NGO), or
company seems currently to be a member of the BIGDC.[39]

Pacific island nations have mostly benefited from the 'Green Silk
Road Envoy training programs', a component of the Green BRI that
aims to foster collaboration between China and BRI partner countries in sustainability policy through activities such as workshops.
Representatives from Samoa, Fiji and Papua New Guinea participated
in a training program between November and December 2019.[40] Two
climate change South–South cooperation training sessions were also
organised for Pacific island countries.[41]

Findings and discussion

One of the things that really stood out for us in undertaking this
research was the difficulty we had in securing participants to talk to.
Of the total number of people contacted (n=37), we received replies
from 43.2 per cent (n=16) and from there, we were able to secure 14
interviews. While the most common form of non-participation was
simply by way of not responding to our initial or follow-up invitations,
we also had some people tell us that they did not want to participate
because of the 'sensitivity' of the subject matter.

It is not clear whether the sensitivity arises concerning the issue
of climate change or the fact that we were interrogating Chinese
engagement, or some combination of the two. Another factor that
may have contributed to the lack of positive responses to our invita-
tion to participate is that the interviews had to be conducted remotely
(via Zoom) due to COVID-19 restrictions. On initial examination,
it appears surprising that there was so little uptake by civil society
given the prominence of climate change as a focus of activity by Pacific
NGOs. However, as became apparent from our discussions, at the

national level the main point of contact is with Chinese contractors.[42] Therefore, it is not surprising that civil society actors do not have many direct insights or observations to provide.

While not necessarily discussed widely in the Pacific context, it is evident that the Chinese domestic agenda and programs significantly affect foreign policy, including diplomatic engagement and development assistance and investments. For example, China continues to be a coal-based economy with a politically powerful coal lobby.[43] Even though lobbying does not operate in the same way as we might understand it in the US or Australia, it remains the case that large coal-mining companies (and politicians from provinces with large resource endowments) are politically influential. This influence flows through into foreign policy announcements and positions, such as we saw happen at COP26 in Glasgow, with a last-minute change to the text of the communiqué due to interventions by the delegations from China and India.[44]

Climate change has been a missing piece of the puzzle when it comes to Chinese engagement with Pacific island countries. This is even though climate change has been the focus of an increasing proportion of Chinese development assistance to the Global South. Although China's foreign aid program included climate elements as far back as 2007, the Chinese National Development and Reform Commission announced the intention to more or less double the quantum of this support in 2012.[45] Similarly, China has become more active in global climate diplomacy forums such as the COP meetings.

China's primary focus when it comes to climate change and the Pacific is on bilateral engagements rather than multilateral or regional efforts. This is not surprising as it aligns with how China engages in other sectors. However, that is not to say that there is no multilateral engagement, and, indeed, there are indications that this may become more significant in the future. Of particular significance in this regard is the inaugural meeting between the Foreign Minister of China, Wang Yi, and the foreign ministers of those Pacific island countries with which China has diplomatic relationships. This was a virtual meeting held in October 2021. Foreign Minister Wang announced at this meeting that his government would establish a China–Pacific Climate Action Cooperation Centre:

> All parties shared the view that climate change is a major challenge facing humanity and are committed to jointly promoting the full and effective implementation of the Paris Agreement and a fair and equitable system of global climate governance for win-win cooperation. China understands the special difficulties of Pacific Island Countries in tackling climate change, and will set up a China–Pacific Island Countries climate action cooperation center and continue to assist Pacific Island Countries as it can in enhancing capacity building to tackle climate change under the framework of South–South cooperation.[46]

In April 2022, Vice Foreign Minister Xie Feng virtually attended an unveiling ceremony of the centre in Laoicheng City, Shandong Province. The choice of location is noteworthy. Some would certainly have expected it to have been located in the Pacific islands region, possibly in Samoa. However, the choice of Shandong Province is significant, given its established provenance as a location of Pacific study and research.[47] The question remains as to the extent to which the work of this centre will be informed by Pacific perspectives and expertise. Similarly, we are yet to learn of the extent to which Pacific academics and other experts will be able to contribute to the work of this centre. Elsewhere, concerns have been raised about the extent to which Chinese think tanks can operate with autonomy,[48] and this is likely to be a question that arises in this context as well.

From the perspective of Pacific officials who work at the regional level, climate change is an integral contact point for engagement with all development partners. In addition, regional interlocutors are more likely to see engagement in relation to climate change as part of a broader, deeper articulation of Pacific interests and concerns:

Everything is related to each other. I don't think you can look at climate policy in isolation. It's linked with the security interests. It's linked with trade and economic interests ... climate and security are linked together ... that's how we look at climate issues ... from a multidimensional lens. [REG 001][49]

A similar view that illustrates the interlinked nature of climate change issues in the region was expressed by a leading civil society participant:

This is the reality of the Pacific islands. You cannot stop the adaptation unless the emissions is [sic] slowing down. You cannot mitigate unless the emission is getting down ... we do adaptation, we do mitigation. But should we have to do more? That's the real question. [VAN 002]

This is perhaps the clearest manifestation of the 'disconnected discourse'. It is not the first time that this apparent disconnect between a regional position and national political imperatives has been identified and it is unlikely to be the last. Given the importance of the challenges of climate change across the region, and the significance of this issue within the current geopolitical discourse, this is a crucial aspect of the data we have collected.

At the bilateral level, when it comes to how Pacific policy-makers engage with Chinese interlocutors in relation to particular projects or investments, climate change is only a factor if it is introduced by the Pacific participants. One of the strongest messages we received from our participants is that China is seen as responsive or reactive to what Pacific countries put forward as their priorities:

The onus is on us, the Pacific Island Countries, to ask China for climate change [funding] ... but at this point in time, yeah, we're not asking for climate change aid. We're asking for infrastructure ... And even if we ask for infrastructure funding, maybe we should expand on the idea ... It should be informed by climate change that would in a way be better. Sustainability of that kind of infrastructure. [SOL 004]

Bilateral relationships between Pacific island countries and China are largely seen as being transactional in nature. Civil society and academic observers expressed a concern that at the national level, those who engage with Chinese officials do not prioritise climate change or environmental concerns:

I don't think our officials really understand the importance of climate change ... Perhaps our leaders just use climate change as the basis to negotiate for funds or development assistance. There is really a lack of understanding of the science or the urgency of the situation. [PNG 001]

This is at odds with how Pacific views are perceived outside the region. In some cases, this may also be counter to how national positions are put forward at regional and/or global levels: 'Our political leaders are just posturing on global platforms'. [PNG 001].

This disconnect is not surprising and has been reflected elsewhere.[50] It speaks to Pacific island countries' complex political economy, which manifests in climate change policy and discourse as it does in other spheres.

A related issue is the extent to which political leaders who engage with Chinese counterparts are guided or informed by wider community views in relation to climate change: 'Papua New Guinean leaders perhaps are not engaging with the wider community especially non-government organisations and civil society groups who are at the forefront of dealing with climate change'. [PNG 001]

When it comes to engagement with civil society on the part of China, this is seen as very low priority in relation to climate change. Several participants reflected that Chinese engagement with civil society groups focused on climate change was insignificant, including in relation to funding research relevant to climate change:

> But I can only share that perspective on how the civil society organisations think. This approach is that even civil society organisations say we never approached them when anything comes up from climate change. We're always going to other countries like the UK, France, or Australia, but never with China. [VAN 002]

Pacific–China engagement in relation to mitigation

Overall, our research indicates minimal engagement between China and Pacific island countries in relation to mitigation issues. There is undoubtedly some awareness that the issue of mitigation is problematic when it comes to domestic policy within China: 'China's really interesting on climate change and in some ways it's not a million miles from Australia in that they are juggling a lot of different constituencies domestically'. [ACA 002]

However, we also noted a perception that reaching 'carbon neutrality' by 2060 can be accepted as 'honest'. And so, advocacy and lobbying in relation to curbing emissions are better directed to those large emitters yet to make meaningful commitments. Conversations with China may be better directed to areas where they are less active such as supporting disaster readiness projects [VAN 002].

A number of our participants indicated that Pacific island leaders are not pressing China to improve their position in terms of cutting emissions. One reason for this was that Papua New Guineans are too respectful or deferential in their dealings with China, as a reflection of that country's economic might: 'They can sometimes hinder big ticket items for [small island developing states], particularly when it comes to emission reduction'. [REG 003]

Our respondents had a range of responses about how they viewed China's global position on climate change. For some, it appears that this is something of a gap in how Chinese engagement is portrayed and understood that 'it's really not clear'. [SOL 003]

However, there was certainly evidence to indicate that some Pacific interviewees are aware of how China is positioning itself on the global stage when it comes to mitigation commitments:

But one of its commitments in COP was that it was no longer going to be financing new coal-fired power stations overseas. Hmm. So that's an interesting one. We haven't got any of them in the Pacific, so it's not terribly relevant to us, but obviously they are. Obviously, finance have been financing it elsewhere and whether those new commitments relate to projects that are already planned or just ones that are not yet planned. [PNG 002]

Pacific–China engagement in relation to adaptation and climate finance

When it comes to adaptation to climate change, several participants noted that there was scope for China to play a more significant role, particularly in relation to technology transfer: 'On the other hand, I mean, clearly when it comes to climate and there are technologies and capacities that China has that if it wants to, it could provide and help extend to Pacific island nations'. [PNG 002]

One of the points raised is that the categorisation of China as a developing country creates a 'quirk' when it comes to climate finance because they are competing for funding from the same envelope that small island developing states, including those in the Pacific, are trying to access. In addition, China's designation as a developing country has allowed them to 'evade' any responsibility or expectation that they would be contributing to climate finance mechanisms such as the Green Climate Fund.

The issue of climate financing overlaps with concerns about the nature of financing between China and Pacific island countries more generally. This, in turn, is significant in relation to the blurring of any demarcation between climate finance and development finance (which is beyond the scope of this study). The risks associated with increased levels of debt are very present in the thinking of Pacific interlocutors, and it is not surprising that a preference for grant funding rather than debt financing was expressed:

> But when it comes to climate finance in general, particularly in the region, grants is the most preferable ... And the fact that when China provides finance, it brings its own people, ... you know, the spill over benefits, really of projects to local communities. You know, it's very much minimal because everything goes back to China, really. [REG 003]

Given that China's work in the region has had such a strong focus on infrastructure, it is not surprising that this was an area of interest in discussions around adaptation to climate change in the Pacific. For example, we heard that there was a need to ensure that infrastructure projects focus on climate resilience or climate proofing. This includes making modifications to projects where required. These concerns easily bleed into wider consternation about large infrastructure projects funded by China, including in relation to quality and local content:

> China is probably wanting to sort of upgrade the status because it's getting a bit of negative feedback from around over the quality of the calibre of some of its projects ... so they're probably going to be open to raising their standards or at least being perceived as raising the standards. [PNG 002]

There are indications that Chinese contractors are aware of the need to ensure that infrastructure in the Pacific is fit for purpose and are open to addressing concerns about climate-proofing if and when they are raised. However, we also heard that there was a need for greater oversight of the companies undertaking these projects, including how they are addressing relevant climate change issues. The significance of local governance structures and systems for getting the best development outcomes from Chinese infrastructure projects has been examined elsewhere, although not with specific reference to climate change aspects or imperatives.[51]

Pacific–China engagement concerning disaster readiness and response

Unlike traditional humanitarian donors such as the US, UK and the EU, established donors that offer a significant amount of funds, experience and policy-making to humanitarian response operations in major catastrophes and complex crises, China conducts its foreign aid differently.[52] Over the previous decade, China's annual humanitarian contributions have ranged from about US$1 million to around US$130 million. Chinese humanitarian aid accounted for less than 1 per cent of the total recorded aid in 2017.[53]

Our conversations with research participants bore this out. There were no references to China having contributed to disaster response in the target countries. That is not to say that China has not contributed to disaster response, because it is certainly the case that they have.[54]

Even while China's foreign policies influence its humanitarian aid, it does not have an established public humanitarian policy beyond the need to assist those in need. Chinese NGOs are still a relative newcomer in terms of international humanitarian aid, despite being a vital element of China's internal disaster management system. In times of crisis, the Chinese government frequently relies on Chinese firms and the Chinese diaspora in the host country to set up activities on the ground.[55]

In 2021, China established three centres to assist Pacific island countries: the Pacific Island Countries Emergency Supply Reserve; Poverty Alleviation and Cooperative Development; and the Pacific Island Countries Climate Change Cooperation Centre.[56] As noted above, this may indicate an intention to expand the amount of multilateral/regional engagement in which China engages in this area.

Another reason that may account for the lack of visibility of China in the field of humanitarian assistance and disaster recovery is that, until very recently, the Chinese military has not been a part of this work. This contrasts with the highly visible interventions through military deployments by countries such as Australia and New Zealand.[57]

One aspect of disaster response that was not mentioned by any of our informants but which is noteworthy is the role of Chinese state-owned enterprises that operate in Pacific island countries and of Chinese community groups, including business associations. It is possible to point to numerous instances of companies and community groups making contributions both in cash and in kind to relief efforts in the countries in which they are resident.[58]

Is China a climate ally for the Pacific?

One of the questions we asked our participants is how China is seen as a 'climate ally' either for individual countries or for the Pacific islands region more generally. The responses to this were mixed and instructive. One of our participants said that he felt that Pacific perceptions had shifted since the COP26 meeting in Glasgow in terms of how China performs on the global stage. He contended that the late intervention by China (and others, including India) to water down the text of the Glasgow Climate Pact had undermined China's climate strategy (to the extent that there is one) in the region.[59]

In this area, as in others, Pacific island countries can use the presence and activity of China as a part of how they seek to exercise leverage over other partners: 'a lot of it does come down to just having an "other" … portraying China as better on climate and better on these issues is a way of shaming Australia and New Zealand into doing more'. [ACA 002]

Although the question we posed was not framed in terms of comparing China with other partners, there was some indication of how respondents saw this as a point of contrast. For example, from our Samoan participant, we heard that people were more likely to think of Australia, the UN, New Zealand or Japan as climate 'allies' for the Pacific.

Opportunities and hopes for the future

Across the board, we heard from our participants that there was room for China to make significant contributions in relation to addressing climate change in the Pacific. For example, we heard from one of our Solomon Islander participants that China could engage more actively with the climate change imperatives contained in communiqués released by the Pacific Islands Forum.[60] 'If you look at the magnitude of the problem and the urgency of the problem that we have, politics aside, there's opportunity to involve China to be a champion.' [REG 003]

Elsewhere, there was hope that high-level interactions had the potential to drive new projects, such as those relating to the use of renewable energy, that would have positive impacts in relation to key climate change issues: 'There is a lot of scope at the leader-to-leader and ministerial level to get some useful projects happening. I think that's where there is more likely to be influence'. [ACA 002]

At the regional level, we also heard that there was scope for China to be a more significant partner in relation to climate change issues: 'China's footprint in terms of climate change mitigation and adaptation support in the region could be enhanced in the future'. [REG 001]

One opportunity for China to contribute to Pacific-led efforts in meeting the challenges of climate change is the Pacific Resilience Facility. China has already provided resources to support some of the scoping work for this initiative, and there are hopes that this will be followed by a strong contribution to the initial capitalisation.[61] Australia and the US have also provided initial funds. The redesigned Facility proposal will be voted on at the 52nd Pacific Island Leaders Meeting in Cook Islands, November 2023.

China is seen as a site of significant technical expertise. There is scope for increased knowledge transfer in key areas such as the use of renewable energy sources and enhanced meteorological services to support disaster preparedness. In addition, as China increases its soft power engagement by way of university scholarships for Pacific island students, there are opportunities to support the development of skills and expertise in climate-focused disciplines: 'China has a lot to offer in terms of its technical and scientific know-how, and it is conducive to Papua New Guinea and developing countries' context'. [PNG 001]

Conclusions

Engagement with China in relation to climate change is a diverse concept, as is so often the way in the Pacific islands region. The nature of the engagement differs between different countries, and the way the engagement operates at the regional level is often different again. This diversity of approach is influenced by several factors, including the maturity of given diplomatic relationships, the attitudes that Pacific officials adopt, and the nature of initiatives that may be under consideration. At this particular time, the geostrategic focus on the Pacific islands region intersects with longstanding discourses, creating opportunity and challenge.

Notes

1 This chapter was adapted from 'Climate Conversations and Disconnected Discourses: An Examination of How Chinese Engagement on Climate Change Aligns with Pacific Priorities', Regional Outlook Paper No. 69, 2022, published by the Griffith Asia Institute.

2 Though not *per capita*.

3 F Urban, 'China's Rise: Challenging the North-South Technology Transfer Paradigm for Climate Change Mitigation and Low Carbon Energy', *Energy Policy*, vol. 113, pp. 320–30.

4 S Sengupta, 'China's Leader, Xi Jinping, Promises to "Strictly Limit" Coal', *New York Times*, 22 April 2021.

5 Y Huang, 'Yanzhong Huang: China's New Rhetoric at COP21', Council on Foreign Relations, 3 December 2015.

6 T Lahiri, 'Xi Jinping to China: Any Harm We Inflict On Nature Will Eventually Return to Haunt Us', *Quartz*, 18 October 2017.

7 C Gang, 'China's Quest for Global Climate Leadership', *East Asia Forum*, 24 June 2021; C Han Springer, 'Ask the Experts: Can China Become a Global Green Leader?' *China Dialogues*, 1 November 2021; M Kaneti, 'China's Vision for Environmental Leadership', *The Diplomat*, 13 December 2021; L Savage, 'The US Left a Hole in Leadership on Climate. China is Filling it', *Politico*, 15 August 2019; J Yang, 'Understanding China's Changing Engagement in Global Climate Governance: A Struggle for Identity', *Asia Europe Journal*, no. 20, 2022.

8 B Lewis, 'China Says Fund for Poorest "Biggest Obstacle" in Climate Talks', *Reuters*, 27 October 2021.

9 D Zhang, 'Assessing China's Climate Change Aid to the Pacific', *In Brief 2020/3*, Department of Pacific Affairs, Australian National University, 2020.

10 M Weigel, *More Money, More Impact? China's Climate Change South-South Cooperation to Date and Future Trends*, United Nations Development Programme, 2022.

11 Ministry of Ecology and Environment, *China's Policies and Actions for Addressing Climate Change*, PRC, 2019.

12 R Harris, 'China's Pacific Climate Pitch Angers Australia, US', *Sydney Morning Herald*, 16 August 2019.

13 XinhuaNet, 'China Vows Closer Ties with Pacific Island Countries', 22 October 2021.

14 Zhang, 'Assessing China's Climate Change Aid to the Pacific'.

15 Lowy Institute, 2022, 'Lowy Institute Pacific Aid Map'.

16 Zhang, 'Assessing China's Climate Change Aid to the Pacific'.

17 Radio New Zealand, 'China Helps Fund Fijian Presidency at COP 23', 15 December 2016.

18 R Herr, *Chinese Influence in the Pacific Islands: The Yin and Yang of Soft Power*, Australian Strategic Policy Institute, April 2019, p. 44.

19 A Westerman, 'Some Pacific Island Nations Are Turning to China. Climate Change Is a Factor', NPR, 23 November 2019.

20 M Clarke, 2019, 'Kiribati Cuts Ties with Taiwan to Switch to China, Days after Solomon Islands', *ABC News*, 20 September 2019.

21 January 2020 to October 2021.

22 Afioga Fiamē Naomi Mata'afa, 'Statement at the General Debate', 76th United Nations General Assembly, 25 September 2021.

23 K Murphy, 'Australia Must Increase 2030 Emissions Target to Help Avoid "Catastrophic" Heating Samoan PM Says', *The Guardian*, 6 October 2021.

24 GS Maribu, 'PNG's Prime Minister Wants to Save His Country's Rainforest: He Can't Do it Alone', *The Diplomat*, 1 October 2021.

25 Solomon Islands Government, 'Gender and Climate Change Inspires Sogavare at Photography Exhibition', 1 October 2020.

26 'Time to Act on Climate Pledge, Pacific Tells PM', *The Australian*, 24 October 2021.

27 L Song, 'Inaugural China-Pacific Foreign Ministers' Meeting Sheds Light on Beijing's Pacific Islands Strategy', East-West Center, 2021.

28 Secretary-General H Puna, 'Remarks: SG Puna at Bilateral with China State Councillor, Foreign Minister HE Wang Yi', Pacific Islands Forum, 29 May 2022.

29 K Tadulala, 'Climate Issues at the Centre of Discussion', *FBC News*, 31 May 2022.

30 Solomon Islands Government, 'Gender and Climate Change Inspires Sogavare at Photography Exhibition'.

31 Solomon Islands Government, 'PM Sogavare Appreciates China's Green Initiatives', 1 October 2020.

32 Consulate-General of the People's Republic of China in Sydney, 'Xi Jinping Speaks with PNG's Prime Minister James Marape on the Phone', 2021.

33 Ministry of Foreign Affairs of the People's Republic of China, 'Xi Jinping Speaks with Fijian Prime Minister Josaia Voreqe Bainimarama on the Phone', 2021.

34 Green Finance and Development Center, 'About the BRI', 2021.

35 J-MF Blanchard and C Flint, 'The Geopolitics of China's Maritime Silk Road Initiative', *Geopolitics*, vol. 22, no. 2, 2017, pp. 223–45.

36 F Ascensão et al., 'Environmental Challenges for the Belt and Road Initiative', *Nature Sustainability*, vol. 1, no. 5, 2018, pp. 206–9; J Hillman and A Tippett, 'The Climate Challenge and China's Belt and Road Initiative', *Council on Foreign Relations*, 31 March 2021; HC Teo et al., 'Environmental Impacts of Infrastructure Development under the Belt and Road Initiative', *Environments*, vol. 6, no. 6, 2019, p. 72; WWF, 'WWF and Greening the Belt and Road Initiative', 2 November 2017.

37 X Liu and MM Bennett, 'The Geopolitics of Knowledge Communities: Situating Chinese and Foreign Studies of the Green Belt and Road Initiative', *Geoforum*, vol. 128, 2022, pp. 168–80.

38 UN Environment Programme, 'The Belt and Road Initiative International Green Development Coalition (BRIGC)', n.d.

39 BRI Green Development Institute, 'Partners', 2021.

40 Zhang, 'Assessing China's Climate Change Aid to the Pacific'.

41 Ministry of Ecology and Environment of the People's Republic of China, 'China's Policies and Actions for Addressing Climate Change', November 2019.

42 For example, China Civil Engineering Construction Corporation, based in Vanuatu.

43 See L Myllyvirta, S Zhang and X Shen, 'Will China Build Hundreds of New Coal Plants in the 2020s?', Carbon Brief, 2020.

44 See F Harvey and R Mason, 'Alok Sharma "Deeply Frustrated" by India and China over Coal', *The Guardian*, 14 November 2021.

45 See T Ma, 'China Upgrades Climate Aid to the Global South', China Dialogue, 20 September 2017.

46 Ministry of Foreign Affairs of the People's Republic of China, 'Joint Statement of China-Pacific Island Countries Foreign Ministers' Meeting', 21 October 2021.

47 See Zhang, 'Assessing China's Climate Change Aid to the Pacific'.

48 See D Zhang, 'The Media and Think Tanks in China: The Construction and Propagation of a Think Tank', *Media Asia*, vol. 48, no. 2, 2021.

49 All names of participants quoted in this section have been kept confidential and are identified only by codes that indicate the person's nationality.

50 See M Dornan, W Morgan, T Newton Cain and S Tarte, 'What's in a Term? "Green Growth" and the "Blue-Green Economy" in the Pacific Islands', *Asia Pacific Policy Studies*, vol. 5, 2018, pp. 408–25.

51 See M Dornan and P Brant, 'Chinese Assistance in the Pacific: Agency, Effectiveness and the Role of Pacific Island Governments', *Asia and the Pacific Policy Studies*, vol. 1, no. 2, 2014, pp. 349–63.

52 Humanitarian Advisory Group et al., *Positive Disruption? China's Humanitarian Aid*, Humanitarian Advisory Group, December 2019, pp. 6–9.

53 J-H Lavey, 'Unpacking China's Overseas Aid Program', *The Interpreter*, 1 May 2020.

54 See Ministry of Foreign Affairs of the People's Republic of China, 'Chinese Ambassador Set Up Tents for the Disaster-Struck Communities', 2015.

55 Humanitarian Advisory Group et al., *Positive Disruption?*

56 P Ligaiula, 'Three New Centres to Assist Pacific Island Countries', Pacific Islands News Association, 17 December 2021.

57 However, this may be changing, as we saw in the recent responses to the undersea volcanic explosion and tsunami in Tonga.

58 See A Roberts, 'CCECC Supports Hola Logistics', *Vanuatu Daily Post*, 2018.

59 See M Jacobs, 'Reflections on COP 26: International Diplomacy, Global Justice and the Greening of Capitalism', *The Political Quarterly*, vol. 93, 2021, pp. 270–7.

60 See, for example, the Kainaki II Declaration for Urgent Climate Change Now, issued by Pacific Islands Forum leaders in 2019.

61 A pledging conference hosted by the UN Secretary-General was held in 2022. He called for initial $1.5 billion capitalisation, and $3 billion was achieved. Current pledges are $9.9 billion. https://www.greenclimate.fund/about/resource-mobilisation/gcf-1.

THE IMPLICATIONS OF CLIMATE CHANGE FOR AUSTRALIAN STRATEGIC AND DEFENCE POLICY IN RELATION TO THE ALLIANCE AND THE PACIFIC ISLAND STATES

Brendan Sargeant

WHEN THE AUSTRALIAN government published the *Defence Strategic Update* in 2020 (2020 DSU), it signalled a more pessimistic view of Australia's strategic outlook. While there are a number of strands to the argument presented in the document, they come down to the reality that the potential threats to Australian security have increased and the timeframe within which they might emerge has reduced. The strategic policy response set out in the 2020 DSU committed to the framework of shape, deter and respond.[1] Australian strategic and defence policy would be directed at shaping the regional environment in ways conducive to its national interests. It would develop the capability to deter potential threats, and it would possess the capacity to respond should a range of threats be realised. The 2020 DSU recognised that the Indo-Pacific is in a period of strategic order transition. The emergence of China as a major regional power and a strategic response by the United States that seeks to place limits on how China might exercise its emerging power has resulted in strategic competition, the outcome of which is uncertain and may take many decades before a new order is established. The 2020 DSU suggests that change of this magnitude is a major crisis.

The other major crisis that has been developing for decades but has increased in intensity in recent years is climate change. In the 2020 DSU, there was only one mention of climate change—as one of several compounding threats to human security.[2] Climate change is an existential crisis because, unchecked, it can destroy the foundations of life as we presently know it. It is a crisis that affects every aspect of national and international life. The challenge for Australia is that the crisis of a changing strategic order and climate are interacting with compounding effects. Australia has never in its post-settlement history had to deal with interacting crises of this magnitude or complexity and, accordingly, will need to develop strategic policy responses that both comprehend the scale of the emerging climate change crisis while meeting the challenge of a changing strategic order. What is becoming evident, particularly if we consider the South Pacific, is that these are not separate challenges. Strategic policy needs to recognise the interaction between the two system-level changes occurring and respond in a way that mitigates the risk that arises from both.

In this chapter, I discuss the Australian strategic and defence policy response to climate change in relation to the US–Australia alliance and the Pacific island states. This is a subset of a larger discussion about the nature of the security challenge that climate change presents.[3] My approach is to begin with a discussion of the guiding assumptions underpinning Australian strategic and defence policy to identify how they reflect and shape a particular perception of the Australian strategic environment and the nature of potential security threats that might arise. From this, I discuss how Australian strategic and defence policy has understood the security challenges of climate change. I then discuss how the US and the countries of the South Pacific understand security and the underpinning assumptions upon which they have built a security narrative that places climate change at its core. Finally, the chapter concludes by discussing how Australia's perceptions of security and the strategic responses that might be appropriate diverge from those of both the US and South Pacific.

Climate change as a strategic force

As a strategic force, climate change manifests in two ways. The first is the changes it brings to the natural environment, with the multitude of consequences that flow. These affect every element of community life, from the nature of the environment within which people live to their economic, social and political security. Climate change also acts as a strategic force in its capacity to reshape perceptions of the utility of the strategic order within which countries function. In an environment where climate change represents an existential threat, traditional security frameworks do not necessarily make sense in terms of the policy priorities that they might mandate.

The challenge of climate change for Australian strategic and defence policy will increase over time as its impact on Australia and regional countries grows. As currently formulated, it is not equipped to respond to the full dimension of the security challenges that climate change will present. Australia's policy response is also increasingly divergent from the policy responses of our most important ally and trading partner, the US, and the Pacific countries in our immediate neighbourhood.

Australian strategic and defence policy: Guiding assumptions

Australian strategic and defence policy has been guided by assumptions about the nature of the world and how it works. The most important of these include the idea that Australian prosperity and security derives from its support for and participation in a strategic order shaped by the predominant power of the US. Another is that Australia's geography functions as a strategic asset, but in certain circumstances, also as the location and vector for security threats. It has also rested on the assumption that maintaining strategic stability across the archipelago to the north through support for state sovereignty strengthens Australian security. These assumptions have shaped how Australian governments have used defence capabilities and engagement to support regional security.

For decades, the overriding goal of defence and strategic policy has been to ensure the strategic stability of the archipelago to Australia's north extending around to the island states of the South Pacific. Policy debates have focused on two major questions. The first is the extent to which defence capabilities should be deployed beyond Australia's shores in order to intervene in crises to forestall the emergence of potential threats closer to Australia. The second has been the extent to which defence capabilities should focus more directly on the defence of Australia. The question that climate change poses is whether assumptions concerning the alliance and Australia's strategic geography are helpful in guiding future policy in an environment where climate change not only operates as a force that changes the nature of the operating environment, but also as a force that changes regional perceptions about the nature of potential security challenges.

The alliance

Successive Australian governments have identified the US–Australia alliance as foundational to Australia's defence capability. Without the alliance, Australia would be much less militarily capable. The *2017 Foreign Policy White Paper* described the alliance as central to Australia's approach in the region, as 'Without strong US political, economic and security engagement, power is likely to shift more quickly in the region and it will be more difficult for Australia to achieve the levels of security and stability we seek'.[4]

At the heart of this relationship is a shared understanding of the nature of the strategic environment and the importance of US strategic primacy to Australian and US interests. One of the key features of Australian strategic and defence policy is the requirement to manage participation in the Indo-Pacific in ways that are broadly congruent with US strategic aims. While there is often disagreement on specific issues, there is broad agreement on how the Indo-Pacific should function and Australia's role within it. These shared interests were reaffirmed during the 2021 Quad meeting, where President Joe Biden emphasised that 'a free and open Indo-Pacific is essential to each of our futures'.[5] Then Prime Minister Scott Morrison reiterated Biden's point, 'the Indo-Pacific that will now shape the destiny of our world in the

21st century', and affirmed Australia's commitment to working with
ASEAN to secure 'an open, inclusive ... and resilient Indo-Pacific'.[6]
One way of reading recent Australian strategic and defence policy is
to see it as an attempt to strengthen Australia's capacity to support US
strategic interests in the Indo-Pacific during a period of major change.

In recent years, US policy in relation to the Indo-Pacific has become
more uncertain in response to political changes in Washington. There
has been pressure on Japan and Korea to contribute more to their
defence. The relationship with the Philippines has been volatile as
President Rodrigo Duterte has played the US against China and vice
versa. There has been a shift in the US strategic policy position in relation
to China, including a stronger posture against China in the South China
Sea. In this environment, Australia has sought to strengthen its ties with
Washington and has been a vocal supporter of continuing US strategic
primacy in the Indo-Pacific. One of the consequences of the Trump
period has been less confidence in US strategic commitment and less
certainty about how the US might respond to a range of potential crises.
The advent of the Biden administration has seen attempts to re-establish
confidence in US strategic engagement. However, the underlying shift
in power relativities between the US and China and the increasingly
adversarial nature of the strategic competition suggest that the strategic
environment will remain volatile and uncertain into the future.

The convergence of perceptions of the strategic environment has
many implications for how Australia might relate to its neighbourhood. Over the years, we have seen various caricatures of Australia as an
uncritical US proxy,[7] a deputy sheriff to the US,[8] a country that adheres
to outdated Cold War frameworks,[9] and so on. These are caricatures
of Australia's position, but they point to a reality that Australia exer-
cises limited agency at the strategic level outside the framework of the
strategic order established and sustained by the US. This means that a
significant focus of defence policy relates to alliance management and
the terms of participation within the alliance, both strategically and
operationally. What this can mean in practice is that a challenge, such
as climate change, that does not easily fall within this strategic policy

framework, may not get the attention that it deserves or is framed in ways that do not speak fully to the challenge it presents.

Strategic geography

The focus of defence policy concerning Australian geographical circumstances is to try and answer the questions: what does our strategic geography enable, and what does it constrain? The answer varies with circumstances, and policy adjusts accordingly. Australia is an island continent spanned by an archipelago that extends from the Indian Ocean to the Pacific and includes the island states of the South Pacific. This archipelago links the North Pacific and the Asian landmass, creating a very complex and diverse environment.

The framework for the development of strategic and defence policy developed in the *1987 Defence White Paper* remains in place with subsequent defence white papers contextualising it within the particular strategic circumstances in play when they were written. The *1987 Defence White Paper* grounded its analysis of Australia's strategic interests in Australia's geography and prioritised force structure development in a hierarchy that had as the first priority the capacity to defend the Australian continent.[10] Its next priority was the security of the near region, which incorporated the archipelago and chain of islands to the north extending around to the southwest Pacific. Its third priority was the ability to contribute to coalition activity in the wider Asia-Pacific region or beyond, depending on government decision-making at the time. While the *2016 Defence White Paper* did not seek to establish in its policy framework priorities between the defence of Australia, Australian security in the region, or engagement in the wider Indo-Pacific and global environment, the 2020 DSU reverted to the more traditional policy framework, established in the *1987 Defence White Paper*.

Paul Dibb, framing the security challenges facing the Pacific as an 'arc of instability', identified Australia's strategic priorities in its immediate neighbourhood. He argued that unstable or weak Pacific states pose a security risk to Australia. He noted in his 1986 *Review of Australia's Defence Capabilities* that the Pacific 'is the area from or through which a military threat to Australia could most easily be posed'.[11] The idea that, under certain circumstances, the geographic structure of the archipelago can amplify threats to Australia has shaped the direction of strategic policy to emphasise stability, the continuation of the existing strategic order, the importance of state integrity, and the importance of maintaining a permissive environment for future Australian Defence Force (ADF) operations.

At the moment, there is considerable anxiety in the Australian Government about the extent to which the increasing Chinese presence is reducing our geographical advantage in Southeast Asia and the South Pacific. However, the more significant issue at stake is the extent to which our perception of our geography conditions our understanding of Pacific island countries' strategic perceptions and security challenges. A focus on strategic geography as a vector for threat reduces our capacity to understand and respond to the agency that those countries might seek to exercise. At a basic level, this can lead to a mismatch of perceptions about the nature of the security environment, the threats that might occur, and the relative priority that we might give to them. Climate change is a security challenge where the divergence of perceptions about the nature of the security challenges it presents can have very significant consequences, both in terms of potential policy responses and capacity for action.

Australian strategic and defence policy framing of climate change[12]

Climate change has been recognised as a factor in defence planning since the *2009 Defence White Paper*. However, while the 2009, 2013 and 2016 Defence white papers recognised climate change as a security risk and a threat multiplier, in the recent *2020 Defence Strategic Update*, climate change was only mentioned once.[13] The 2020 DSU positioned climate change as part of a broader range of threats of human security, and suggested the response of defence planning be increased disaster response and resilience measures.[14] As noted in the introduction to this book, the Australian government's *2023 National Defence Strategic*

Review (DSR) identified climate change as a core national security issue.[15] However, the DSR still offers too little in terms of clarity on the climate challenge or the steps to be taken to prepare for and deal adequately with the crises that climate change is likely to bring.[16] For example, the role of the ADF in response to cascading climate crises is the subject of hot debate and national consultation. Currently, the ADF is the government's primary non-financial means to assist state- and territory-led crisis responses, should it be requested. The Defence Strategic Review recommended that the ADF should only be used as the last resort for domestic aid to the civil community, so it can remain battle-ready. The Albanese government is searching for viable crisis response alternatives to the ADF and an ability to draw on enhanced latent industrial capacity to uplift its capability when needed.[17]

Prior to 2020, successive white papers had positioned climate change as a factor that is affecting the nature of the ADF operating environment and a source of increased risk both to capability and to the capacity to operate. While these papers acknowledged the increased security risk of climate change, they built on an established policy framework which is guided by an understanding that the regional environment is subject to natural disasters that may require crisis intervention of which strategic purpose has been to maintain stability and support for the existing strategic order. As the *2000 Defence White Paper* noted, 'ADF units, including Reserve units, make a major contribution to disaster relief in Australia and our immediate neighbourhood'.[18] The *2009 Defence White Paper* similarly identified that 'Given our size and resources, Australia will be expected to take a leadership role within the South Pacific if these states are overwhelmed by a natural or man-made crisis'.[19]

Each successive document emphasised that many countries in the region were especially vulnerable to the effects of climate change. The *2009 Defence White Paper* noted that 'The security effects of climate change are likely to be most pronounced where states have limited capacity to respond to environmental strains'.[20] As a result, the 2009 document argued that they may require external assistance to manage and respond to the consequences of climate change.[21] The *2013 Defence White Paper* similarly acknowledged that the major challenges facing the region would be 'compounded by the effects of climate change'[22] as the risks associated with resource insecurity may be exacerbated by climate change.[23] The 2013 document argued that this would lead to an increased demand for humanitarian assistance, disaster relief and stabilisation operations from the ADF over coming decades.[24] Similar to the 2009 and the 2013 Defence white papers, the *2016 Defence White Paper* noted the centrality of climate change to Australian defence and strategic planning in the coming decades, identifying it as one of the 'Six Key Drivers' that will shape Australia's strategic environment. The paper identified climate change as a factor that will contribute to instability for some countries in the South Pacific, and dedicated ADF resources to 'mitigating the destabilising effects that climate change will have'.[25]

These strategic documents position the Defence policy response, including deployment of the ADF, to the likely increase in natural disasters across the Indo-Pacific as one of management and mitigation. It argues that the ADF will, over time, adapt its capabilities to this changing environment. This policy governs how Defence understands and manages its training and operating environment within Australia, and how it might need to put in place systems and processes that account for changes wrought by climate change. It also includes recognition that Defence will have an increased role in responding to what is likely to be an increasing suite of major disasters resulting from the impact of climate change on the natural and urban environment. However, it does not include a recognition that the capacity and capability of the ADF to respond to natural disasters can be affected by its commitment to its priorities, both domestic and international. The Royal Commission into natural disaster arrangements following the 2020 bushfires has highlighted this issue. It identified the ADF as central to Australia's ability to fight bushfires. While the ADF has been positioned as central to disaster relief both in Australia and in the Pacific, as the Royal Commission acknowledged, responding to domestic natural disasters is not the role of the ADF as the ADF has finite capacity and capability.[26]

Current policy places climate change and its effects in a similar category to such endogenous forces as cyber-attacks and terrorism. These are threats that emerge as elements of the operating environment, but do not represent a fundamental change to the environment to the extent that might challenge the role, function or major capabilities of the ADF. More broadly, the emergence of climate change in strategic policy documents does not suggest that climate change is considered as a factor or a force that might challenge some of the underpinning assumptions that shape policy. In this respect, current policy does not see it as a strategic force that needs to be accounted for. The focus of strategic policy continues to be the preservation and defence of Australia's interests in the existing strategic order and the development of the capacity to resist state-level coercion through the deployment of military force.

How the Pacific islands frame climate change

Pacific islands do not see regional security through the same lens as Australia. As the Secretary-General of the Pacific Islands Forum, Meg Taylor, stated, 'the highest priority for our region is climate change mitigation and adaptation'.[27] The Pacific islands have developed different conceptions of security and have used different enabling metaphors to construct an alternative framing and narrative. This has in turn influenced their own sense of agency and community in developing strategic responses to security challenges, of which the most important is climate change. At the core of Australia's strategic relationship with Pacific island states, there is a very different perception about the nature of the challenge that climate change represents for security and the policy responses that might be appropriate.

An important statement about the nature of the South Pacific strategic environment was issued by the Pacific Islands Forum Leadership Summit in Tuvalu in 2019.[28] The Kainaki II Declaration for Urgent Climate Change Action Now, 'Securing the Future of Our Blue Pacific', articulated a very different framing of the strategic environment within which these islands are located. The strategic environment was described as the ocean, as 'the Blue Pacific Continent'.[29] This enabling idea serves to reposition and reframe the oceanic environment in relation to the islands that exist within it. It challenges the idea that security is just a question of state sovereignty that can be satisfied within the confines of the interests of the individual nation-state. It recognises that the prosperity and agency of individual countries depends on the maritime environment that they are located within, and that this dependency is inextricably linked with the interests of other countries in that environment. The health and state of that environment is the critical determinant of the capacity of those countries to prosper and achieve security in the broadest sense. It repositions the security discussion to one of the state of the ocean environment that surrounds these countries, and within this context climate change becomes the overriding security concern because of the existential threat that it represents.

The logic of the reality of climate change in conjunction with the understanding of the ocean as the strategic environment requires that security rests on an understanding of interdependence, rather than the capacity for independent action. The security of each country is bound up in the security of the whole, which rests on the foundation of an ocean that is healthy. This perspective reframes priorities and puts into a different perspective many of the traditional enablers of state sovereignty and security. If climate change is the existential threat, then all other policy frameworks that might shape security agendas become subordinate. The test for strategic and defence policy in this context is the contribution that it makes to the mitigation of the climate change threat, and the capacity for effective response should threats be realised. It also recognises that not all threats that might arise from climate change are amenable to traditional defence policy responses.

This understanding of the oceanic environment also reframes the understanding of the broader Indo-Pacific strategic environment. To the extent that the Indo-Pacific is an arena for emerging strategic competition and a struggle for establishment of the future strategic order, the question for policy in the South Pacific is the extent to which this struggle will support or detract from its ability to respond to climate change.

Many of these ideas find expression in the Boe Declaration on Regional Security, issued by the Pacific Islands Forum in 2018, which presents an expanded conception of security, 'inclusive of human security, humanitarian assistance, prioritising environmental security, and regional cooperation in building resilience to disasters and climate change'.[30] It assumes strategic interdependence between the countries that have signed up to it, which includes Australia. It also recognises, and this has been repeated many times by leaders within the South Pacific, that no country can deal with climate change alone, but that it has to be a collective effort. Notwithstanding Australia being a signatory to the declaration, the framing of climate change as a strategic issue is at variance with the priority that Australia would give to it.

The impact of climate change on Australian strategic and defence policy

There has been much discussion in policy and academic circles about the scale and nature of change in the Indo-Pacific strategic environment, but no disagreement that major change is occurring. The two big drivers of change, as discussed above, are climate change and the changing strategic order. Climate change, along with population growth and the pressure on natural resources, is creating enormous stresses on the biosphere. These changes are interacting with change in the strategic order in unpredictable and compounding ways.

Climate change is a challenge for strategic and defence policy in a multitude of ways. Climate change is a feature of changes in our regional strategic environment. At a minimum, climate change increases the size of unknown strategic risk. Climate change is also shaping the environment in which change is occurring. Perhaps the most important feature about climate change, both as a force, and as a defining feature of the emerging strategic and operating environment, is that it challenges traditional frameworks for strategic policy. It does this in two ways. First, climate change is a force that will create potential political and social upheaval, which may require intervention by Australia, including with the use of the ADF. The dilemma for defence policy is how it adapts the force to respond to a potential spectrum of threat that spans traditional nation-state conflict and the exercise of coercion, through to the capacity to support response to political, social and economic fragility and potential state breakdown.

Perhaps most importantly, climate change is a system-wide challenge which no single country can resolve without the assistance of other countries. Climate change emphasises the interdependencies of countries and the need to respond in an integrated way that ensures that each country's individual response strengthens the response of all countries. As a security issue, climate change challenges traditional security frameworks that privilege national interests over the collective interest. Traditional security frameworks bias policy towards national responses that focus on the manifestations of climate change, rather than the causes.

Australian strategic policy has adopted the enabling idea of the Indo-Pacific. At one level, the Indo-Pacific idea is a conceptual framework that seeks to reposition China in the region's strategic architecture. In this sense it is an idea that brings the Pacific islands into view as a location of competition, rather than as countries with individual agency. As the *2017 Foreign Policy White Paper* stated, the stability and economic progress of the Pacific region are of fundamental importance to Australia.[31] Former Prime Minister Morrison, during a visit to Solomon Islands in May 2019, stated that 'The Pacific is front and centre of Australia's strategic outlook'.[32] The challenge for defence policy in this context is to reconcile the requirement to develop policies that respond to the reality of China's increasing presence and strategic contestation in the near region while at the same time responding to the very different strategic and security perceptions of the Pacific island states.

For Australia, the principal vehicle for achieving stability in the region is through the Pacific Step-Up, which recognises and responds to the challenges in the region as identified by Pacific leaders and communities. The Department of Foreign Affairs and Trade has described the Pacific Step-Up as one of Australia's 'highest foreign policy priorities'.[33] The Pacific Step-Up is particularly focused on strengthening climate and disaster resilience, sustaining economic growth, and supporting the promotion of healthy and educated populations. It is a significant policy response to security challenges for Pacific island states, driven as much by strategic competition with China as it is a response to the needs of individual countries.

In very traditional terms, the challenge that China presents is the potential for the exercise of coercive power that raises the level of potential threat against Australia and its interests. Australian policy has always worked to prevent the emergence of a foreign power in the near region that has the capacity to directly or indirectly threaten Australia. The potential for China to establish a strategic position in the near region goes directly against very longstanding perceptions of Australia's strategic interests and how they might be sustained. However, from the perspective of the Pacific islands, the major threat to security arises from the reality of climate change. The Boe Declaration outlined the centrality of climate change as a security threat: 'We reaffirm that climate change remains the single greatest threat to the livelihoods, security and wellbeing of the peoples of the Pacific and our commitment to progress the implementation of the Paris Agreement'.[34]

The central concern of the Pacific islands is climate change, both as an existential threat of sea level rises that make life on the Pacific islands unsustainable, and as a cause of natural disasters, which in their increasing frequency and intensity are likely to make normal life impossible. Climate change is a threat to the functioning of societies at every level. For the Pacific islands, great power competition is very much a secondary concern. To the extent that Australia is unable to recognise this reality and incorporate it into its policy frameworks, its approach will continue to lack credibility. This in turn will place limits on the nature of the strategic relationship with the Pacific islands and the capacity to develop broad agreements on the nature of the security environment.

The focus of the 2020 DSU was very much on the emergence of an environment where the strategic order was changing and the potential for state-on-state conflict was increasing. This suggests that policy frameworks for understanding the strategic implications of climate change have not shifted, and that the prevailing perspective is that climate change will affect the operating environment but will be less relevant to the main strategic preoccupation, which is the changing strategic order. For the Pacific islands, this suggests that there will continue to be little scope for the development of a shared perspective on the nature of the security environment and the challenges facing it. Australian and Pacific island perceptions are likely therefore to continue to diverge, and this will create a continuing strategic opening for China.

In this respect, not only is climate change a biophysical force in the world, but it is also an arena for a political struggle concerning the perception of how the strategic order should work. For some states, such as the Pacific islands, the reality of climate change is so overwhelming in its implications, it is a major, if not the major, consideration in shaping strategic policy. For other states, like Australia, current strategic and defence policy focuses on the first element, but not the second.

The impact of climate change on the alliance

The Biden administration has placed climate change as its overriding strategic priority. In its presentation of the challenge, it has argued that it is a challenge that no single country can deal with by itself, and that no national level policy can mitigate the impact of climate change on an individual country. In his Inaugural Address, President Biden identified seven policy areas as immediate priorities, positioning the climate crisis directly after the COVID-19 crisis.[35] One week after taking office, President Biden signed an *Executive Order on Tackling the Climate Crisis at Home and Abroad*. Biden described the executive order as necessary to 'confront the existential threat of climate change'.[36] The executive order presents a whole-of-government approach to deal with the climate crisis that threatens the 'ability to live on this planet'.[37]

John Kerry, the Special Presidential Envoy for Climate, echoes Biden's rhetoric of describing climate change as an existential security threat and 'among the most complex and compelling security issues that I think we have ever faced'.[38] In an address to the UN Security Council in 2021, Kerry described climate change as 'the challenge of all of our generations' and 'so massive, so multi-faceted, that it's impossible to disentangle it from other challenges that the Security Council faces'.[39] Reiterating the urgency of climate change, Defense Secretary Lloyd Austin stated, 'today, no nation can find lasting security without addressing the climate crisis'.[40]

The opening remarks of the US Secretary of State, Antony Blinken, at the Leaders' Summit on Climate in April 2021, emphasised the need for global cooperation. He argued, 'no country can overcome this existential threat alone. We're in this together. And what each of our nations does or does not do will not only impact people of our own country, but people everywhere'.[41] The language of the Biden administration is very similar to the language of the countries of the South Pacific, which describes climate change as 'the single greatest threat to the livelihoods, security and wellbeing of the peoples of the Pacific'.[42] The Kainaki II Declaration of August 2019, was the strongest collective statement the Pacific Islands Forum leaders have ever issued on climate change. In the declaration, the leaders noted 'escalating climate change-related impacts, coupled with the intensification of geostrategic competition, is exacerbating the region's vulnerabilities'.[43]

With the Biden administration's focus on responding to climate change as the overwhelming strategic priority of the present moment, it is still an open question as to the extent to which this shift in global strategic priority by that administration will call into question the framing of security challenges, particularly in the context of climate change. The administration has positioned China as a strategic competitor but noted that it will need China's cooperation if it is to develop a truly global response to climate change. As the 2021 US–China Joint Statement Addressing the Climate Crisis stated, 'The United States and China are committed to cooperating with each other and with other countries to tackle the climate crisis, which must be addressed with the seriousness and urgency that it demands'.[44]

It is an open question as to whether this emerging feature of US strategic policy might reframe an understanding of the nature of the security challenge in the South Pacific from the perspective of the US, and the extent to which this might in turn influence Australian policy and perceptions of the security environment.

The language that former Prime Minister Morrison used, as set out in key speeches, framed the Australian approach, particularly with his emphasis on climate change being like COVID-19—a challenge that is being dealt with by countries in their own individual ways, presenting climate change as a national issue. Morrison framed climate change as a technological challenge and one that requires capacity and capability building as opposed to a whole-of-government response.[45] This puts Australia in contrast to the US. In an address to the OECD Council, Morrison stated, 'Performance on climate change matters at least as much as ambition on climate change', and that 'Above all though, the defining issue, I believe, for the global economy and regional stability, is the security and prosperity environment that is created by ensuring we address the great powers strategic competition that is occurring within the Indo Pacific region'.[46]

Morrison, like the 2020 DSU, positioned regional stability as separate from climate change, while the US and Pacific perceive them as inextricably linked. Morrison views climate change as requiring a 'technological solution', one which is led by the market. He presented climate change as not just the role of 'advanced economies', stating, 'Carbon emissions don't have national accents. They don't speak with that wonderful Irish lilt or an Australian twang'. As such, he suggested technology is the solution, technology that all countries can adopt. He shifted the focus from individual actions from countries to action from technology companies.[47] Morrison, in a statement to Parliament House, drew attention to the two countries' responses to climate change: 'like President-Elect Biden, we are committed to developing new technologies to reduce global emissions as we tackle climate change'.[48] Morrison again positioned climate change as a technological challenge and not an existential threat.

Conclusion

It is a legitimate question to ask whether strategic and defence policy can address the challenge of climate change given that it is a much larger strategic challenge than can be dealt with through the application of strategic and defence policy alone. In this sense, the focus on adaptation and capacity for crisis response may represent a feasible approach. There is some validity to this argument, particularly as Australian strategic and defence policy has been designed to deal with a certain set of challenges arising out of the interaction of states within a larger strategic system. However, climate change as a strategic force changes the nature of the system because if unchecked it puts all countries within that system at risk. There is consequently an overriding imperative to recognise the reality of interdependence, and to acknowledge that giving expression in action to this interdependence may be a more pressing requirement than the traditional focus on the preservation of state sovereignty. In other words, there is perhaps the need for a strategic policy that mandates a much larger conception of security and the reimagining of the role of strategic and defence policy in the face of climate change.

There will continue to be an emerging strategic environment of contestation between powers. There will continue to be a requirement for countries to support their security through the development of defence capability. There will continue to be a struggle to establish a new strategic order across the Indo-Pacific. However, the challenge that climate change presents is that it demands that these challenges are seen in a different and larger strategic context. The purpose of this would be to enable the development of policies and approaches that recognise the interdependency of countries and the larger imperative to take action to guarantee the survival of all countries.

As presently formulated, the Australian strategic and defence policy does not recognise the interdependency that is emerging as the governing strategic policy framework within the international community to guide the development of national level policy and approaches to climate change. In this respect, the challenge of climate change continues to be subordinate to the challenge of a changing strategic order. The argument of this chapter is that these challenges are convergent, and that climate change is the more significant challenge when considered over the longer term. Given the direction of US policy and the reality of the increasing impact of climate change, it is arguable that Australian approaches, including its framing of security and its positioning of defence within that framework, is increasingly not fit for purpose. In relation to the Pacific islands, this means that, increasingly, Australian strategic and defence policy will lack credibility because it is only a partial response to the strategic challenges that they face, and that Australia's role as a security provider will be steadily diminished.

Notes

1 Department of Defence, *2020 Defence Strategic Update,* Defence Publishing Service, Canberra, 2020.
2 Ibid., p. 16.
3 M McDonald, 'Climate Change and Security: Towards Ecological Security?', *International Theory,* vol. 10, no. 2, 2018, pp. 153–80.
4 Department of Foreign Affairs and Trade, *2017 Foreign Policy White Paper,* Foreign Affairs and Trade Publishing Service, Canberra, 2017, p. 4.
5 J Biden, 'Remarks by President Biden, Prime Minister Modi of India, Prime Minister Morrison of Australia, and Prime Minister Suga of Japan in the Virtual Quad Leaders Summit', The White House Briefing Room, 12 March 2021.
6 S Morrison, 'Remarks by President Biden, Prime Minister Modi of India, Prime Minister Morrison of Australia, and Prime Minister Suga of Japan in the Virtual Quad Leaders Summit', The White House Briefing Room, 12 March 2021.
7 B Westcott, 'Malcolm Fraser Calls for an End to the Australian-US Alliance', *Sydney Morning Herald,* 13 May 2014.
8 The 'deputy sheriff' phrase was first coined in 1999 after Howard failed to swiftly deny an Australian media report that he would accept that role for maintaining security in the region as part of his US alliance. G Henderson, 'Howard Should End Confusion on Foreign Policy', *The Age,* 3 June 2003.
9 ABC News, 'China Tells Australia to Abandon its "Cold War mentality" while Criticising Our Politicians,' 29 April 2021.

10 Department of Defence, *1987 Defence White Paper*, Australian Government Publishing Service, Canberra, 1987.

11 P Dibb, *Review of Australia's Defence Capabilities*, Australian Government Publishing Service, Canberra 1986, p. 4.

12 This section has been updated by the editors.

13 Department of Defence, *2020 Defence Strategic Update*, p. 16.

14 Ibid.

15 Australian Government, *2023 National Defence Strategic Review*, Commonwealth of Australia, Canberra, 2023, p. 17.

16 R Glasser, 'The ADF Will Have to Deal with the Consequences of Climate Change', *The Strategist*, 28 April 2023.

17 Department of Home Affairs, 'Alternative Commonwealth Capabilities for Crisis Response, Discussion Paper', August 2023. See also S Harris Rimmer, 'How to Defend Australians: A Heterodox Approach', Centre of Gravity series, 2020.

18 Department of Defence, *2000, Defence White Paper*, Defence Publishing Service, Canberra, 2000, p. 53.

19 Department of Defence, *2009, Defence White Paper*, Defence Publishing Service, Canberra, 2009, p. 54.

20 Ibid., pp. 39–40.

21 Ibid., pp. 40.

22 Department of Defence, *2013, Defence White Paper*, Defence Publishing Service, Canberra, 2013, p. 15.

23 Ibid., pp. 18–19.

24 Ibid., pp. 18–19.

25 Department of Defence, *2016 Defence White Paper*, Defence Publishing Service, Canberra, 2016, p. 48.

26 Commonwealth of Australia, 'Chapter 7: Role of the Australian Defence Force', *Report of the Royal Commission into National Natural Disaster Arrangements*, Commonwealth of Australia, Canberra, 2020, p. 189.

27 M Taylor, 'Remarks by the Secretary General, Dame Meg Taylor, at the 3rd China–Pacific Island Countries Economic Development and Cooperation Forum', Pacific Islands Forum, 21 October 2019.

28 Pacific Islands Forum, Kainaki II Declaration for Urgent Climate Action Now, 15 August 2019.

29 Ibid.

30 Pacific Islands Forum, Boe Declaration on Regional Security, 5 September, 2018.

31 Department of Foreign Affairs and Trade, *2017 Foreign Policy White Paper*.

32 S Morrison, 'Visit to Solomon Islands, United Kingdom and Singapore', Media Release, 27 May 2019.

33 Department of Foreign Affairs and Trade, 'Pacific Step Up: Stepping up Australia's Engagement with Our Pacific Family', September 2019.

34 Pacific Islands Forum, Boe Declaration on Regional Security.

35 J Biden, 'Inaugural Address by President Joseph R. Biden, Jr.', The White House Briefing Room, 20 January 2021; J Biden, 'The Biden-Harris Administration Immediate Priorities', The White House, 2021.

36 J Biden, 'Remarks by President Biden Before Signing Executive Actions on Tackling Climate Change, Creating Jobs, and Restoring Scientific Integrity', The White House Briefing Room, 27 January 2021.

37 J Biden, 'Executive Order on Tackling the Climate Crisis at Home and Abroad', The White House, 27 January 2021.

38 J Kerry, 'Secretary Kerry Participates in the UN Security Council Open Debate on Climate and Security', US Department of State, 23 February 2021.

39 Kerry, 'Secretary Kerry Participates in the UN Security Council Open Debate on Climate and Security'.

40 L Austin, 'Secretary Austin Remarks at Climate Change Summit', US Department of Defense, 22 April 2021.

41 A Blinken, 'Opening Remarks at the Virtual Leaders Summit on Climate', US Department of State, 22 April 2021.

42 Pacific Islands Forum, Boe Declaration on Regional Security.

43 Pacific Islands Forum, Kainaki II Declaration for Urgent Climate Action Now.

44 'U.S.-China Joint Statement Addressing the Climate Crisis', Press Release, US Department of State, 17 April 2021.

45 S Morrison, 'Press Conference—OECD Council, Paris', Media Release, 16 June 2021.

46 Ibid.

47 Ibid.

48 S Morrison, 'Statement—Australian Parliament House, ACT', 9 November 2020.

A CLIMATE AGENDA FOR AUSTRALIA'S PACIFIC DEVELOPMENT, DIPLOMACY AND DEFENCE ENGAGEMENT

Melissa Conley Tyler

O N 21 MAY 2022, Australia elected a new government. It also elected a record number of Greens and community independents running on a platform of climate action.[1] This result was widely interpreted as an expression of frustration with the previous government's inaction and lack of ambition on climate goals. To add to the public mood, just a few weeks later much of Australia was hit by an energy crisis—adding urgency to the calls to move quickly away from fossil fuels.[2]

The new government's election commitments included an emissions reduction of 43 per cent below 2005 levels by 2030, investment in solar banks and community batteries, rewiring the energy grid, promotion of clean energy exports and manufacturing, encouraging take-up of electric vehicles and conducting a climate change risk assessment.[3] Less than a month after the election, Australia notified the United Nations of a revised emissions reduction goal,[4] making news around the world.[5]

Nowhere was the change in government more transformative than in relations with the Pacific. There had been no secret about Pacific island countries' views about Australia's lack of climate ambition. For example, Australia's behaviour at the 2019 Pacific Islands Forum meeting in watering down the language around climate action in the final communiqué was heavily criticised by Pacific leaders,[6] with Tuvalu's Prime Minister Enele Sopoaga saying Australia's Pacific Step-Up would 'not mean anything ... unless we deal with the issue of climate change. It's as serious as that'.[7]

Only four days after being sworn in as Minister for Foreign Affairs, Penny Wong visited Fiji to speak to the Pacific Islands Forum Secretariat to herald 'a new era in Australian engagement in the Pacific'.[8] She put climate action at the centre of her remarks, promising: 'This is a different Australian Government. We will stand shoulder to shoulder with our Pacific family in response to this crisis'.

Minister Wong repeated similar sentiments in her visits to Samoa[9] and Tonga[10] and to New Zealand[11] and Solomon Islands.[12] She stressed the 'change in direction' on climate[13] by a government with 'a very different view on climate change to our predecessors'.[14] She said the government sees itself having 'ground to make up'[15] after 'a lost decade on climate action'.[16] And she presented the focus on climate issues as responding to the will of the people: 'the Australian people have voted for a government and a parliament that is supportive of more ambitious action on climate change. And that is what we will do at home and in the world'.[17] These messages were reinforced by Prime Minister Anthony Albanese at the Pacific Islands Forum Leaders' Summit in July.[18]

The initial response from Pacific leaders was very positive. Prime Minister Fiamē Naomi Mata'afa of Samoa stated:

> We're very pleased in Samoa, and no doubt the Pacific region, that with the new Australian Government, the policy shift brings them closer to alignment with the Pacific advocacy for climate change. We feel that this will strengthen the Pacific position on climate change.[19]

Prime Minister Siaosi Sovaleni of Tonga responded in similar terms:

> We are particularly pleased with the Australian Government's recognition that climate change is an existential threat, including to the security of our islands. We are pleased to learn of Australia's effort to reduce carbon emissions and increase the share of renewable energy.[20]

One of the memorable images of the Pacific Islands Forum Leaders' Summit was Solomon Islands Prime Minister Manasseh Sogavare hugging Prime Minister Albanese.[21]

The question will be how to build on this positive momentum so that climate action becomes something that ties Australia and the Pacific closer together rather than pushing them apart.

During 2022, I led a program consulting with more than 140 experts in Australia and the Pacific on how Australia can shape a shared future with the Pacific across its defence, diplomacy and development cooperation.[22] This resulted in an Asia-Pacific Development, Diplomacy & Defence Dialogue (AP4D) options paper on what it looks like for Australia to be an effective climate ally with the Pacific.[23]

Below, I outline the eight-part agenda set out in this AP4D options paper and look at how much of this has been evident in the Albanese government's first two months in office. It shows a new government determined to change direction on climate and improve relations with the Pacific, very much in line with the AP4D vision of Australia as a Pacific climate ally.

There remain issues that Australia will need to work on, given that many of the challenges and blockages that the previous government faced still exist. This means Australia will need to maintain its focus on how it can be a climate ally and embed this in all the arms of statecraft with which it engages the Pacific.

Declaratory policy

The first pathway recommended by the AP4D options paper focuses on changing Australia's declaratory policy to put the effects, impacts and root causes of climate change as Australia's central foreign policy concern in the Pacific:

> The Australian Government changes its declaratory policy on climate, signalling a shift to a new approach. This would include reaffirming the Boe Declaration[24] and Kainaki II Declaration,[25] which both assert that climate change is the single greatest threat to the Pacific region.

Climate change is the primary security issue for Pacific island countries and, due to their geographies, is an existential threat. Australia's comprehension of what is at stake for Pacific island countries is critical to its own regional security objectives. This requires taking Pacific concerns seriously and approaching climate change as a major regional priority requiring massive, urgent action.

The new government has made a point of stating this clearly and unequivocally. The words of Minister for Foreign Affairs Wong's first speech are worth quoting at length to show the way she acknowledged Pacific frustration and declared a new way forward:

> As Australia's first ever Climate Minister, I know the imperative that we all share to take serious action to reduce emissions and transform our economies. Nothing is more central to the security and economies of the Pacific. I understand that climate change is not an abstract threat, but an existential one. It's right there in the Pacific Island Forum's Boe Declaration on Regional Security from 2018 ...
>
> You've been saying this for a long time. Pacific leaders were saying this to me when I was Climate Minister over a decade ago. You've been crystal clear and consistent. You've led the global debate.
>
> I understand that—under past governments—Australia has neglected its responsibility to act on climate change. Ignoring the

calls of our Pacific family to act. Disrespecting Pacific nations in their struggle to adapt to what is an existential threat. Whether it manifests in rising sea levels in Pacific Island countries, or in disastrous bushfires and catastrophic flooding back at home in Australia, we can see that climate change is happening across the Pacific family.

I want to assure you that we have heard you. As our election last weekend showed—Australians understand the imperative of acting on climate change. The climate crisis loomed as one of the key concerns to the Australian people. There is a huge groundswell of support for taking real action on the climate crisis in Australia ... and the new Government is firmly committed to making it happen.[26]

This was reinforced when Prime Minister Albanese spoke in Suva about 'the very real threat of climate change has to our Pacific Islanders neighbours—for countries like Tuvalu and Kiribati, it is a threat to their very existence',[27] and contrasted this with the previous government and its 'argy-bargy about whether climate change was real or not'.[28]

Climate and energy policy

The second pathway recommended in the AP4D option paper focuses on Australia's own energy and climate policies:

Australia announces an ambitious emissions target for 2030, in line with key partners including the United States, Europe, United Kingdom and the G7. Australia adopts climate and energy policies that gives market operators certainty about Australia's climate ambitions and sends a strong signal to the market that investment in renewables is viable and profitable.

Australia establishes regional targets for decarbonisation in 2030 and 2050 as part of the 2050 Strategy for the Blue Pacific. This would involve a timeline to phase out coal as a domestic energy source, as well as a recognition that coal will have a limited lifespan as an export commodity.

Australia's economic and political settings have not matched Australia's foreign policy priorities in the Pacific. The reluctance of successive Australian governments to set ambitious emissions reduction targets has hindered Australia's diplomatic efforts in the Pacific. Given the importance of these issues to the Pacific, Australia's domestic energy policy effectively became its foreign policy within the region.

Pacific leaders believe that Australia has signed up to a series of regional agreements on climate and should meet these commitments regardless of the domestic pressure within Australia on energy policy.

Energy policy has been the 'third rail' of Australian domestic politics, slowing Australia's transition towards renewables. At the federal political level, Australia's approach to climate change has been impacted by the economics of coal and natural gas being its second and third largest exports.

The election result was a sign that the consensus in favour of climate action is strengthening. Polling shows that Australians are conscious of vulnerability to climate change and there is widespread recognition of the climate crisis.[29]

In her first speech in the Pacific, Minister for Foreign Affairs Wong set out the changes that the Pacific will see in Australia's climate and energy policy:

> The Albanese Government was elected on a platform of reducing carbon emissions by 43 per cent by 2030 and reaching net zero by 2050. We won't just say this—we will enshrine it in law and submit a new Nationally Determined Contribution to the UNFCCC very soon.
>
> We are committed to transitioning to a low carbon economy, moving to cleaner, cheaper energy. Our plan will see the proportion of renewables in Australia's National Energy Market

increase to 82 per cent by 2030. It's a plan to boost renewable energy, create jobs and reduce emissions.[30]

This means that Australia has an energy policy that is committed to transitioning away from the use of fossil fuels for domestic energy consumption. There may be an increasing realisation that exports of fossil fuels have a limited lifespan and that new sources of export revenue need to be found before demand for fossil fuels in international markets falls.

Certainly, the government has clearly stated a vision of Australia becoming a major exporter of renewable energy, with Prime Minister Albanese in Suva stressing the opportunity for Australia to become a 'renewable energy superpower'.[31] Australia's emergence as a renewable energy superpower would allow it to reconcile its economic needs with its foreign policy in the Pacific, enhancing Australia's global standing, as well as respect and trust within the Pacific.

Climate diplomacy

The third pathway recommended in the AP4D option paper focuses on Australia acting as an ally with the Pacific in international climate diplomacy:

> Australia works with Pacific island countries to undertake meaningful collective diplomacy on climate change, working as an ally for climate action on the global stage. It supports the Friends of Climate and Security Group in the United Nations Security Council. This should include issuing a regional declaration at the Pacific Islands Forum calling on all countries to submit nationally determined contributions consistent with limiting warming to 1.5C.
>
> Australia and Pacific island countries co-host a Conference of the Parties (COP) meeting as a demonstration of Australia's commitment to the targets set by the Paris Agreement, as well

as affirmation that Australia is a dedicated member of the Pacific family.

Pacific island countries have been at the forefront of global concern about climate change since the scientific consensus emerged in the mid-1980s.[32] They demonstrated diplomatic leadership by forming an alliance of mutual interest and concerns with island states in the Caribbean and the Indian Ocean in 1990 (the AOSIS), while the following year the South Pacific Forum (as the Pacific Islands Forum was then called) released a statement stating that climate change posed a major risk to the region.[33] Pacific island countries were instrumental in putting climate change on the agenda at the UN Security Council, while Pacific leaders have become highly experienced in climate negotiations.[34]

The Pacific's leadership on climate issues was recognised by Minister for Foreign Affairs Wong in her first speech, noting that 'Pacific nations have championed their interests on the international stage—and led international thinking on issues such as climate'.[35] She shared her experience of seeing Pacific leadership in action:

> I remember when I was Minister for Climate Change between 2007 and 2010 that the voices of the Pacific were so strong and so authentic and spoke with so much power because for you climate change isn't abstract, it's not a political argument—it's real.[36]

She went on to commit Australia to becoming a leader in climate diplomacy and to work collectively with the Pacific: 'It's why we will work to regain Australia's role as an international leader on climate change. We will reinstate the role of Australia's Ambassador for Climate Change. And we have proposed a bid to co-host a future UN Conference of the Parties with Pacific Island countries'.

In particular, the proposal to co-host a future COP suggests that Australia is joining the Pacific in a regional diplomatic bloc that can drive global ambition on climate change mitigation. This positions

Australia as a constructive partner working with the Pacific in a model of shared leadership, and as a genuine part of Pacific regionalism as an integral and invested part of the Pacific neighbourhood.

Prime Minister Albanese noted 'the support of all of, every single one of, the island nations support for our bid for a Conference of the Parties on climate change to be held with Australia and the Pacific'.[37] This suggests Australia is no longer isolated from the international consensus on climate action and enhances its status on the global stage by working together with the Pacific. Connected and combined, Australia and the Pacific have a strong international voice on climate action.

Dialogue and links

The fourth pathway recommended in the AP4D option paper focuses on Australia creating dialogue and building on existing links:

> The relationship with Pacific peoples is a key focus of Australia's First Nations Foreign Policy.
>
> Australia builds on the good practice relationships that exist between Australia's climate science organisations and Pacific equivalents—including CSIRO, Geoscience Australia and the Bureau of Meteorology—and through higher education and technical training.[38]
>
> Australia establishes an annual discussion within the Pacific with a specific climate focus: 'a 1.5 Track Dialogue for 1.5 Degrees'.

Out of these, the government committed to implementing a First Nations Foreign Policy that 'incorporates First Nations identities, perspectives and practices into Australia's overseas engagement' as part of its election platform.[39] Minister for Foreign Affairs Wong highlighted this in her first speech in the Pacific:

> We will move to enshrine an Indigenous Voice to Parliament in this term of government ...

And in my own portfolio as Foreign Minister, we will develop a First Nations approach to foreign policy. We will appoint Australia's inaugural First Nations Ambassador—who will lead a new office within DFAT.

And on a range of other fronts we will be working to enhance the role and position of First Nations peoples, both at home and overseas.[40]

She also brought it up during her visit to New Zealand, noting her host country's depth of wisdom on Indigenous perspectives on foreign policy and areas Australia can learn from.[41]

This provides a valuable opportunity. The relationship between Australia's First Nations and Pacific peoples is a missing pillar of Australia's relations with the Pacific, with Pacific communities signalling that they want to collaborate more with First Nations people. Indigenous knowledge can be a critical component in this knowledge-building. For example, Indigenous perspectives on environmental guardianship complement the Blue Pacific concept, focusing on collective and individual responsibilities for caring for Country.[42]

Interestingly, scientific links were not mentioned by the Minister for Foreign Affairs or the Prime Minister in their featured media appearances in the Pacific,[43] suggesting it is not as much of a focus, perhaps as a mature area of cooperation.[44]

Prime Minister Albanese has spoken of the importance of 'engagement and people-to-people relations' to build mutual understanding with the Pacific, including floating the idea of more sporting links in rugby union and rugby league.[45]

Disaster risk and response

The fifth pathway recommended in the AP4D option paper looks at Australia's role in disaster preparedness and response:

Australia should conduct a national review of climate risks. This should subsequently be extended by collaborating with Pacific island countries and New Zealand on a regional climate risk assessment.

Australia needs to build local disaster response capacity given that longer and larger disaster seasons are going to challenge the region. Localisation will be an imperative.

Defence can promote greater civil-military cooperation and involvement of first responders including fire and emergency services. It should promote greater climate disaster response interoperability between Australia and the Pacific, as has occurred with the FRANZ arrangement.[46]

Disaster response is an area where Australia and the Pacific have shared interests and opportunities to work together. With Australian communities suffering major weather events, there is growing awareness of the shared experiences of Australians and their Pacific neighbours. Climate is part of mainstream defence debate in Australia, with the Australian Defence Force often called upon to respond to extreme weather events.[47] From the Pacific side, there is recognition of Australian funding for disaster response and for community adaptation over at least two decades.

Minister for Foreign Affairs Wong conveyed a strong message on mutuality:

One of the most powerful examples of the depth of our bond is the way our Pacific brothers and sisters have come to Australia's aid—during the Black Summer bushfires and more recently during our devastating floods.

It shows that we do what families do. We are there for each other in good times and in bad.[48]

This shows an understanding that the relationship is not just one-way and that there is an opportunity to build on this for mutual learning, with the Pacific contributing local knowledge and innovations in the areas of environmental management and climate adaptation.

Climate finance

The sixth pathway recommended in the AP4D option paper focuses on Australia's role in assisting the Pacific to access climate finance:

> Australia rejoins the Green Climate Fund (GCF) which has become a major funder of climate projects in the region. As well as increased finance, this also provides the opportunity for Australia to advocate for reform to GCF governance as it applies to Pacific island countries. Currently, the preferred ways of working of Pacific countries in relation to climate change, particularly in support of direct access pathways to climate finance, is not well supported by GCF rules and regulation. Australia could use its diplomatic influence and development financing expertise to reform these practices.
>
> Given Pacific countries' huge needs for climate finance, Australia should support a range of financing modalities. This should include the Pacific Resilience Fund recently established by the Pacific Islands Forum and the Regional Pacific Nationally Determined Contribution (NDC) Hub.

Pacific countries face a large climate finance gap, with demand for financing of climate adaptation far exceeding existing opportunities. There is also a lack of transparency and coherence in climate financing. The Green Climate Fund has become the dominant climate fund in the Pacific since it started approving projects in 2015. It has proven difficult for Pacific island countries to directly access financing through this mechanism, with low rates of accreditation and spending.[49] This means that often funding is not getting to the local level in the Pacific.[50]

Minister for Foreign Affairs Wong acknowledged the importance of the issue in the Pacific in her first speech in Fiji: 'That's why we have announced an Australia-Pacific Climate Infrastructure Partnership to support climate-related infrastructure and energy projects in Pacific countries and Timor-Leste ... We will offer quality, climate resilient infrastructure'.[51]

However, Australia went to the Pacific Island Forum Leaders' Summit without a position on the specific question of rejoining the Green Climate Fund. Following the Summit, Minister for Foreign Affairs Wong stated, 'We have not made a final decision', and that she would work through it with Minister for Climate Change and Energy Chris Bowen.[52]

This may well have been deliberate, as a way to ask Pacific leaders how Australia can best support green finance and then to be seen to be listening and responding in its eventual policy decision.

Migration

The seventh pathway recommended in the AP4D option paper focuses on long-term planning around migration:

> Australia needs to prepare for the future in its migration poli-
> cies, tackling the problem of climate mobility as a serious issue
> given the need for people movement to major economies and
> within the region. Safe migration pathways need to be discussed
> and a new regional convention of refugees may be needed. The
> desire to maintain community bonds and culture may require
> a new model that allows Pacific communities to retain nation-
> hood within Australia's political structure. Australian leaders
> should plan for the need to prepare the domestic population for
> an influx of people from the Pacific.

In the Pacific, the comprehensive effects of climate change are dislo-cating communities and affecting both human and traditional security calculations. Low-lying regions face the prospect of wholesale migration as islands become uninhabitable.[53] Across the region there are impacts on employment, resource availability, food security and emergency ser-vices. For fragile states there is the danger of complete state failure.

There is a deep concern among Pacific island countries about migra-tion as a form of adaptation. Relocating is not the best or preferred option, especially given the cultural ties of Pacific peoples to their homelands. Migration as a form of adaptation also shifts the responsibility of adaptation away from carbon emitters to individuals and families.

This makes it a fraught topic of discussion.

The current focus in the migration space is on labour mobility and pathways to permanent migration. These were the subject of another AP4D paper on Pacific economies and societies.[54]

In Minister for Foreign Affairs Wong's first speech in the Pacific she focused on labour mobility and on pathways to permanency, as set out in the ALP's election policy:

> We will ensure that those Pacific Islanders who come to work in Australia are treated fairly—with better conditions. We will allow workers to bring their families.
>
> And we will create the Pacific engagement visa—to provide a pathway to permanency for 3,000 members of our Pacific family per year.[55]

She focused on longer-term stays, on the ability to bring family and on pathways to permanency in her media appearances in Fiji,[56] Samoa,[57] Tonga[58] and Solomon Islands.[59] This was clearly a topic of great interest and one that has been welcomed.

Similarly, in his appearances in Fiji, the Prime Minister focused on the Pacific Australian Labour Mobility scheme (including expanding it to services and enabling family members to accompany workers) and new pathways to permanent residency.[60] He spoke warmly about the election commitment to create pathways 'to make people from the Pacific permanent Australian Citizens ... to give people more security', saying 'there will always be a role for temporary migration, but I am someone who believes people should have a stake in the country they live'.[61] Some of the win-win benefits of labour mobility he mentioned—such as building people-to-people relations—could be used to argue for further migration pathways in the future.

At some point, discussion around migration may need to look at longer term issues, but at present the focus is on using migration to provide economic benefits in terms of skills and remittances and to contribute to the longer-term aim of building a sense of Pacific family.

Loss and damage

Finally, the eighth pathway in the AP4D options paper is on the emerging issue of loss and damage:

> Australia should continue to engage with Pacific island countries in the emerging debate calling for reparation for loss and damage caused by carbon emitters. There are likely to be continuing calls as a question of climate justice. With outstanding issues following the Glasgow Conference of the Parties (COP), there is an opportunity for Australia-Pacific collaboration to be part of this debate.

The issue of climate change is all-encompassing in the Pacific. It permeates everything, given its existential nature. There is a shared sense across the region of the importance of climate change as a security threat and an understanding of the loss and damage that climate change will cause. Most recently, there have been attempts to quantify this loss and damage.[62]

This area hasn't been mentioned by the new government, in speeches or doorstops in the region. It is likely that it is a topic that Australia will have to continue to engage with as international discussions continue over the term of the government.

The path ahead

The analysis above shows that the new government has implemented key parts of the vision of Australia as a climate ally with the Pacific developed by the Asia-Pacific Development, Diplomacy & Defence Dialogue (AP4D) through consultations with more than 140 experts in Australia and the Pacific.[63] There have been strong declarations of a change in climate policy—'We will end the climate wars in Australia'[64]—and concrete changes in Australia's climate and energy policy. Australia has shown that it wishes to act as an ally with the

Pacific in international climate diplomacy and is signalling the desire to build dialogue and people-to-people links, including through labour mobility and migration pathways and through a First Nations Foreign Policy. There have been positive statements on mutual learning around disaster risks and on ways to facilitate climate finance.

The Pacific Islands Forum Leaders' Summit in July 2022 showed how much of a change Australia's new approach to climate action had made to its relations with the Pacific—but also gave a hint of issues ahead. Australia signed up to a communiqué mentioning 'the current climate emergency',[65] in contrast with 2019, when it was accused of watering down the language in a marathon meeting which reportedly led to shouting and tears.[66] Australia also backed Vanuatu's bid to seek a legal opinion from the International Court of Justice on climate change. Commentators noted that the new Prime Minister 'brought a refreshing change in Australia's tone and attitude to the forum'.[67] Pacific leaders welcomed Australia's new emissions reduction targets and supported Australia's proposal to co-host a future UN Conference of the Parties with Pacific island countries. There was a palpable sense of greater alignment, with the shift in tone being welcomed by regional leaders.[68] Ahead of the Forum, Tuvalu's Foreign Minister, Simon Kofe, described a sense of being 'on the same page'.[69] Australia's new stance appears to have created the desired reset in relations.[70]

However, even amid this celebratory atmosphere,[71] there were calls for Australia to go further. Fiji's Prime Minister Frank Bainimarama tweeted:

> Australia's new climate pledge is a step-up that Fiji has long sought—but out of the duty I owe every young person in the Pacific, I have urged @AlboMP to go further for our family's shared future by aligning Australia's commitment to the 1.5-degree target.[72]

One obvious area of difference was Australia's stance on new coal and gas developments. The new government's position is that it is willing to approve new developments within its emission reduction targets and environmental standards.[73] The Pacific consensus is for the position the Greens took into the election, of no new fossil fuel developments. While Prime Minister Albanese has said that this wasn't raised with him during the Leaders' Summit[74]—and Minister for Foreign Affairs Wong has said that Pacific leaders hadn't asked her for this commitment—it has definitely been advocated by former Pacific leaders and climate activists.[75]

This suggests that, positive as the initial reaction to the new government has been, in the medium term there will continue to be friction. Pacific island countries have made clear their commitment to strong climate action: 'Pacific countries know they're in a fight for survival, and any country that wants their support must show it's serious about tackling climate change'.[76] In the remainder of its term, the Albanese government is likely to see continuing calls for Australia to increase its climate ambition. It will remain a key issue for the Pacific, and Australia should expect pressure to progressively increase its ambition over time.

Conclusion

Climate change is a shared experience Australia has with the Pacific. Through rising sea levels, changes in weather patterns and more extreme weather events, climate change is creating severe disruption to both Australian and Pacific communities.

Since the May 2022 election, there are positive signs of Australia becoming a constructive partner for the Pacific on the mutual challenge of climate change. There are signs of a realisation that for Australia to become an effective climate ally with the Pacific it needs to do more than simply position itself as a first responder to natural disasters. Australia needs to revisit its own contribution to climate change as a major emitter and fossil fuel exporter through an ambitious domestic climate policy and work with Pacific island countries through processes of multilateral diplomacy to drive global ambition to reduce emissions.

Using the AP4D's agenda for what this looks like in practice it is possible to see much positive momentum from the new government in pursuing a vision that aligns with the ideal of Australia as a climate ally with the Pacific. While it won't all be plain sailing ahead—with Australia likely to continue to face pressure around the speed of its transition away from fossil fuels—it is much more positive than it looked in 2021.

The changes in Australia's climate position—and the way this has been expressed—suggest that the new Australian government is attempting to pursue a Pacific diplomacy that is based on mutuality and respect, including for Pacific concerns on climate change, with an understanding that Australia's security and Pacific security are interlinked.[77] It is a vision where a shared future for the Pacific family is shaped using all Australia's arms of statecraft, putting 'more energy and more resources into the Pacific ... to engage more closely and to listen respectfully'.[78] This enables Australia to promote, in Prime Minister Albanese's words, 'our shared interests in a peaceful, prosperous and resilient region and to addressing the pressing challenges our region faces'.[79]

As Minister for Foreign Affairs Wong puts it:

Nothing will change our geography, our proximity. Nothing will change the fact that our future is intertwined ... Today, I was keen to use this opportunity to start to underscore our commitment to doing our part to strengthen our Pacific Family. Central to this is action on climate change. But as I have outlined, we will draw on all elements of our relationships to achieve our shared interests in building a stable and prosperous region, where rules and sovereignty are respected. As fellow members of the Pacific Family, our security and prosperity is truly a thing we achieve together, or not at all.[80]

Coordinated climate action is an opportunity for Australia's development, diplomacy and defence engagement to work together in an integrated way to build a shared future with the Pacific.

Notes

1 A Klein, 'Australia Votes for Stronger Climate Action in "Greenslide" Election', *New Scientist*, 23 May 2022.

2 G Whiteside, 'Plans for Australia's First Offshore Wind Farms Forge Ahead as Energy Crisis Continues', ABC News, 23 July 2022.

3 Australian Labor Party, *Powering Australia*, 2022. For a comparison of the climate policies that parties took to the 2022 election see Climate Council, 'Australian Political Party Platform Analysis—2022 Federal Election'.

4 Department of Industry, Science and Resources, 'Australia Submits New Emissions Target to UNFCCC', 16 June 2022.

5 For example, T Turnbull, 'Climate Change: Australia Signs New Carbon Emissions Target', BBC, 16 June 2022.

6 K Lyons, 'Fiji PM Accuses Scott Morrison of "Insulting" and Alienating Pacific Leaders', *The Guardian*, 16 August 2019.

7 K Lyons, 'Australia Waters Down Pacific Islands Plea on Climate Crisis', *The Guardian*, 16 August 2019.

8 P Wong, 'A New Era in Australian Engagement in the Pacific', 26 May 2022.

9 P Wong, 'Joint Press Conference—Apia, Samoa', 2 June 2022.

10 P Wong, 'Joint Press Conference—Nuku'alofa, Tonga', 3 June 2022.

11 P Wong, 'Joint Press Conference with New Zealand Foreign Minister Nanaia Mahuta', 16 June 2022.

12 P Wong, 'Press Conference—Honiara', 17 June 2022.

13 P Wong, 'Joint Press Conference—Apia, Samoa', 2 June 2022.

14 P Wong, 'Joint Press Conference with New Zealand Foreign Minister Nanaia Mahuta', 16 June 2022.

15 Ibid.

16 P Wong, 'Doorstop Interview Suva', 27 May 2022.

17 P Wong, 'Joint Press Conference—Nuku'alofa, Tonga', 3 June 2022.

18 A Albanese, 'Doorstop Interview Suva', 14 July 2022.

19 P Wong, 'Joint Press Conference—Apia, Samoa', 2 June 2022.

20 P Wong, 'Joint Press Conference—Nuku'alofa, Tonga', 3 June 2022.

21 E Ransley and C McLeod, '"Need a Hug": Anthony Albanese Meets Solomon Islands PM for First Time', News.com.au, 13 July 2022.

22 Asia-Pacific Development, Diplomacy & Defence Dialogue, *Australia and the Pacific: Shaping a Shared Future*, Canberra 2022. This program was funded by the Australian Civil-Military Centre.

23 Asia-Pacific Development, Diplomacy & Defence Dialogue, *What Does it Look Like for Australia to Be an Effective Climate Ally with the Pacific*, Canberra, 2022.

24 Pacific Islands Forum, Boe Declaration on Regional Security, September 2018.

25 Pacific Islands Forum, 'Kainaki II Declaration for Urgent Climate Action Now', August 2019.

26 P Wong, 'A New Era in Australian Engagement in the Pacific'.

27 A Albanese, 'Doorstop Interview Suva', 14 July 2022.

28 A Albanese, 'Doorstop Interview Suva', 15 July 2022.

29 The Australia Institute, *Climate of the Nation 2021, Tracking Australia's Attitudes Towards Climate Change and Energy,* October 2021.

30 P Wong, 'A New Era in Australian Engagement in the Pacific'.

31 A Albanese, 'Doorstop Interview Suva', 14 July 2022.

32 G Carter, *Establishing a Pacific Voice in the Climate Change Negotiations,* in G Fry and S Tarte (eds), *The New Pacific Diplomacy,* ANU Press, Canberra, 2015, pp. 205–22.

33 South Pacific Forum, *22nd South Pacific Forum, Palikir, Pohnpei, Federated States of Micronesia, 29–30 July: Forum Communiqué,* 1991.

34 F Manoa, 'The Pacific Small Island Developing States (PSIDS)' Early Advocacy on Climate and Security at the United Nations', Griffith Asia Insights, 27 May 2021.

35 P Wong, 'A New Era in Australian Engagement in the Pacific'.

36 P Wong, 'Doorstop Interview Suva', 27 May 2022.

37 A Albanese, 'Doorstop Interview Suva', 14 July 2022.

38 Australia Aid, *Australia Pacific Climate Partnership,* ClimateWise.

39 Australian Labor Party, *First Nations,* 2022.

40 P Wong, 'A New Era in Australian Engagement in the Pacific'.

41 P Wong, 'Joint Press Conference with New Zealand Foreign Minister Nanaia Mahuta'.

42 J Blackwell and J Ballangarry, *Indigenous Foreign Policy: A New Way Forward?,* AFFPC Issues Paper Series, issue 1, April 2022.

43 See, for example, A Albanese, 'Doorstop Interview Suva', 14 July 2022; and A Albanese, 'Doorstop Interview Suva', 15 July 2022.

44 See, for example, Department of Foreign Affairs, 'SciTech4Climate: Harnessing Science and Technology to Support Climate Resilience in the Indo-Pacific', n.d.

45 Albanese, 'Doorstop Interview Suva', 14 July 2022.

46 Ministry of Foreign Affairs and Trade, *The FRANZ Arrangement,* October 2014.

47 Department of Defence, *2020 Defence Strategic Update,* July 2021.

48 P Wong, Speech to the Pacific Islands Forum Secretariat, Suva, Fiji, 26 May 2022.

49 International Monetary Fund, *Unlocking Access to Climate Finance for Pacific Island Countries,* Departmental Papers, 2021.

50 International Federation of Red Cross and Red Crescent Societies, *World Disasters Report 2020, Come Heat or High Water, Tackling the Humanitarian Impacts of the Climate Crises Together,* 2020.

51 Wong, 'A New Era in Australian Engagement in the Pacific'.

52 Albanese, 'Doorstop Interview Suva', 14 July 2022.

53 K Lyons, 'IPCC Report Shows "Possible Loss of Entire Countries within the Century"', *The Guardian*, 10 August 2021.

54 Asia-Pacific Development, Diplomacy & Defence Dialogue, *What Does it Look Like for Australia to Be a Generational Partner for Pacific Economies and Societies.*

55 Wong, 'A New Era in Australian Engagement in the Pacific'.

56 Wong, 'Doorstop Interview Suva'.

57 Wong, 'Joint Press Conference—Apia, Samoa'.

58 Wong, 'Joint Press Conference—Nuku'alofa, Tonga'.

59 P Wong, 'Press Conference—Honiara', 17 June 2022.

60 A Albanese, 'Doorstop Interview Suva', 15 July 2022; Albanese, 'Doorstop Interview Suva', 14 July 2022.

61 Albanese, 'Doorstop Interview Suva', 14 July 2022.

62 World Economic Forum, 'Has Vanuatu Just Made the Most Significant Change to Any Country's Climate Change Commitments?', 15 August 2022.

63 Asia-Pacific Development, Diplomacy & Defence Dialogue, *What Does it Look Like for Australia to Be a Generational Partner for Pacific Economies and Societies.*

64 Wong, 'A New Era in Australian Engagement in the Pacific'.

65 Pacific Islands Forum, *51st Pacific Islands Forum, Suva, Fiji, 11–14 July 2022, Forum Communiqué*, 2022.

66 J Collins, 'What Happened at the Pacific Islands Forum', *The Interpreter*, 15 July 2022.

67 J Wallis, A Powles and S Middleby, 'Australia and New Zealand Have a Golden Opportunity to Build Stronger Ties in the Pacific—But Will they Take it?', *The Conversation*, 20 July 2022.

68 T Newton Cain and S Armbruster, 'Smiles in Suva: The 51st Pacific Islands Forum Leaders' Meeting', DevPolicy, 19 July 2022.

69 K Lyons, 'Australia at Odds with Neighbouring Nations on New Coal and Gas Projects at Pacific Islands Forum', *The Guardian*, 12 July 2022.

70 W Morgan, 'Will Australia's New Climate Policy Be Enough to Reset Relations with Pacific Nations?', Griffith Asia Insights, 11 July 2022.

71 One commentator noted that the summit 'was talked up as the friendliest ever' and noted the 'happy vibe': G Dobell, 'Geopolitics Looms Larger than Ever at Pacific Islands Forum Summit', *The Strategist*, 18 July 2022.

72 F Bainimarama, 13 July 2022, https://twitter.com/FijiPM/status/154718686 1453737984. Others spoke of 'smiles in Suva'.

73 J Branco, 'Labor Rejects Greens Bid for End to New Coal and Gas Projects', 9 News, 27 July 2022.

74 S Dziedzic, 'Pacific Leaders to Declare "Climate Emergency" in PIF Statement, Praise Australia's Move to Lift Emissions Reduction Target', ABC News, 15 July 2022.

75 Lyons, 'Australia at Odds with Neighbouring Nations on New Coal and Gas Projects at Pacific Islands Forum'.

76 W Morgan, 'Pacific Islands Are Back on the Map, and Climate Action Is Not Negotiable for Would-Be Allies', *The Conversation*, 18 July 2022.

77 Wong, 'Press conference—Honiara'.

78 Wong, 'Joint Press Conference—Apia, Samoa'.

79 'Pacific Islands Forum Leaders' Meeting', Media Release, 12 July 2022.

80 Wong, 'A New Era in Australian Engagement in the Pacific'.

AUSTRALIA'S STRATEGIC CULTURE AND CLIMATE CHANGE

Mark Beeson

I F THE POLICY-MAKING elites of any country ought to know something about climate change, it's Australia's. After all, Australia is a country of 'droughts and flooding rains', as Dorothea Mackellar famously put it. Recently, however, 'weather events' that were thought to occur once in one hundred years now seem to happen every two or three.[1] Lives are routinely upended, if not lost, as a direct consequence of a rapidly changing climate that is affecting the driest continent on the planet more adversely than most. Under such circumstances, governments of all political persuasions might struggle to respond effectively to an unprecedented environmental crisis that threatens to definitively end the idea that Australia is 'the lucky country'. But it's also not unreasonable to expect Australia's leaders to at least *try* to address environmental problems, rather than continuing with a strategy of business as usual, which has brought the world to the very brink of potentially irredeemable catastrophe.[2]

While many of the obstacles to developing effective and sustainable environmental policies have international origins—especially the difficulty of addressing seemingly insurmountable collective action problems—some are entirely home grown. To be sure, climate change is one issue area that no country can deal with in isolation, but it's noteworthy that there is a striking disconnect between domestic and international policy. Although it may be difficult to separate 'inside' from 'outside' when it comes to policy-making in a supposedly global era, this hasn't stopped political leaders from trying, or from privileging notionally national concerns above the international variety. Given the disjuncture between the historically arbitrary nature of national borders and the transnational nature of the natural environment, however, efforts at isolated national climate mitigation are doomed to fail.[3] Paradoxically, this has not stopped some of Australia's political leaders from trying to use this as an excuse for continuing inaction and even the pursuit of national policies that the relevant scientific community has identified as irresponsible and dangerous.[4]

This all takes some explaining. After all, the first duty of political leaders is to ensure the safety of the nation and its people. Pursuing policies that are considered to do precisely the opposite in the (not very) long-term seems to fly in the face of responsible policy-making that takes account of the sorts of clear and present dangers that security specialists usually fret about. If being burned to death, drowned, or merely seeing one's livelihood and the future of one's offspring going up in smoke isn't a real and tangible threat to security, it's difficult to know what is. This claim looks doubly plausible in a country like Australia that faces no direct, immediate security threat of the sort that generations of military planners have spent their lives planning for.[5] One possible answer to this paradox, I suggest in what follows, is that Australia's 'strategic culture' encourages security analysts and the policy-makers they advise to prioritise improbable traditional threats from other states, rather than the very real, immediate and increasingly visible danger posed by unmitigated climate change. The concomitant 'opportunity costs' of this sort of thinking, I argue, are immense, unjustifiable and, if they continue, likely to culminate in economic, political, social and—yes—even traditional security crises as the world descends into a Darwinian struggle for survival.[6] I develop this rather deflating but all-too-plausible thesis by firstly looking at the general relationship between security and the environment, and then by considering the consequences of Australian policy-makers' short-sighted and self-absorbed approach to the greatest collective action problem the world has ever faced.

Climate change and security

At this moment in human history it is no longer controversial to suggest that unmitigated climate change and environmental degradation are problems. On the contrary, there is an overwhelming consensus about the causes of climate change and even their possible impact over the next few decades.[7] To be sure, the further out one looks, the more uncertain some of the modelling and predictions become, but most informed observers agree that we are facing a challenge that threatens the very basis of human civilisation, especially the progressive, liberal variety.[8] As potential security problems go, they don't get much more serious. To be fair, this possibility has not entirely escaped the notice of strategic elites around the world either. Since the early 2000s, the idea that climate change might pose a threat to world peace has, according to Adger,[9] 'become accepted wisdom in foreign and defense ministries around the world'. And yet while there have been some suitably alarming policy documents and reports produced by leading defence establishments that reflect the emerging conventional wisdom,[10] possible responses have been depressingly familiar.

At one level this is entirely unsurprising: it is not the responsibility of agencies such as the Pentagon, for example, to develop strategies to combat climate change. The primary task of military establishments is to respond to traditional security threats that emanate from their counterparts in other states.[11] Even if some of the drivers of potential inter-state conflict and possible wars of the future are seen to be novel and rapidly changing, the responses are still overwhelmingly predicated on the logic of military threats and competition. What is more surprising, perhaps, is that the governments to which militaries are notionally responsible in democracies, at least, quite literally continue to buy into the logic of war and inter-state conflict, despite the fact that the latter has become gratifyingly rare.[12] True, there is no shortage of conflict, mayhem and coercion in the world, but they are frequently confined within the notional borders of failed states. In yet another paradox, some of the most powerful states that have been least affected by conflict or environmental degradation remain the most enthusiastic exponents of old-fashioned geopolitics and purchasers of advanced military hardware.[13] Finding a possible explanation for this conundrum involves a brief theoretical digression and consideration of the culture from within which strategic policy emerges.

Recognising a threat when you see one

Given the relative novelty of the climate problem when seen in the long-run, perhaps we shouldn't be too surprised that getting 'environmental issues' on the policy agenda has proved difficult, alarmingly slow and politically contested.[14] There has been no shortage of 'virtue signalling' on the part of states that enjoy the luxury of taking such issues seriously, but for all the talk of 'joined up government' in the West, there has often been a noteworthy disjuncture between rhetoric and reality. In some important cases, there has even been an active repudiation of the scientific consensus by powerful vested interests and compliant national governments.[15] The administration of former President Donald Trump is the most consequential and baleful example of this possibility. Not only did the Trump administration undermine his own country's efforts to tackle climate change and restructure the domestic economy, it also made the chances of developing an effective international response that much more difficult.[16]

However, it is not only the well-documented efforts of powerful economic interests and their mutually rewarding links to the domestic political class that accounts for the difficulty of shifting the conventional wisdom and injecting urgency into the climate change challenge. On the contrary, despite scholarly alarm about the possible links between deteriorating environmental conditions and security threats, some academics were resistant to the idea that the 'traditional' security agenda should be expanded to include environmental issues as this might make the subsequent definition of security too wide to be analytically useful.[17] And yet, it is not unreasonable to suggest that if people don't *feel* secure, this is, and ought to be, one telling indicator of the failure of states to actually provide security for the populations they claim to represent and protect. While there has been a good deal of lip service paid to the idea of 'human security' and its possible importance as a more accurate indicator of people on the receiving end of security policies of one sort or another, actually realising such goals has proved difficult.[18] In yet another paradox, one of the areas in which real 'progress' has been made—in widespread improvements in living standards in China, for example—has also been responsible for a potentially catastrophic decline in water security, soil productivity, air quality, and a host of other vital environmental indicators.[19]

The United States and China are also, of course, the two most important actors in the world when it comes to dealing with climate change and virtually any other international issue one might care to mention. They are especially consequential countries when it comes to the environment, because they are the two largest emitters of the sorts of greenhouse gases that are responsible for global warming. Without agreement between the US and China to act on environmental issues in a cooperative and constructive way, it is difficult to see how the actions of other countries could really make that much difference to a collective action problem that necessitates hitherto unseen and frankly unimaginable levels of cooperation.[20] While there are some tentative indications that the leaders of the 'G2' actually recognise this,[21] it is not clear they are capable of overcoming their growing international competition which threatens to bring about a very old-fashioned and dangerous set of security challenges.

Consequently, there are two particularly important, interconnected reasons why the bilateral relationship between the US and China is especially crucial at this juncture. First, and most problematically, there is an intensifying geopolitical competition between the world's two greatest powers, which makes cooperation inherently problematic.[22] Both states labour under the illusion that they are fulfilling historical missions and the standard bearers of different forms of political and economic governance.[23] The US is currently preoccupied with trying to reclaim its role as leader of the 'rules based international order', while China is busily trying to develop its own alternative version.[24] Significantly, China is both resentful of the historical privileges and impact of American hegemony and keen to cultivate supporters of its own by leveraging its growing geo-economic power. For many analysts in both China and the US, the chances of outright conflict between the two superpowers has never been higher.[25]

The second reason that relations between China and the US are especially fraught, therefore, is because the vast majority of policy-making elites in both countries subscribe to a view of the world in which conflict is endemic and national security continues to be determined largely by the possession of superior weapons systems.[26] Despite much academic innovation in recent years, what international relations scholars describe as 'realism' continues to dominate the thinking and actions among strategic elites in both the US and China, and the overwhelming majority of the so-called 'international community', for that matter. Indeed, in yet another paradox, the routinely invoked idea of the international community is strikingly at odds with the realist view of an ungoverned, self-help system where states must rely on their own resources to ensure security and the capacity to influence and/or deter others. Ideas about the nature of possible threats and the best ways of countering them reflect the distinctive 'strategic cultures' of different countries.[27] Despite some noteworthy differences, the strategic cultures of different states share some surprisingly durable and influential views about the best ways of achieving security. It is worth spelling out just what a potential obstacle such inherited views and traditions are when it comes to dealing with new problems such as climate change.

Strategic culture and its consequences

Culture of all sorts is a still a relatively neglected aspect of the study of international relations. Given that China and the US are very different countries and at least some of these differences can be attributed to their distinctive historical experiences, it is important to consider what kind of role culture might play in this. Geertz famously defined culture in general as an 'historically transmitted pattern of meanings embodied in symbols, a system of inherited conceptions expressed in symbolic forms by means of which men communicate, perpetuate, and develop their knowledge about state breakdown or crisis'.[28] The point to emphasise is that cultural traditions and historical legacies can explain the distinctive ideas that some countries have about their national identities and even their role in the international system. The US is the most consequential example of this possibility in recent history, but it is impossible to understand the attitudes of China's current leadership or of many Chinese people more generally, for that matter, without taking account of the so-called 'century of shame' caused by European imperialism.[29] Attitudes towards Hong Kong and Taiwan in particular are the direct result of this traumatic and humbling period. The leadership of China may subscribe to a broadly conceived realist worldview, but it is one that is imbued with distinctively Chinese characteristics and specific national goals.

One way of conceptualising such differences and accounting for the different priorities national military establishments attach to various ideas and policies is through the lens of strategic cultures. The possible significance of differing strategic cultures and the impact this may have on national strategy was dramatically highlighted during the Cold War when George Kennan's famous 'long telegram'[30] warned of the impact of the Soviet Union's deep-seated anxieties about security, which were the engrained product of a unique historical experience. Nor are such differences simply a curiosity of interest to military historians either. On the contrary, apart from the potential impact of such ideas on traditional security issues, they also have the potential to profoundly influence domestic policy agendas and the attitude states may have to development and the environment. It is important to remember just how much importance both the Soviets and China under Mao Zedong attached to economic development at all costs, not least because of the possible role it might have in underwriting national military security.[31]

The consequences for the natural environment in both countries were simply appalling.

The idea that distinctive and different national strategic cultures might be significant was highlighted by Graham Allison's seminal analysis of the Cuban missile crisis,[32] which drew attention to the potentially pivotal role of individuals and the contingent historical context in which they operated. Colin Gray developed this notion to analyse the very different strategic cultures that existed in the US and the Soviet Union, and the possible impact of socialisation processes in determining attitudes towards apparently common 'structural variables' such as nuclear weapons.[33] While this may seem somewhat unremarkable in hindsight, it still marks a major departure from most forms of realist thinking, especially the pared-back 'parsimonious' version developed by Kenneth Waltz[34] and his followers which studiously ignores domestic differences when analysing strategic behaviour and the respective priorities of policy-makers.

Analysts who do take strategic culture seriously, do so because it highlights the importance of

> a set of shared beliefs, and assumptions derived from common experiences and accepted narratives (both oral and written), that shape collective identity and relationships to other groups, and which influence the appropriate ends and means chosen for achieving security objectives.[35]

Such definitions highlight the way in which at least some varieties of international relations theorising have evolved to take account of and explain the influence of the social construction of reality—even the strategic reality. The possible importance of distinguishing between putative friend and enemy and the profound impact this might have on the attitudes of policy-makers is startlingly clear when we consider that Canada and the US have the longest undefended border in the world. It really makes a difference who the neighbours are and how policy-makers expect them to behave as a consequence. Even in rather narrowly conceived military terms, therefore, Bradley Klein suggests that strategic culture may be thought of as describing

> the state's war-making style, understood in terms of its military institutions and its accumulated strategic traditions of air, land and naval power. But strategic culture is more than mere military style, for it emerges from an infrastructure of technology and an armaments sector. Most importantly, it is based upon the political ideologies of public discourse that help define occasions as worthy of military involvement.[36]

Klein was writing towards the—entirely unpredicted—end of the Cold War and was consequently preoccupied with the production of (American) hegemonic power and the manner in which great powers were embedded in a web of international relationships, 'both diplomatic and economic'. It is not only the failure of mainstream strategic analysts to foresee the collapse of the Soviet Union and the (short-lived) triumph of the US-led international order that makes Klein's analysis look remarkably prescient, however. On the contrary, in the intervening 30 years or so we have witnessed the similarly unforeseen 'rise of China' and the monumental failure of American grand strategy—not least because American strategic thinkers disastrously failed to recognise or take seriously the distinctive cultural and social context of the countries they tried to transform in the Middle East.[37]

The Blob

The presidency of George W Bush will forever be associated with the calamitous intervention in Iraq, which must be considered one of the greatest strategic failures in American history. One might be forgiven for thinking that this episode would have marked the proverbial turning point in American strategic thinking, not least because of the ruinous cost in blood and treasure that it inflicted on the US itself.[38] And there is some merit in this argument. The presidency of another Republican leader, Donald Trump, suggests that individuals not only make a difference in determining domestic *and* foreign policy outcomes and objectives, but that they can also materially affect the way even the most powerful states interact with the world. Trump's transactional, America-first approach to foreign policy is a notable departure from Bush's and even Barak Obama's.[39] And yet, having said that, the election of Joe Biden has led many commentators in the US to claim that the world will see a return to geopolitical business as usual, as the so-called 'Blob' reasserts its influence on American foreign and strategic policy.[40] Given the influence of the US on Australian foreign policy it is worth saying something about the continuities, disjunctures and even the continuing primacy of what is still the most powerful state in the world and the notional guarantor of Australia's security.

In retrospect, the Bush administration's disastrous war in Iraq looks a good deal less aberrant than the chaotic, unpredictable domestically driven foreign policy that developed under Trump. After all, George Washington's famous admonition about the dangers of 'foreign entanglements' notwithstanding, the history of the US has been punctuated by frequent and often violent interventions overseas. Indeed, it is frequently claimed that the US has been at war for more than 90 per cent of its history as an independent nation.[41] For a country that sees itself as the quintessential expression of good governance, liberalism, enlightened values and a role model for the world, this is a somewhat surprising historical record that takes some explaining. A generous interpretation might be that defending freedom and defeating despots is something that only the US has been able to do in the modern era, and that this is part of *America's* national identity,[42] even if it is frequently overlooked by scholars from that country. Whatever one thinks of that claim, it is generally the case that analysts in the US see it as an essentially benign hegemon and a force for good in the world.[43] The fact that much of the world—including the former Soviet Union and more recently and consequentially China, of course—see America's dominance in very different terms is another reminder of just how historically contingent and different such perspectives can be.

The intensifying economic and strategic competition with China is likely to reinforce American efforts to curb China's influence and reassert the primacy of the US. Whether this will actually be feasible, given the high levels of interdependence that exist between the two rivals and the diminished material position of the US relative to China, is another question.[44] What we can say with some confidence is that the Blob, or America's foreign policy establishment and the received wisdom that permeates it, has become re-ascendant under Biden, and this is a good thing according to its many defenders. Brands et al. suggest that:

> the foreign policy establishment is not a closed cabal, American statecraft has not been a giant failure, and scrapping professionalism for amateurism would be a disaster ... the establishment's practical track record has been impressive, with some well-known fiascos outweighed by many quiet successes. And the current [Trump] administration's foreign policy blunders—including in its response to the current pandemic—demonstrate what happens when the establishment's experience and expertise are rejected. In short, the Blob is not the problem. It is the solution.[45]

However, when the recent record of the US is considered, the 'fiascos' are arguably far more striking and consequential than the 'quiet successes'. It is for this reason that some prominent American realists argue that 'today's foreign policy elite is a dysfunctional caste of privileged insiders who are frequently disdainful of alternative perspectives and insulated both professionally and personally from the consequences of the policies they promote'.[46] Some commentators go further and argue that 'with respect to China, the foreign policy establishment's world view, and the discursive practices it employs, make it unlikely that the USA will be able peacefully to accommodate China's rise'.[47]

To be fair, there are signs that the foreign policy establishment recognises the folly of some policies and the necessity of others: the decision to pull out of Afghanistan and the importance attached to making progress on climate change mark a significant recalibration of America's foreign policy priorities.[48] And yet even those who may welcome either or both of these developments would have to concede that such changes were adopted without consulting key allies or considering the difficulties they may cause the leaders of countries such as Australia. In yet another paradox, Australia's historical relationship with the US is causing problems for one of America's staunchest allies and supporters. As we shall see, this is arguably a consequence of the ideational hegemony of Australia's own version of the Blob, which is a product of its own very distinctive strategic culture.

Strategic culture with Australian characteristics

Australia is a country like no other. True, much the same claim could be made about any other state, perhaps, but no other country enjoys the exclusive possession of an entire continent. Australia's relative immunity to the recent COVID epidemic has dramatically highlighted the advantages of being an island continent. One might be forgiven for thinking, therefore, that being relatively isolated and a long way from some of the world's strategic flashpoints might have given Australian policy-makers a heightened sense of security, even relative invulnerability. Nothing could be further from the truth. On the contrary, from its relatively recent origins as a notionally independent country, Australian policy-makers have felt anxious, strategically isolated and in need of the support of what former Prime Minister Robert Menzies famously called 'great and powerful friends'. Indeed, so influential was this sense of insecurity and reliance on the help of more powerful allies, that despite its independent status, Australian policy-makers did not take responsibility for their own foreign policy until the exigencies of war forced them to during World War II.[49]

A sense of isolation, vulnerability, distance from like-minded friendly powers, and a pervasive ambivalence—and ignorance—about 'Asia' were, therefore, the principal early influences on the development of Australian strategic thinking.[50] While this may have been understandable—even forgivable—given Australia's modern origins

there is a continuing fear of 'abandonment', which invariably trumps concerns about 'entrapment' or the possibility that weaker states may feel obliged to behave in ways that they otherwise might not, all other things being equal. Paying the 'insurance premium' that is presumed to ensure continuing American military support has seen Australia participate in wars in Korea, Vietnam, Iraq, Afghanistan and even Syria, where possible Australian strategic interests seem implausibly remote, to put it mildly. But as one of the leading analysts of alliance politics points out, 'commitment weakens bargaining power. The more firmly one is committed to the alliance, the less credible, and therefore the less effective, are threats to withdraw support from the ally or abandon the alliance'.[55]

Consequently, generations of Australian policy-makers and the security specialists who advise them have felt they had little choice other than to actively recommit themselves to the alliance, no matter how remote the supposed threat to Australia may actually have been. Not only is this 'bandwagoning' behaviour at odds with what mainstream international relations theory might lead us to expect, it reinforces the dominance and leverage of the more powerful alliance partner.[56] Even when the notoriously unreliable, erratic figure of Donald Trump—who had little sympathy for, or commitment to, even longstanding allies in Europe—demonstrated just how uncertain this strategy might be, Australian policy-makers went out of their way to curry favour and demonstrate their dependability, no matter who occupied the White House.[57]

A number of points are worth making about the Trump presidency articular and the role of the US more generally in this context. The idea that smaller states might enjoy increased bargaining hat reflects their possible independence and status as potential tes' seems unavailable to enthusiastic alliance supporters such lia who risk being taken for granted by the US. The currently le idea that less powerful states might 'hedge' or even play at power against another,[58] always looked like a triumph of experience, but in Australia's case it is simply not plausible that Australia would not actively support the US, much less side with China. Put differently, for all of the claims made about Australia's ability to act as an independent 'middle power', its political leaders and strategic analysts generally lack the political will or imagination to act or even think differently.[59]

Second, the US alliance system has been a deeply embedded and institutionalised part of the security architecture of the region of which Australia has been a part for more than half a century. As Victor Cha points out, the 'hub and spokes' relations that the US established in East Asia after World War II meant that 'it exercised near-total control over the foreign and domestic affairs of its allies, and it created an asymmetry of power that rendered inconceivable counterbalancing by these smaller countries, on their own or in concert with others'.[60] Moreover, in Australia's case in particular, the relationship has been consolidated by the creation of key institutions and regular bilateral meetings which gave crucial ballast to the alliance, despite the fact the ANZUS Treaty itself notoriously failed to oblige either nation to do more than 'consult' in the unlikely event of a direct threat to either country.[61] Indeed, the only occasion on which the ANZUS Treaty has been invoked was when John Howard offered Australian support in the wake of the attacks on the World Trade Center.

A possible third point to make is more contingent and perhaps less enduring, or even a source of tension with Joe Biden in the White House: the Morrison and Trump administrations had similar views when it came to climate change and the continuing importance of fossil fuels. Importantly, neither the Morrison government nor the Trump administration considered climate change to be something they needed to address, much less a direct threat to the security of the nation and its people.[62] Since the election of Joe Biden the priorities of the US appear to have changed quite dramatically, the influence of the Blob notwithstanding. The question now is not only whether Australia's strategic culture under Prime Minister Albanese will pose a possible obstacle to addressing environmental issues, but whether it will actually damage relations with the country's most important ally.[63] The bipartisan support for AUKUS suggests that alliance politics are still dominant.

Future threats aren't what they used to be

One of the most significant consequences of the distinctive strategic culture that has emerged in Australia is its resistance to change. Perhaps we should not be surprised that security planners and analysts trained to think of security primarily in military terms might find it difficult to think about the nature of threats from other causes. But as Bloomfield and Nossal[64] point out, even an effort to make Australia more strategically self-reliant in traditional military terms was 'half-hearted', and a consequence of a form of what might be described as ideational path-dependence:

> When decision-makers were faced with the challenge of changing objective circumstances, therefore, the old strategic traditions were, in a sense, 'ready-made', easily understandable, and culturally palatable.[65]

While a degree of intellectual inertia may be a familiar feature of large organisations where conformity and adherence to the conventional wisdom are seen as desirable qualities, it is important to recognise that such behaviours are a consciously reinforced and cultivated part of strategic thinking generally in Australia. This is particularly true of the inviolable place of the alliance as the central part of Australia's overall security posture.[66]

One of the reasons the alliance—and all of the thinking that it inspires among Australia's strategic elites—remains so dominant is that it is institutionalised in highly influential organisations and networks that are specifically designed to reinforce its authority and influence. While participants in bodies such as the Australian American Leadership Dialogue (AALD) might not see themselves as actively involved in the 'social construction of reality', in many ways that's precisely what they are doing. As Vince Scappatura[67] notes, however, 'the AALD departs from other [Track 2] initiatives or "epistemic communities" to function more like a pro-American lobby group engaged in an effort to protect Australia's "special relationship" with the US'. Much the same observation could be made about the more formal 'Track 1' AUSMIN talks, in which the foreign and defence ministers of the US and Australia meet each year.[68] While these have been an important mechanism for 'alliance maintenance' and socialising participants into the existing normative and conceptual order, ironically enough they may be about to become a source of tension rather than ideological consensus.

While strategic thinking in Australia remains preoccupied with traditional security threats, there are credible signs that the Biden administration has recognised that such views are no longer an accurate reflection of the challenges that actually face the world. The very fact that members of the Blob in the US realise that security is no longer something that individual countries or even limited alliances of states can achieve acting alone may prove to be something of a watershed in strategic thinking and priorities. Joe Biden's 2021 'climate summit' revealed major differences between his administration and the former Morrison government on the importance attached to climate change as a key threat, and the willingness of his government to try and do something about it. Importantly, the US placed direct pressure on the former Morrison government to play a more active and effective part in addressing climate change and greenhouse gas emissions.[69] Australia's principal ally, in other words, was helping to turn Australia into an international outlier, if not pariah, when it comes to fostering international cooperation to deal with the greatest collective action problem the world has ever seen.

But the former Morrison government in particular found it hard to respond to Biden's shift, and instead focused on AUKUS. On the one hand, the Coalition is hostage to its own 'base' and the powerful vested interests that have been such an important source of political donations for the conservative side of politics for many years.[70] On the other hand, however, some of the principal sources of strategic advice, such as the

Australian Strategic Policy Institute, are still prioritising very traditional-looking threats that revolve primarily around the rise of China. It is not unreasonable to assume that the reason ASPI invariably recommends investing more in military hardware as the best policy has at least some connection to the fact that the organisation receives lavish finding from major weapons manufactures and the federal government.[71] At the very least, there would seem to be a potential conflict of interest and real questions about ASPI's ability to objectively respond to what ought to be a rapidly shifting calculus of concern.

As a consequence of Australia's distinctive history and the pervasive sense of strategic insecurity that pervades a very small 'epistemic community' of like-minded experts, its strategic culture has proved durable and relatively impervious to change.[72] When combined with a limited number of powerful and influential media outlets that support both the alliance relationship with the United States *and* a policy agenda that privileges economic development over environmental threats, then it is not hard to see why some ideas about security may prove difficult to change, despite Australia experiencing some of the most unambiguous deleterious impacts of climate change. Even before the loss of crucial seats to 'teal' candidates in the 2021 election, there were signs that even in the Coalition's electoral heartland sentiment about the reality of climate change may be changing in the face of continuing environmental catastrophes.[73] The question is whether the Dutton opposition, in particular, and the small group of strategic experts that advises it, are capable of recognising the profound shift in the very real threats that confront Australia, its people, and the existing economic paradigm—in which coal remains very significant.

If the overwhelming scientific consensus about the dangers of climate change is not sufficient, perhaps the new economic opportunities that some think are available to Australia may influence thinking in the Dutton shadow government. There is no shortage of plausible-looking models for turning Australia into a renewable energy superpower,[74] after all. And yet the Morrison government and now Dutton opposition in particular have proved resolutely impervious to advice of experts—when they come from outside the existing community of influential lobbyists, political donors and the epistemic community that continues to dominate debates about strategic policy, at least. But even this latter group may find it hard to reconcile a continuing privileging of traditional threats from other nation-states when the country that is seen as the bedrock of national security is pressuring Australians and their policy-makers to change. If the US can seemingly overturn the assumption that its grand strategy remains constant,[75] then it is not unreasonable to assume that Australia may have to fall into line as it always does when its more powerful alliance partner demands it.

Conclusion

Despite the very visible, increasingly frequent and destructive impact of climate change on Australia, Coalition governments in particular have been reluctant to commit themselves to addressing it in a serious way. At the same time, however, resources can be found—even in the midst of a major economic downturn—to purchase expensive weapons systems that many think will be outdated before they are ever delivered and unlikely to influence the behaviour of possible adversaries. Such views are entirely in keeping with the conventional wisdom among Australia's small but influential strategic community, which continues to pay next to no attention to what is arguably the single greatest threat to the security of ordinary Australians there has ever been. Even the most thoughtful Australian analysts continue to focus exclusively on conventional security: Hugh White's 2019 opus, *How to Defend Australia*, for example, contains not a single reference to either the environment or climate change in the index.[76] Even scholars dedicated to the pursuit of peace and the repudiation of militarism, such as Alex Bellamy, fail to take climate change into account when thinking about how we collectively avoid war.[77]

Ironically enough, however, it has dawned on at least some realists that 'the world's great powers are far more threatened by climate change than they are by each other'.[78] There are some signs that the magnitude of the threat to states of all varieties is finally being recognised, too: the

Biden administration's apparently sincere and well-intentioned recent multilateral initiatives represent an important change in the thinking that underpins security policy in what is still the world's most powerful state. This has major implications for ostensible friend and notional foe alike. Given the forbiddingly truncated timeframe in which to actually act effectively and overcome major obstacles to collective action, it may also be the last chance we have. The fact that even close, otherwise enthusiastically supportive allies such as Australia remain reluctant to join this effort is, however, a painful reminder of just how difficult the challenge actually is, and how many otherwise well-informed supposed experts still fail to grasp the existential threat climate change poses.

If the leadership of one of the most fortunate countries in the world is not prepared to share the burden of addressing climate change and the concomitant need to rapidly and radically restructure economic activity and our overall relationship to the natural environment, it is difficult to see why the likes of India, Indonesia or even China should. In the increasingly likely event that we collectively fail to do so, it will be of little comfort to be proved correct about the pernicious, short-sighted and misguided impact of our strategic culture.

Notes

1   L Hughes et al., *Summer of Crisis*, Climate Council, 2020.
2   A Morton, 'Australian Scientists Warn Urgent Action Needed to Save 19 "Collapsing" Ecosystems', *The Guardian*, 26 February 2021.
3   M Beeson, *Rethinking Global Governance*, Palgrave, Basingstoke, 2019.
4   S Holmes à Court, 'When it Comes to Emissions, the "Too Small to Matter" Argument Is Absurd, Reckless and Morally Bankrupt', *The Guardian* 9 January 2020.
5   M Beeson, *Environmental Anarchy? International Security in the 21st Century*, Bristol University Press, Bristol, 2021.
6   G Dyer, *Climate Wars: The Fight for Survival as the World Overheats*, Oneworld, Oxford, 2010.
7   W Steffen et al., 'Trajectories of the Earth System in the Anthropocene', *Proceedings of the National Academy of Science*, vol. 115, no. 33, pp. 8252–9.
8   A Lieven, *Climate Change and the Nation State: The Case for Nationalism in a Warming World*, Oxford University Press, Oxford, 220, p. 116.

9   WN Adger, 'Climate Change, Human Well-Being and Insecurity', *New Political Economy*, vol. 15, no. 2, pp. 275–92, 280.

10 KM Campbell et al., *The Age of Consequences: The Foreign Policy and National Security Implications of Global Climate Change*, Center for Strategic and International Studies, Washington.

11 R Brooks, *How Everything Became War and the Military Became Everything: Tales from the Pentagon*, Simon & Schuster, New York, 2017.

12 S Pinker, *The Better Angels of Our Nature: Why Violence Has Declined*, Viking, New York, 2012.

13 I Ghosh, 'Mapped: The Countries with the Most Military Spending', *Visual Capitalist*, 24 September 2020.

14 F Fischer, 'Knowledge Politics and Post-Truth in Climate Denial: On the Social Construction of Alternative Facts', *Critical Policy Studies*, vol. 13, no. 2, pp. 133–52.

15 PJ Jacques, 'A General Theory of Climate Denial', *Global Environmental Politics*, vol. 12, no. 2, pp. 9–17.

16 T Nichols , *The Death of Expertise: The Campaign Against Established Knowledge and Why it Matters*, Oxford University Press, Oxford, 2017.

17 D Deudney, 'The Case Against Linking Environmental Degradation and National Security', *Millennium: Journal of International Studies*, vol. 19, no. 3, 1990, pp. 461–76.

18 R Paris, 'Human Security: Paradigm Shift or Hot Air?', *International Security*, vol. 26, no. 2, 2001, pp. 87–102.

19 EC Economy, *The River Runs Black: The Environmental Challenge to China's Future*, Cornell University Press, Ithaca, 2004.

20 M Beeson and F Li, 'China's Place in Regional and Global Governance: A New World Comes into View', *Global Policy*, vol. 7, no. 4, 2016, pp. 491–9.

21 SL Myers, 'Despite Tensions, U.S. and China Agree to Work Together on Climate Change', *New York Times*, 17 April 2021.

22 L Wei and B Davis, 'China's Message to America: We're an Equal Now', *Wall Street Journal*, 12 April 2021.

23 F Zhang, 'The Rise of Chinese Exceptionalism in International Relations', *European Journal of International Relations*, vol. 19, no. 2, 2013, pp. 305–28.

24 M Beeson and S Xu, 'China's Evolving Role in Global Governance: The AIIB and the Limits of an Alternative International Order', in K Zeng, *Handbook of the International Political Economy of China*, Edward Elgar, Cheltenham, 2019, pp. 345–60.

25 G Allison, *Destined for War: Can America and China Escape Thucydides's Trap?*, Houghton Mifflin Harcourt, Boston, 2017.

26 AI Johnston, *Cultural Realism: Strategic Culture and Grand Strategy in Chinese History*, Princeton University Press, Princeton, 1995; RD Blackwill,

and AJ Tellis, *Revising US Grand Strategy Toward China*, Council on Foreign Relations, New York, 2015.

27 A Bloomfield, 'Time to Move On: Reconceptualizing the Strategic Culture Debate', *Contemporary Security Policy*, vol. 33, no. 3, 2012, pp. 437–61.

28 C Geertz, *The Interpretation of Cultures*, vol. 5019, Basic Books, New York, 1973, p. 89.

29 WA Callahan, *China: The Pessoptimist Nation*, Oxford University Press, Oxford, 2010.

30 G Kennan, 'The Sources of Soviet Conduct', in JF Hoge and F Zakaria (eds), *The American Encounter: The United States and the Making of the Modern World*, Basic Books, New York, 1997, pp. 155–69.

31 J Shapiro, *Mao's War Against Nature: Politics and the Environment in Revolutionary China*, Cambridge University Press, Cambridge, 2001; CE Ziegler, *Environmental Policy in the USSR*, University of Massachusetts Press, Amherst, 1990.

32 GT Allison, *Essence of Decision: Explaining the Cuban Missile Crisis*, Little, Brown and Company, New York, 1971.

33 CS Gray, 'National Style in Strategy: The American Example', *International Security*, vol. 6, no. 2, 1981, pp. 21–47.

34 KN Waltz, *Theory of International Politics*, McGraw-Hill, New York, 1979.

35 J Glenn, 'Realism Versus Strategic Culture: Competition and Collaboration?' *International Studies Review*, vol. 11, no. 3, 2009, pp. 523–51, 530.

36 BS Klein, 'Hegemony and Strategic Culture: American Power Projection and Alliance Defence Politics', *Review of International Studies*, vol. 14, no. 2, 1988, pp. 133–48, 136.

37 AJ Bacevich, *The Limits of Power: The End of American Exceptionalism*, Metropolitan Books, New York, 2008.

38 JE Stiglitz and LJ Bilmes, *The Three Trillion Dollar War: The True Cost of the Iraq Conflict*, WW Norton, New York, 2008.

39 M Beeson, 'Donald Trump and Post-Pivot Asia: The Implications of a "Transactional" Approach to Foreign Policy', *Asian Studies Review*, vol. 44, no. 1, 2020, pp. 10–27.

40 E Ashford, 'Build a Better Blob: Foreign Policy Is Not a Binary Choice Between Trumpism and Discredited Elites', *Foreign Affairs*, 29 May 2020.

41 C Oord, 'Believe it or Not: Since its Birth the USA Has Only Had 17 Years of Peace', *War History Online*, 2019.

42 T Smith, *America's Mission: The United States and the Worldwide Struggle for Democracy in the Twentieth Century*, Princeton University Press, Princeton, 1994.

43 M Mandelbaum, *The Rise and Fall of Peace on Earth*, Oxford University Press, Oxford, 2019.

44 C Layne, 'This Time it's Real: The End of Unipolarity and the Pax Americana', *International Studies Quarterly*, vol. 56, no. 1, 2012, pp. 203–13.

45 H Brands, P Feaver and W Inboden, 'In Defense of the Blob: America's Foreign Policy Establishment Is the Solution, Not the Problem', *Foreign Affairs*, 29 April 2020.

46 SM Walt, *The Hell of Good Intentions: America's Foreign Policy Elite and the Decline of US Primacy,* Farrar, Straus and Giroux, New York, 2018, p. 93.

47 C Layne, 'The US Foreign Policy Establishment and Grand Strategy: How American Elites Obstruct Strategic Adjustment', *International Politics,* vol. 54, no. 3, 2017, p. 260–75, 261.

48 A Gearam, 'With Afghan Pullout, Biden Aims to Reset Global Agenda', *Washington Post,* 13 April 2021.

49 TB Millar, *Australia in Peace and War: External Relations, 1788–1977,* ANU Press, Canberra, 1978.

50 A Burke, *In Fear of Security: Australia's Invasion Anxiety,* Pluto Press, Sydney, 2001.

51 A Capling, 'Twenty Years of Australia's Engagement with Asia', *The Pacific Review*, vol. 21, no. 5, 2008, pp. 601–22.

52 JD Wilson, 'Rescaling to the Indo-Pacific: From Economic to Security-Driven Regionalism in Asia', *East Asia*, vol. 35, no. 2, 2018, pp. 177–96.

53 D Walker, *Anxious Nation: Australia and the Rise of Asia 1850–1939,* University of Queensland Press, St Lucia, 1999.

54 M Fraser, *Dangerous Allies*, Melbourne University Press, Melbourne 2014.

55 GH Snyder, *Alliance Politics*, Cornell University Press, Ithaca, 2007, p. 168.

56 SM Walt, 'Alliances in a Unipolar World', *World Politics,* vol. 61, no. 1, 2009, pp. 86–120.

57 P Karp, 'Scott Morrison Accused of "Pandering" to Trump and Damaging Relations with Biden', *The Guardian*, 20 January 2021.

58 JD Ciorciari, 'The Variable Effectiveness of Hedging Strategies', *International Relations of the Asia-Pacific*, vol. 19, no. 3, 2019, pp. 523–55.

59 M Beeson and R Higgott, 'The Changing Architecture of Politics in the Asia-Pacific: Australia's middle power moment?', *International Relations of the Asia-Pacific*, vol. 14, no. 2, 2014, pp. 215–37.

60 VD Cha, *Powerplay: The Origins of the American Alliance System,* Princeton University Press, Princeton, 2016, p. 4.

61 C Fernandes, *Island Off the Coast of Asia: Instruments of Statecraft in Australian Foreign Policy,* Rowman & Littlefield, Lexington, 2018.

62 A Morton, 'Malcolm Turnbull Says Morrison Was "Dazzled and Duchessed" by Trump on Climate Policy', *The Guardian*, 24 November 2020.

63 F Jotzo, 'The US Climate Target Blows Australia's Out of the Water', *The Guardian,* 23 April 2021.

64 A Bloomfield and KR Nossal, 'Towards an Explicative Understanding of Strategic Culture: The Cases of Australia and Canada', *Contemporary Security Policy*, vol. 28, no. 2, 2007, pp. 286–307, 295.

65 Ibid., p. 294.

66 V Scappatura, *The US Lobby and Australian Defence Policy*, Monash University Publishing, Melbourne, 2019.

67 V Scappatura, 'The Role of the AALD in Preserving the Australia–US Alliance', *Australian Journal of Political Science*, vol. 49, no. 4, 2014, pp. 596–610, 600.

68 M Wesley, 'The Canberra–Washington Bubble', *The Saturday Paper*, 1 August 2020.

69 A Morton and K Murphy, 'Biden Administration Says Australia Needs to Cut Greenhouse Gas Emissions Sooner', *The Guardian*, 22 April 2021.

70 G Pearse, *High & Dry: John Howard, Climate Change and the Selling of Australia's Future*, Viking, Camberwell, 2007; P Riordan and J Smyth, 'Australian Mining Lobby's Power Endures Despite Wildfire Crisis', *Financial Times*, 17 February 2020.

71 M Reubenstein, 'ASPI Rakes in Millions of Dollars from Commonwealth Government Contracts While Publicly Driving the "China Threat" Narrative', Michael West Media, 1 July 2020.

72 N Bisley, *Australia's Strategic Culture*, National Bureau of Asian Research, Washington, 2016.

73 J Smyth, 'Australia Calls Emergency Meetings as Climate Crisis Intensifies', *Financial Times*, 9 February 2019.

74 R Garnaut, *Superpower: Australia's Low-Carbon Opportunity*, Black Inc., Melbourne, 2019.

75 P Porter, 'Why America's Grand Strategy Has Not Changed: Power, Habit, and the US Foreign Policy Establishment', *International Security*, vol. 42, no. 4, 2018, pp. 9–46.

76 H White, *How to Defend Australia*, La Trobe University Press, Melbourne, 2019.

77 Alex Bellamy, *World Peace: And How We Can Achieve it*, Oxford University Press, Oxford, 2019.

78 A Lieven, *Climate Change and the Nation State: The Case for Nationalism in a Warming World*, Oxford University Press, Oxford, 2020, p. xii.

RECONCILING REGIONAL SECURITY OUTLOOKS IN THE ASIA-PACIFIC

Sandra Tarte

PREVAILING NARRATIVES OF security in the Pacific have been framed as a contest between the so-called Indo-Pacific security narrative, with its China-threat focus, and the human security and environment focus of the so-called Blue Pacific narrative. The main purpose of this chapter is to explore areas of convergence as well as divergence in these regional security narratives. It examines the possibilities of cooperation arising from the Boe Declaration adopted by the Pacific Islands Forum in 2018. By advancing an expanded concept of security, this Declaration highlights that some degree of convergence has taken place at the declaratory, if not conceptual, levels. I suggest that the current geopolitical environment provides opportunities for Pacific states to drive their agenda by leveraging the complementary security interests of major external powers in the region. However, strategic competition between the major powers could in the long term be counterproductive to achieving the region's climate change goals and ambitions.

The emergence of China as a regional power in the Pacific has led to a new era of geopolitical rivalry in the region, with the United States, Australia, Japan and New Zealand, among others, launching major policy initiatives for the Pacific islands.[1] This enhanced engagement has been driven by a narrative based on geostrategic security concerns. Changes in regional geopolitics have coincided with the emergence of a more assertive, independent and innovative diplomacy by Pacific island states.[2] This paradigm shift in Pacific diplomacy positioned the region to advance a quite different regional security narrative, based on an expanded concept of security and focused on climate change. This is captured in the Boe Declaration on regional security adopted by Forum leaders at their summit in Nauru in 2018.[3]

As stated, these regional developments have been framed as a contest between divergent security paradigms: the Indo-Pacific security narrative and the Blue Pacific narrative.[4] Underpinning such a framing is the question of whether one or the other will eventually prevail. But such representations also highlight the problem of how to 'bridge the divide'[5] and to ensure these narratives 'don't talk past each other'.[6] This reflects the broader significance of contending security narratives, which expose tensions in the foreign policies of regional powers and potentially undermine strategic interests and partnerships.[7]

Australia, being a member of the Pacific Islands Forum, has come under particular pressure. As the former Tuvalu Prime Minister declared: 'We cannot be regional partners under this step-up initiative—genuine and durable partners—unless the Government of Australia takes a more progressive response to climate change'.[8] This point was underscored by Oxfam in its background briefing report to the 2019 Forum summit: 'If Australia is to remain a valued and trusted member of the Pacific family, and with that retain the ability to have a say in the region's future, then it must begin responding to the number one priority of Pacific island countries—climate change'.[9] So how to 'bridge the divide'?

Contending narratives

The growing presence and power of China in the Pacific has triggered significant policy responses from traditional Pacific powers, namely the US, Australia, New Zealand and Japan.[10] A key feature of these responses has been the framing of the wider region as Indo-Pacific—as opposed to Asia-Pacific. This is seen as an important feature of the new geopolitics of the Pacific and aims to unite key allies in the region. From the US point of view, Indo-Pacific strategy is also 'about competing with the Belt and Road Initiative, pushing back in the South China Sea, and negotiating or renegotiating bilateral trade deals'.[11]

The security narrative that has underpinned and framed these initiatives essentially reflects a 'traditional geopolitical view of security'.[12] China is perceived as a 'strategic competitor', aspiring to 'regional hegemony' in the Indo-Pacific. Increased US engagement in the Pacific islands aims to 'preserve a free and open Indo-Pacific, maintain access, and promote our status as security partner of choice'.[13] Pacific island states are therefore encouraged to remain wedded to traditional partners; and by implication to exclude China. This recalls the 'strategic denial' posture of the Cold War era.[14]

Within this narrative, security threats to the Pacific islands have been defined in terms of their vulnerability to economic and political influence from China. This is seen to arise in the context of increasing Chinese loans to support infrastructure development in the Pacific. Alluding to this concern, the New Zealand Ministry of Defence stated: 'Steep debt burdens associated with infrastructure projects have potential implications for influence, access and governance'.[15] Portraying Chinese loans as a potential threat to Pacific islands' sovereignty feeds into the narrative of the Free and Open Indo-Pacific strategy, which is aimed in part at 'preserving small states' sovereignty'.[16]

This perspective of China as a threat has been challenged by Pacific island leaders, who instead see opportunities for development assistance, security cooperation and market access. As the Pacific Islands Forum Secretary-General stated: 'Forum Island countries have been excluded from the sorts of financing, technology and infrastructure that can enable us to fully engage in a globalised world. Many countries see the rise of China and its increasing interest in the region as providing an opportunity to rectify that'.[17] China is also viewed as a more amenable development partner, with 'less stringent processes for getting large infrastructure projects implemented'.[18]

To strengthen regional solidarity and to amplify the region's voice and influence, the Pacific Islands Forum has adopted a collective identity known as Blue Pacific. If there is an agenda behind the Blue Pacific identity it is about empowerment. There has been a very deliberate attempt to challenge notions of small, vulnerable and fragile—as the dominant characterisations of the island states—with a counter-narrative emphasising the collective strength of 'large ocean states'. The Blue Pacific narrative also challenges the portrayal of the Pacific islands as 'passive collaborators or victims of a new wave of colonialism'.[19]

The Blue Pacific identity frames the Pacific's own security narrative and agenda. Within this narrative, security is by definition comprehensive and multidimensional. This is captured in the discourse around climate change. Over time, climate change has come to be defined as posing an existential threat, leaving no doubt about what action was needed: 'The survival of vulnerable small island developing states can only be guaranteed if there is concerted global effort to reduce greenhouse gas emissions to maintain the temperature increase below 1.5 degrees Celsius'.[20] In this context, the large polluters are seen to be responsible for the principal threat to the region. In 1997, the Smaller Islands States group within the Pacific Islands Forum condemned Australia for opposing strict reductions of greenhouse gas emissions.[21] This position has gained strength in recent years. Indeed, a defining feature of the new Pacific diplomacy has been the willingness of Pacific leaders to speak truth to power—in calling out political leaders of their much larger developed partners, and Australia in particular. The 2019 Pacific Leaders' Forum provides a number of examples of this.[22]

The above discussion raises the question of how the Pacific's regional security priorities on climate change—and human security more broadly—can be advanced alongside the geopolitical and geostrategic priorities of the region's major external powers. Past examples of security cooperation provide some evidence of compromise and of cooperative security.

Evidence from the past

Pacific island states count as their major regional security achievements the South Pacific Nuclear Free Zone of 1985 and the Regional Assistance Mission to Solomon Islands (RAMSI) from 2003 to 2017.[23] The Multilateral Fisheries Access Agreement between the US and Pacific island countries, adopted in 1987, which ended the so-called 'tuna wars' between the US and the region, can also be counted as a key security achievement.[24] What is significant about these is that they 'succeeded' despite divergent security perspectives and imperatives of the major players. Contending narratives on security, in other words, did not preclude cooperation to achieve common or complementary objectives.

The South Pacific Nuclear Free Zone (Treaty of Rarotonga), adopted in 1985, is regarded as one of the key regional security achievements in the Pacific—a contribution to global as well as regional nuclear non-proliferation. But it was also a compromise, the product of competing interests and priorities of Forum member states. While some Forum member states were staunchly anti-nuclear (including New Zealand in the mid-1980s), others sought to balance their opposition to nuclear testing and waste dumping with their relationships with the US (they included Fiji and Tonga). The main architect of the treaty was Australia, which proposed a limited nuclear-free zone, one that it believed would not conflict with the strategic interests of its ally (the US) by not proscribing nuclear armed vessels transiting the region or visiting ports. This proposal was initially opposed by four Pacific island countries (Papua New Guinea, Solomon Islands, Vanuatu and Nauru), which advocated for a more comprehensive nuclear-free zone. But in the end consensus prevailed and the treaty was adopted.[25]

It could be argued that the treaty met the minimum requirements of a nuclear-free zone, thus to some extent defusing regional anti-nuclear pressures. US concerns that it would encourage anti-nuclear feeling in the region were largely dispelled. While the US refused to accede to the treaty's protocols (a situation that continues to this day), it nevertheless respected them. French nuclear testing continued, intermittently, for a further 11 years. But France eventually acceded to the treaty protocols—joining China and Russia.

Strategic interests and Cold War geopolitics were more explicitly evident, and effectively used by the Pacific, in the context of the 1987 Multilateral Treaty on Fisheries between the governments of certain Pacific island countries and the US government. The treaty was significant in that it successfully addressed the very different yet complementary security agendas of the US and Pacific island states. The so-called 'tuna wars' of the early to mid-1980s had been fuelled by US refusal to recognise coastal state sovereign rights to tuna occurring within Exclusive Economic Zones. This led to some Pacific island states apprehending and confiscating US tuna boats caught fishing within their waters without a licence, action that triggered retaliatory measures by the US government. It was not until two Pacific island states (Kiribati and Vanuatu) concluded bilateral fisheries access agreements with the Soviet Union, in 1985 and 1986 respectively, and others (Fiji and Papua New Guinea) mooted the possibility of doing the same, that regional negotiations with the US made any significant progress. With US government funding, the 1987 treaty secured unprecedented financial returns for the region, and guaranteed fishing access to the US tuna fleet. It also greatly enhanced maritime surveillance and enforcement. Meanwhile, neither bilateral access agreement with the Soviet Union was renewed.[26]

RAMSI is held up as the most prominent example of regional security cooperation—encapsulating a 'truly Pacific approach' to restoring law and order, peace and stability. But its genesis lay not in the deterioration of security in Solomon Islands per se, but in Australia's assessment of the global security context—namely the war on terror. Indeed, it is possible that RAMSI—which relied on Australian leadership and resources—may never have happened had the international situation been different. Two earlier requests to Australia for assistance had in fact gone unheeded. RAMSI was a product of Australia's strategic interests in stabilising a 'porous and undeveloped region'.[27] This in turn formed part of its contribution to the US-led war on terror. The use of regional multilateralism (RAMSI) rather than a unilateral intervention was due in part to the influence of other Forum members—most notably New Zealand. This intervention was legitimised by the request from the Solomon Islands government and carried out under the mandate of a regional mechanism known as the Biketawa Declaration. RAMSI thus became a 'Pacific model' of cooperative intervention, based on a regional mandate and the formal legal agreement of the elected government, in this case the Parliament of Solomon Islands.[28]

The above examples point to the way different security narratives and agendas came together to deliver outcomes broadly acceptable to all regional parties. Can the same occur with the Boe Declaration?

Possibilities of the Boe Declaration

The Boe Declaration has as its starting point 'an expanded concept of security'. In keeping with the priorities of the Pacific states, the declaration 'reaffirms that climate change remains the single greatest threat to the livelihoods, security and wellbeing of the peoples of the Pacific' and reaffirms the region's 'commitment to progress the implementation of the Paris Agreement'.[29] Defining climate change as 'the single greatest threat' provides significant weight to the Pacific in shaping the security narrative in the region.[30] It also provides leverage to the Pacific island states in their efforts to influence the policies and actions of the world's largest emitters of greenhouse gases. These include fellow Forum member Australia as well as Forum Dialogue partners the US and China. All are expected to align their security engagement around the priority areas of the Boe Declaration.[31]

At the same time, this initiative provides an opportunity to advance the geopolitical agenda of Western powers. This is through the commitments made under the Boe Declaration for stronger regional security architecture; for improved coordination among existing security mechanisms; and for shared security analysis, assessment and advice. For Australia and New Zealand in particular, this presents an opportunity to bolster their influence over regional security cooperation. Both Australia and New Zealand are members of the Forum

Subcommittee on Regional Security—established under the Boe Declaration—and Australia funded the attendance of Pacific island delegations to its first meeting in 2019. Australia is also funding related security initiatives such as the Pacific Fusion Centre and the Australia Pacific Security College.[32]

Although not stated explicitly, it is understood that by strengthening—if not cementing— their place in the regional security architecture, Australia and New Zealand can minimise, or contain, the influence of China. They can also ensure the Pacific remains tethered to Australia, New Zealand and other traditional security partners through the defence ties that such arrangements facilitate.

Australia and other traditional partners have thus aligned their security engagement with the region around the priority area of the Boe Declaration that calls for the strengthening of national security capacity. This is evident through the maritime surveillance efforts of the US, Australia, New Zealand and also Japan—such as US Ship-rider agreements and Australia's Pacific patrol boat program. Promoting partnerships, interoperability and 'burden sharing' is a key component of this strategy. Since 2017 major Western allies with interests in the Pacific—the US, Japan, Australia and New Zealand—have strengthened their joint security dialogues and cooperation with respect to the island states. Security dialogues have focused on strengthening port security, enhancing information sharing, and building institutional collaboration and military-to-military cooperation.[33]

This approach corresponds with the geopolitical narrative and agenda of shoring up the so-called rules-based order: capacity building serves to bolster Pacific island states' defence and law enforcement capabilities, and therefore sovereignty and territorial integrity. This approach also has the underlying objective of maintaining—or reclaiming in the case of Fiji—their position as security partners of choice.

There is evidence that Pacific island states have taken advantage of this geopolitical imperative to drive their own broad-based security agenda. Enhancing the capacity of national maritime, defence and law enforcement agencies provides the island states with the ability to counter cross-border threats from transnational crime, and illegal, unreported and unregulated (IUU) fishing, as well as to respond to climate change threats—namely humanitarian and disaster response. This is one dimension of climate security.

An example of complementary security agendas at work is the Black Rock training camp in Fiji. Australia is providing assistance to develop the former Fiji military forces camp into a regional training centre—dedicated to peacekeeping, disaster preparedness and humanitarian response. For Australia, this development is seen as a 'symbol of our partnership, a long-term and enduring commitment ... [It aims] to increase the interoperability between our militaries as well as our police forces' and build people-to-people ties.[34] Australia will also be funding a Maritime Essential Services Centre in Fiji, to facilitate maritime security coordination within Fiji and throughout the region.

Fiji's ambitions are to provide a regional training facility for other Pacific island states, and also to develop its own capacity to be a 'security partner of choice' in the region. While it has turned to Australia for support, Fiji remains open to overtures from other willing partners, including China and Indonesia.[35]

Supporting Pacific island national security capacity around maritime law enforcement, disaster response and border control reflects a shared interest in strengthening state sovereignty and territorial integrity.

This provides a basis for convergence between the security agenda of major partners and that of the Pacific island states. But there is a related point of convergence that derives from the security-related imperatives of responding to climate threats both within the region and beyond—the climate emergency. These threats include those to the stability and viability of Pacific island states and more broad-based and systemic crises impacting on the region's partners and neighbours. There is thus a security imperative to support the Pacific's mitigation and adaptation efforts. This underpins one of Australia's key justifications for aid to the region, which is the Pacific's 'high vulnerability to the impacts of climate change and natural disasters'.[36]

There are indications that regional partners are now going further, by integrating climate change into their own defence planning and decision-making. New Zealand, for example, has taken significant steps towards aligning defence, if not domestic, policies to the Boe Declaration's key priorities. The 2018 Strategic Defence Policy Statement for the first time recognised climate change as 'a major driver of military operations'. A follow-up Defence Assessment report released in December 2018, titled 'The Climate Crisis', described climate change as posing a significant threat to both national and regional security. New Zealand has thus taken 'a proactive approach in promoting global recognition of climate change as a security risk'.[37] The US, under the Biden administration, has also explicitly linked climate change and security. This is underscored by former Secretary of State John Kerry's appointment as Special Presidential Envoy for Climate, a Cabinet-level position that is housed within the National Security Council.[38]

Conclusion

Pacific states have gradually succeeded in pushing climate change to the forefront of the regional security narrative and paradigm, where it is now defined both as an existential threat and as a threat multiplier. It is exacerbating, among other things, the damage and risks caused by nuclear waste; and adversely impacting fisheries and agriculture and thus food security. The current pandemic, with its unprecedented health and economic security shocks, has augmented this security narrative. As Fiji's Minister for the Economy declared: 'COVID-19—like climate change—is a transboundary threat and one that again signals the need to proactively shape the vision for the future we want'.[39]

This discussion has suggested that the current geopolitical environment provides opportunities for the Pacific to drive their agenda by leveraging the complementary security interests of major external powers in the region. Indeed, it could be argued that geopolitical tensions—stemming from China's rising influence in the region—have benefited the Pacific's efforts to address climate change and related security priorities such as maritime security and disaster preparedness.

Competition with China in what is recognised as a 'region of strategic geopolitical importance' has encouraged key partners, such as Australia and New Zealand, to endorse the security narrative of the Boe Declaration, and led to greater security collaboration. Meanwhile, the policy of 'strategic denial' has been bolstered to some extent, as China continues to be excluded from key dialogues such as Joint Heads of Pacific Security meetings, an initiative under Australia's Pacific Step-Up.[40]

However, continuing geopolitical tensions and strategic competition between the major powers could in the longer term prove counterproductive to achieving the region's climate change goals and ambitions. Ultimately what is needed is 'greater ambition on climate action' by the world's major emitters. This arguably requires more cooperation, not less, among all the major powers. Much may depend on the Biden administration and on the prospects this raises for strengthening multilateral approaches to tackling the climate crisis and to promoting engagement with China in this endeavour.

On the one hand, the US under a Democrat administration has reengaged with the Paris Agreement, with Special Presidential Envoy for Climate John Kerry, vowing 'to treat the climate crisis as the urgent national security threat it is'.[41] But there are no indications that geopolitical tensions are likely to be reduced with China. United States' concerns about China's role in the Pacific are, if anything, becoming more alarmist. This has led to new aid commitments to the region, including a $200 million package announced in November 2020 as well as proposals for a US military presence in Papua New Guinea and Palau.[42]

So, how to tackle the climate crisis and overcome geopolitical tensions? This requires both the US and China moving beyond a paradigm of strategic competition and embracing a common status of 'responsible stakeholder'. As one commentator observed: 'By linking geopolitics and climate, the United States and China have an opportunity to improve the prospects of both'.[43]

At the regional level, the Pacific may be well positioned to advance this link between geopolitics and climate through the Blue Pacific narrative. As described in an Oxfam report, Blue Pacific 'captures the growing geostrategic and economic significance of the region, and cements a powerful narrative of self-determination based on Pacific values'.[44] Within this narrative a 'friends to all approach' has been adopted by Pacific island leaders as the 'accepted modality for engagement and for building relationships and partnerships'.[45] This could provide the basis for building a more open and inclusive regional order; where the complementary security interests of all states are prioritised and advanced.

Notes

1   W Morgan, *Winds of Change: Pacific Islands and the Shifting Balance of Power in the Pacific Ocean*, SGDIA Working paper Series, No. 10, University of the South Pacific, Suva, 2019; W Morgan, 'Oceans Apart: Considering the Indo Pacific and the Blue Pacific', *Security Challenges*, vol. 16, no. 1, 2020, pp. 44–64; J Wallis, J Batley and R Seaton, *How Does the 'Pacific' Fit into the 'IndoPacific'? The Changing Geopolitics of the Pacific Islands: Workshop Report*, 2019, Department of Pacific Affairs Working Paper 2019/1.

2   G Fry and S Tarte, 'The New Pacific Diplomacy: An Introduction', in G Fry and S Tarte (eds), *The New Pacific Diplomacy*, ANU Press, Canberra, 2015, pp. 3–19.

3   Pacific Islands Forum, *49th Pacific Islands Forum, Yaren, Nauru, 3–6 September, 2018: Forum Communiqué*, 2018.

4   G Fry, *Framing the Islands: Power and Diplomatic Agency in Pacific Regionalism*, ANU Press, Canberra, 2019, p. 270.

5   T Newton Cain, 'Let's Hear it for the Boe', *Security Challenges*, vol. 16, no. 1, 2020, pp. 32–6.

6   J Wallis, 'Competing Pacific Narratives', *East Asia Forum*, 20 January 2019.

7   M O'Keefe, 'The Militarisation of China in the Pacific: Stepping Up to a New Cold War?', *Security Challenges*, vol. 16, no. 1, 2020, pp. 32–6, 94–112; Morgan, 'Oceans Apart', pp. 44–64.

8   S Dziedzic, 'Tuvalu Prime Minister Enele Sopoaga Says Australia's Climate Change Inaction Undermines its "Pacific Pivot"', ABC News, 4 December 2018.

9   Oxfam, *Save Tuvalu, Save the World: The Climate Crisis and the Pacific*, a background briefing for the Pacific Islands Forum, Tuvalu 12–16 August 2019, p. 5.

10   Morgan, *Winds of Change*; Wallis, Batley and Seaton, *How Does the 'Pacific' Fit into the 'Indo-Pacific'?*

11   GB Poling, 'For Lack of a Strategy: The Free and Open Indo-Pacific', *War on the Rocks, Texas National Security Review*, 13 November 2019.

12 Fry, *Framing the Islands*, p. 268.

13 US Department of Defense, *Indo-Pacific Strategy Report*, 1 June 2019, p. 21.

14 Fry, *Framing the Islands*, pp. 265, 268.

15 New Zealand Ministry of Defence, *Strategic Defence Policy Statement*, Wellington, 2018, p. 24.

16 US Department of Defense, *Indo-Pacific Strategy Report*, p. 41.

17 M Taylor, 'Keynote Address, University of the South Pacific, Port Vila, Vanuatu', 8 February 2019, Pacific Islands Forum, in G Smith and T Wesley-Smith (eds), *The China Alternative: Changing Regional Order in the Pacific Islands Symposium*, ANU Press, Canberra, 2021.

18 R Regenvanu, 'Keynote Address, University of the South Pacific, Port Vila, Vanuatu', 8 February 2019, Pacific Islands Forum, in G Smith and T Wesley-Smith (eds), *The China Alternative: Changing Regional Order in the Pacific Islands Symposium,* ANU Press, Canberra, 2021.

19 M Taylor, Keynote Address, University of the South Pacific.

20 Pacific Islands Forum Secretariat, *Supplementary Brief on Climate Change and Disaster Risk Reduction*, Suva, 2015.

21 Greenpeace, *'True Security': Achieving a Peaceful, Secure and Prosperous Pacific*, a Report for Greenpeace Australia Pacific for the 2005 Pacific Islands Forum, Suva, 2005.

22 Frank Bainimarama, 'Keynote Address at the Sautalaga Event of the 50th Pacific Islands Forum, Tuvalu', 12 August 2019; T Newton Cain, 'Australia Shows Up in Tuvalu and Trips Over', *East Asia Forum*, 30 August 2019.

23 M Taylor, 'Opening Remarks by Meg Taylor DBE, Secretary General, Pacific Islands Forum at the Biketawa Plus Security Declaration Workshop', Pacific Islands Forum, Suva, 18 June 2018.

24 J Tarai, 'The New Pacific Diplomacy and the South Pacific Tuna Treaty', in Fry and Tarte (eds), *The New Pacific Diplomacy*.

25 Fry, *Framing the Islands*, pp.181–2.

26 Tarai, 'The New Pacific Diplomacy and the South Pacific Tuna Treaty', pp. 237–48; S Tarte, *Japan's Aid Diplomacy and the Pacific Islands*, National Center for Development Studies and Institute of Pacific Studies, Canberra and Suva, Sandra, 1998, pp. 101–3.

27 AusAID, *Pacific Regional Aid Strategy 2004–2009*, 2004.

28 See Solomon Islands National Parliament, *The Facilitation of International Assistance Act,* 17 July; N Baker, 'New Zealand and Australia in Pacific Regionalism', in Fry and Tarte (eds), *The New Pacific Diplomacy*, pp. 137–48, 142–3; Fry, *Framing the Islands*, pp. 258–9; S Ratuva, *Contested Terrain: Reconceptualising Security in the Pacific*, ANU Press, Canberra, 2019, p. 80.

29 Pacific Islands Forum, *49th Pacific Islands Forum: Forum Communiqué*.

30 Fry, *Framing the Islands*, p. 271.

31 M Taylor, 'Remarks by the Secretary General, Dame Meg Taylor, at the Launch of the Boe Declaration Action Plan', Pacific Islands Forum, Suva, 15 October 2019.

32 Morgan, *Winds of Change*.

33 See Australia New Zealand United States Inaugural Pacific Security Dialogue, Joint Statement, 8 June 2018.

34 S Morrison, 'Remarks at Blackrock Camp, Fiji', 18 January 2019.

35 One PNG News Online, 'Fiji's Call for a "Pacific Brigade" Rejected: ADF', 26 November 2019.

36 S Ratuva, *Contested Terrain*, p. 92.

37 New Zealand Government, 'Defence Climate Change Implementation Plan Released', Media Release, 9 December 2019.

38 O Milman, 'John Kerry Named as Joe Biden's Special Climate Envoy', *The Guardian*, 24 November 2020.

39 K Tadulala, 'Sayed-Khaiyum Stresses the Need to Address Transboundary Threat', *FBC News*, 22 November 2020.

40 Radio New Zealand, 'Pacific Security Leaders Share COVID-19 Lessons', 14 November 2020.

41 Milman, 'John Kerry Named as Joe Biden's Special Climate Envoy'.

42 Radio New Zealand, 'US Offers Counter-China Funding for Pacific Nations', 26 November 2020.

43 E Ingleson, 'After the Election Strategic Competition Won't Save the United States and China', *East Asia Forum*, 1 November 2020.

44 Oxfam, *Save Tuvalu, Save the World*, p. 5.

45 M Taylor, 'Keynote Address to 2018 State of the Pacific Conference', 8 September 2018, Pacific Islands Forum; C Pratt, 'Strengthening the US-Pacific Islands Partnership', Opening Remarks to the Center for Strategic & International Studies US-Pacific Dialogue, Pacific Islands Forum, 4 March 2019.

CLIMATE CHANGE AND MARITIME BOUNDARIES

Pacific responses and implications for Australia

Rebecca Strating and Joanne Wallis

MARITIME BOUNDARIES ARE important for Pacific island states, for which resource-rich maritime areas are a vital source of revenue and central to their identity as 'large ocean states'[1] in the 'Blue Pacific'.[2] In this chapter we consider how climate change, and particularly rising sea levels, challenges the maritime entitlements of Pacific island states. The 1982 United Nations Convention on the Law of the Sea (UNCLOS), already under pressure from states contesting (or ignoring) its provisions, appears incapable of resolving the issues presented by climate change to maritime boundaries without substantial amendment or the development of new norms or customary law. We analyse how Pacific island states are responding to these legal and political challenges through collective maritime boundary diplomacy. The chapter concludes by identifying the implications of these challenges for Australia and its responsibilities as a member of the 'Pacific family'.

Maritime boundaries in the Pacific

Pacific island states view the seas as central to the scope and exercise of state sovereignty. The stability of Pacific maritime resource entitlements rests on the viability and legitimacy of maritime boundaries and the international legal regime that underpins them. The rights of Pacific island states to resources in the seabed and water column, such as oil, gas, minerals and fish, derive from the zoning regime established in the third convention of UNCLOS in 1982.[3] The maritime zones set out under UNCLOS provide a graduated set of sovereign rights to coastal states. Article 3 provides that each state has sovereign rights over their territorial seas up to 12 nautical miles seaward of their coastline. Within this area, states have rights that closely approximate territorial sovereignty. States are in principle free to enforce any law, regulate any use and exploit any resource, although navigating states retain certain transit rights in this zone, including to 'innocent passage'.[4] Coastal states are also empowered to implement limited rights in an area beyond the territorial sea known as the 'contiguous zone', extending for 24 nautical miles from their shores, for the purpose of preventing certain violations and enforcing police powers.[5]

One of the most significant legal innovations in UNCLOS is the Exclusive Economic Zone (EEZ) set out in Part V. The EEZ regime is of particular importance to Pacific island states given that many depend economically on fisheries resources, and it was advocated by Pacific leaders during UNCLOS negotiations.[6] It recognises rights of coastal states to jurisdiction over the resources in an area extending 200 nautical miles from their baselines.[7] Coastal states have the right to exploit, develop, manage and conserve all resources found in these waters, including fish, on the ocean floor and in the subsoil. Coastal states also retain jurisdiction over marine scientific research, artificial islands and structures, as well as responsibility for the management of resources within this zone. UNCLOS delivers significant benefits for Pacific island states that have small land masses. It is estimated to have given Pacific island states rights to over 30 569 000 square kilometres of EEZ area,[8] in contrast to their combined landmass of 552 789 square kilometres (84 per cent of which is Papua New Guinea).[9] This constitutes about 28 per cent of EEZ claims worldwide.[10] For example, although Tuvalu has only 26 square kilometres of land, it has a maritime area covering more than 900 000 square kilometres. Cook Islands has 600 square kilometres of land, but a maritime area of approximately 2 million square kilometres.

Fisheries are a critical industry for economic development and sustainability for many Pacific island states. They provide revenue from licences and access agreements, an important source of food and income, and employment.[11] Subsistence fisheries, for example, provide 50 per cent to 90 per cent of the animal protein diet for populations living in remote and rural settings.[12] Fisheries are one of the few non-aid sources of foreign income for smaller states, such as Kiribati, Tuvalu and Marshall Islands. The Pacific Ocean is the richest in terms of commercial fisheries, and the Western and Central Pacific tuna fishery is the largest in the world.[13] In 2014, Gillet found that the volume of all fisheries and aquaculture production in the region 'was about 2.0 million metric tonnes (mt), worth US$3.2 billion'.[14] The region's tuna fisheries have more recently been valued at around US$6 billion (in 2018).[15]

Hydrocarbons and minerals in the seabed are governed by the continental shelf regime. Under article 77 of UNCLOS, states hold exploration and exploitation rights to living sedentary species and non-living resources of the seabed and subsoil such as hydrocarbons and minerals over their continental shelves.[16] In many cases, maritime boundaries may perform dual functions insofar as they delimit the EEZ and continental shelf, however this is not always the case. States may in some circumstances claim an extended continental shelf of 350 nautical miles. While deep-sea mining has not started in the Pacific (or elsewhere), Pacific island states may seek to secure their continental shelf boundaries to ensure the exploration and exploitation of deep sea mineral resources. Seabed mining presents another potential future source of revenue as technology for locating and extracting these minerals improves, particularly as many of the minerals critical to supporting renewable energy technology are found in the seabed.[17] However, there are also concerns that such mining would have adverse environmental impacts on maritime ecosystems, fisheries and biodiversity.

Climate change challenges to the Pacific islands' maritime boundaries

Through rising sea levels and altering coastlines, climate change is likely to affect Pacific island states' maritime entitlements under UNCLOS. Under article 5, coastal states usually have 'normal' baselines that coincide with the 'low-water line along the coast as marked on large-scale charts officially recognised by the coastal State'.[18] These baselines are what maritime entitlements—including EEZ, contiguous zone and continental shelf—are measured against. Natural coastlines are 'impermanent features'[19] and as coastlines change, baselines move; that is, baselines are ambulatory.[20] The key legal issue for low-lying states, including many in the Pacific islands, is that several of their normal baselines are vulnerable to inundation as sea levels rise. This raises the question of whether these states should be able to fix these baselines (and consequently their maritime boundaries) under UNCLOS before they are eroded or inundated due to climate change.

Sea level rise may also lead to the reclassification of land features, with potential implications for claims under UNCLOS. Different categories of land features generate different maritime entitlements. An atoll must have naturally formed islands that are above high tide in order to support a maritime claim.[21] An island, 'a naturally formed area of land, surrounded by water, which is above water at high tide', can generate the full suite of maritime entitlements, including up to a 200 nautical mile EEZ and continental shelf.[22] In contrast, rocks are features incapable of sustaining 'human habitation or economic life of their own', and are only entitled to a 12 nautical mile territorial zone, but no EEZ or continental shelf.[23] Low-lying elevations, that is, 'a feature exposed at low tide but submerged at high tide',[24] are not entitled to a territorial sea, EEZ or continental shelf, and can only generate a 500-metre safety zone. In practical terms, this means that if due to coastal erosion or inundation an 'island' is reclassified as a rock or low-lying elevation, it is no longer capable of generating EEZ and continental shelf claims. The effects of sea level on the maritime boundaries of Pacific island states are unlikely to be uniform. Marshall

Islands, Tokelau, Tuvalu and Kiribati are wholly, or almost entirely, made up of low-elevation atolls and reef features, which means they are at greater risk of their maritime territory disappearing.[25]

Sea level rise may also have implications for archipelagic status. Archipelagic states are those that have legal rights to draw straight baselines around a cluster of islands and reefs, provided that the ratio of the area of the water to the area of the land is between 1 to 1 and 9 to 1.[26] Within archipelagic waters, states hold similar rights to internal waters, except that innocent passage must be allowed. If land features that are used as basepoints are rendered uninhabitable, this may alter the capacities of states to claim archipelagic status. UNCLOS states that archipelagic baselines 'shall not be drawn to and from low-tide elevations, unless lighthouses or similar installations which are permanently above sea level have been built on them or where a low-tide elevation is situated wholly or partly at a distance not exceeding the breadth of the territorial sea from the nearest island'.[27] Taking the Republic of Marshall Islands as an example, half a metre sea level rise would threaten the habitability of key atolls that help form its coastal baselines as an archipelagic state by rendering them low-tide elevations.[28] If the Ujelang, Enewetak, Bokak and Bikar low-lying atolls are found to have no EEZ claim, this would signify a 'major contraction' in Marshall Islands' maritime area, including threatening the world's largest shark sanctuary.[29] A 1-metre sea level rise could result in an EEZ area of 100 000 square nautical miles becoming high seas and providing new rights to other states, resulting in Marshall Islands losing income derived from fishing licences, which comprises nearly 15 per cent of its GDP.[30] Kiribati is also vulnerable to climate-induced sea level rise, and inundated territory may threaten the archipelagic status of the Gilbert Island chain, with attendant loss of significant maritime area.[31] If the Line Islands and the Phoenix Islands became submerged, it is estimated that Kiribati would lose around 460 000 square nautical miles of EEZ.[32]

UNCLOS does not provide that the declared maritime jurisdictions of states will continue to be respected once they begin to be altered by climate change. This has left scholars and practitioners examining legal options, particularly as there is recognition of 'the inequity of a situation where small island states that have contributed the least to the greenhouse gas emissions that are causing anthropogenic climate change, might, under the current rules of international law, suffer the first and most serious impacts of sea level rise'.[33] Both the International Law Association and the International Law Commission have established groups to study the issue. One option is the emergence of a new principle of customary international law fixing baselines at their current positions. This has found favour with some international law experts, who argue that if the purpose of UNCLOS was 'to create and maintain stability, certainty, and fairness in the governance of oceans, then a freezing of the baselines or the outer limits of maritime zones would be a consistent—and most just—means to preserve endangered states' rights to their marine resources'.[34] However, this view faces the challenge that, even if Pacific island states can demonstrate sufficient state practice in support, it may be difficult for them to secure sufficient acceptance of it by other states to constitute *opinio juris*. Other alternatives face similar political challenges, such as the possibility of securing agreement to a protocol to the 1994 UN Framework Convention on Climate Change, an amendment to UNCLOS, a decision of the meeting of the state parties to UNCLOS, a resolution of the UN General Assembly, or an advisory opinion from the International Tribunal on the Law of the Sea in favour of fixing baselines. Alternatively, it has been proposed that small island states could include artificial islands as defined territory.[35] Maintaining existing land territory and consequently maritime jurisdiction by using preservation methods is currently acceptable, as UNCLOS allows states to physically protect their baselines through techniques such as seawalls, moles (including piers, breakwaters or causeways) and harbours.[36] However, the proposed solution of permitting artificial islands as 'defined territory' would have potentially deleterious consequences for the management of other maritime disputes, such as those in the South China Sea where artificial island build-up is affecting both the strategic situation and the capacities of smaller Southeast Asian powers to access their maritime entitlements under international law.

The Westphalian ideal of a territorialised nation-state is coming under challenge through climate change, not just due to sea level rise but other developments that make the land uninhabitable, such as soil salination and compromised freshwater sources. The loss of habitation may affect the maritime boundaries of Pacific island states as this is crucial to distinguishing between an 'island' and 'rock', with implications for EEZ and continental shelf claims. Although binding only on the parties to the dispute, the decision of the Tribunal in the *South China Sea Arbitration* between the Philippines and the People's Republic of China set a stringent threshold for islands to generate maritime jurisdiction, most notably in its criteria for what constitutes habitation and economic activity.[37] If such a criteria were more widely applied, this could have implications for the maritime zoning around land features that are no longer habitable due to the effects of climate change. There has already been consideration of possible relocation of citizens of low-lying atoll states and their sense of nationhood and sovereignty in response to the loss of territory.[38] Some have proposed a new legal category for a post-climate international order for de-territorialised or landless nation-states, or the 'nation ex-situ'.[39] Others have sought to provide a normative 'global justice' approach to the issue of ambulatory baselines.[40] The issue of maritime zoning provokes different questions about how a de-territorialised state might continue to be 'quasi-territorial' through the maritime jurisdiction nations may continue to assert if maritime boundaries are fixed.

Pacific island states' responses

Pacific island states have responded to the challenges of climate change to their maritime boundaries with a high level of regional solidarity and international activism under the auspices of the Pacific Islands Forum, reflecting a broader process of international assertiveness described as the 'new Pacific Diplomacy'.[41] This reflects an increasing emphasis on a 'partnership approach' and 'collective outcomes and impact' by

Forum leaders.[42] Since 1974, Pacific island states have been working together to redraw and publicly declare their maritime baselines and boundaries. This has been done to pre-empt arguments that climate change-induced sea level rise will change their baselines and maritime jurisdictions. Consequently, there is a determined 'regional move to secure the present spatial scope of its maritime jurisdiction against the threat of future sea level rise'.[43]

These efforts have accelerated over the last 20 years. Notably, in 2010 the Pacific Islands Forum developed a Framework for a Pacific Oceanscape, which provided that the Pacific island states should, 'in their national interest', deposit coordinates and charts delineating their maritime jurisdictions with the UN.[44] Indeed, Action item 1B of that Framework is titled 'Regional Effort to Fix Baselines and Maritime Boundaries to Ensure the Impact of Climate Change and Sea Level Rise Does Not Result in Reduced Jurisdiction of Pacific Island Countries and Territories'. This explicitly states that: 'This could be a united regional effort that establishes baselines and maritime zones so that areas could not be challenged and reduced due to climate change and sea level rise'.[45] These commitments have been echoed in subsequent regional declarations. In the 2014 Palau Declaration, Forum leaders called for 'strengthened regional efforts to fix baselines and maritime boundaries to ensure that the impact of climate change and sea level rise does not result in reduced jurisdiction'.[46] In 2015, Polynesian leaders called for the states parties to the UN Framework Convention on Climate Change to acknowledge the importance of EEZs for island states and to 'permanently establish the baselines ... without taking account of sea level rise'.[47] In 2018, the Parties to the Nauru Agreement signed the Delap Commitment on Securing Our Common Wealth of Oceans in which state signatories commit to 'pursue legal recognition of the defined baselines established under the United Nations Convention on the Law of the Sea to remain in perpetuity irrespective of the impacts of sea level rise'.[48]

This commitment was restated at the 2019 Pacific Islands Forum leaders' meeting; their communiqué identified 'a collective effort to develop international law with the aim of ensuring that once a [Forum] Member's maritime zones are delineated in accordance with UNCLOS, that Member's maritime zones cannot be challenged or reduced as a result of sea-level rise and climate change'.[49] To advance this goal, in September 2020 the Pacific Islands Forum convened a regional conference on 'Securing the Limits of the Blue Pacific: Legal Options and Institutional Responses to the Impacts of Sea Level Rise on Maritime Zones'. When she opened the conference, Dame Meg Taylor, then Secretary-General of the Forum, emphasised the importance of a regional response, noting that 'our identity and advocacy as a collective is absolutely vital'.[50] The conference concluded with a commitment to 'secure maritime zones against sea level rise', to 'ensure that maritime laws recognize maritime boundaries as secure' and to work 'to develop regional norms for sea level rise and maritime zones'.[51] At the October 2020 Forum foreign ministers' meeting, leaders agreed to develop a 'regional normative declaration for Leaders' consideration in 2021' and endorsed, in principle, the idea of establishing a Forum Officials Committee Specialist Sub-Committee on Sea-Level Rise in Relation to International Law.[52]

Individual Pacific island states have also taken the initiative. Tuvalu intends to require all states that form relations with it to 'recognise the statehood of the nation as permanent and its existing maritime boundaries as set regardless of the impact of sea-level rise'.[53] The Tuvaluan government has urged other Pacific island states to 'take unilateral action to enact policies and legislation that support the legal proposition put forward by Forum Leaders in their meeting in Tuvalu in 2019', with a particular focus on establishing state practice in order to develop customary international law.[54] Other Pacific states have followed this approach by adopting legislation that purports to fix their maritime jurisdictions. This approach is also favoured by the International Law Association Committee on Sea Level Rise and International Law, which in 2018 endorsed a recommendation that established baselines or maritime zones, or both, be fixed and that there be no requirement to recalculate them based on sea level rise.[55]

In order for Pacific island states to declare fixed baselines under UNCLOS they first have to be mapped and maritime boundary disputes resolved. To achieve this, since the early 2000s the Pacific Islands Regional Maritime Boundaries Project has provided assistance to Pacific island states to clarify the extent of their maritime jurisdictions, including: depositing information about their maritime boundaries with the Secretary-General of the UN, as required by UNCLOS; preparing a continental shelf submission for the UN Commission on the Limits of the Continental Shelf; updating maritime zones legislation; and delineating the limits of their maritime zones, including drafting and negotiating maritime boundaries treaties.[56] The Project has involved a partnership between the Pacific community and the Australian government, with the support of the Forum Fisheries Agency (FFA), Global Resource Information Data Network, the Commonwealth Secretariat and the University of Sydney, and a range of relevant Australian government agencies. Although the FFA had been working since the 1990s to establish territorial sea baselines, when the Project began, many maps and charts being used by Pacific states were outdated and had often been produced by third countries; for example, Fiji and Papua New Guinea relied on British Admiralty charts.[57]

The Project has assisted Pacific island states to use geographic information systems to declare their maritime zones using geographic coordinates. This is significant, because it 'has the potential to establish a body of regional state practice which may have a more wide-ranging impact on the law of the sea. This is because this practice "fixes" the outer limits rather than leaving them as "ambulatory".[58] In the Pacific islands, the distance from the baseline is 'being determined at a particular point in time, and then declared using coordinates.'[59] This means that the distance from the ambulatory baseline no longer determines the outer limits of maritime territory. Instead, it is determined by baselines set at a particular point in time and enshrined in legal instruments.

The Project has also provided a forum for Pacific island states to negotiate the delimitation of the estimated 49 maritime boundaries between them.[60] This has seen the number of maritime boundary agreements in the region double in recent years; almost three quarters have been negotiated and 13 remain outstanding.[61] These agreements 'have all been based on principles of equidistance'.[62] In their 2018 communiqué, Pacific Islands Forum leaders 'committed to progressing the resolution of outstanding maritime boundary claims'.[63] They reaffirmed this commitment in their 2019 communiqué.[64] Tuvalu and Kiribati have also passed domestic legislation replacing low tide line as the baseline with 'a system of fixed geographic coordinates'.[65]

As at October 2020, the following states had lodged continental shelf submissions with the UN Commission on the Limits of the Continental Shelf: Cook Islands, Fiji, Federated States of Micronesia, Papua New Guinea, Solomon Islands, Palau, Tonga, Tuvalu, Tokelau and Kiribati, as well as Australia, New Zealand and France (on behalf of its territories).[66] Several of these submissions overlap. France and Vanuatu also dispute sovereignty over Matthew and Hunter Islands.[67] As described above, continental shelves are important because coastal states exercise sovereign control over them for the purpose of exploration and exploitation of natural resources, particularly oil and gas.[68] Significantly, according to UNCLOS, continental shelf submissions have the effect of '*permanently* describing the outer limits of its continental shelf',[69] suggesting that—once declared and submitted—Pacific island states' continental shelves would not change despite the effects of rising sea levels.[70] However, this is relevant only to the continental shelf and not the EEZ, which relates to fishing rights and responsibilities beyond the 12 nautical mile territorial sea.

Over the last decade, within the auspices of the Pacific Islands Forum, Pacific island leaders have begun to frame Pacific island states as 'large ocean island states' (LOIS),[71] or 'Big Ocean Countries'.[72] Their intent has been to provide an alternative framing that emphasises resilience and potential as a counter to framings that focus on Pacific island states' vulnerability. This reframing has taken shape in the concept of the 'Blue Pacific', officially characterised at the 2017 Forum leaders' meeting as 'a long-term Forum foreign policy commitment to act as one "Blue Continent"'.[73] However it reflects ideas that had appeared in the Forum's 2014 Framework for Pacific Regionalism.[74] When he opened the 2017 meeting, the Samoan Prime Minister, Tuila'epa Sa'ilele Malielegaoi, said that the Blue Pacific identity emphasises 'Exercising a sense of common identity and purpose linked to the ocean'.[75] Malielegaoi expanded on his understanding when speaking at the UN, observing that 'the Pacific Ocean has provided our island communities their cultural and historical identity and attachment since time immemorial'.[76] Notably, while Australian and other Western discourse typically understands the ocean as a barrier which separates and isolates states, the Blue Pacific narrative seeks to 'reframe the region away from the enduring narrative of small, isolated and fragile, to a narrative of large, connected and strategically important ocean continent'.[77] Reflecting this narrative, Forum leaders are working to develop a '2050 Strategy for the Blue Pacific Continent'.[78] The use of the word 'continent' is significant, suggesting an understanding of Pacific island states as the 'largest oceanic continent in the world', with the ocean connecting 'cultures, identities, resources and development aspirations'.[79] This picks up on longstanding thinking in the region, as in 1949 Albert Norman criticised the 'chauvinistic policies' of Europeans who perceived the 'waters of the South Pacific' as 'separating each "island" group' and creating 'the impression that this society is broken up and hopelessly separated from its essential parts'. Colonisation enhanced this impression as European powers '"claimed" for their own the visible peaks of land'.[80] Norman called for the 'social reclamation of the world's seventh "continent" and its people' to 'free the land of these bonds, to restore the essential regional viewpoint and unity, to overlook the dividing waters, to see the land and its people as united', in response.[81]

However, the extent of regional support for this reframing can be overstated. Although the Micronesian member states ultimately decided not to withdraw from the Pacific Islands Forum in 2022 over their concerns about the selection of the next Secretary-General, the fact that they even made this threat indicates both that regional solidarity is not unproblematic and that there may be underlying concerns about the extent to which the Forum has presented itself as playing a central role in speaking for the region.

Implications for Australia

The impact of climate change on the maritime boundaries of Pacific island states will have a number of consequences for Australia. First, Australia shares—although to a less significant degree—the challenge that rising sea levels pose to maritime boundaries. Australia has the third largest EEZ in the world, partly because of its large land mass, but also due to its islands and atolls. Australia's islands and atolls in the Torres Strait, Coral Sea and the Cocos Keeling atoll islands in the Indian Ocean face the same vulnerabilities to climate change as Pacific island states, which may have consequences for Australia's maritime boundaries. This might explain why Australia endorsed the 2014 Palau Declaration, which called for 'strengthened regional efforts to fix baselines and maritime boundaries to ensure that the impact of climate change and sea level rise does not result in reduced jurisdiction', and has been supporting Pacific island states' efforts to map and settle their maritime boundaries. As part of Australia's Pacific Step-Up policies, in 2019 it committed A\$3.5 million to the Pacific community to 'address the risks to maritime boundaries from sea-level rise and climate change related impacts'.[82]

Yet there are tensions between how Australia and Pacific island states perceive their maritime boundaries. Australia's own practice is based on an ambulatory conception of EEZ boundaries; the location of the territorial sea baseline moves with the low water line and the coasts' physical character as land determines maritime claims.[83] In contrast, the Pacific Islands Forum's Blue Pacific narrative reflects the ongoing process of 'maritime territorialization' in the Pacific islands, whereby maritime area is treated as 'the equivalent of land territory in the conception of what constitutes sovereignty', that is, 'the seas are becoming increasingly viewed as analogous to land'.[84] By mapping and settling their maritime boundaries under UNCLOS, Pacific island states are making clear that for them, the sea is sovereign territory 'that can be cut off and measured against spatial categories and placed in a national and global territorial grid defined by latitudes and longitudes'.[85] The Blue Pacific narrative highlights how maritime 'sovereignty claims have evolved from being about material resources to ideational "symbolic" politics that link maritime spaces to national identity, and position "sea territory" as necessary for completing sovereignty and independence'.[86] This goes further than the regime enshrined by UNCLOS, which does not grant coastal states full territorial sovereignty—including the right to prevent the incursion of other states—over their maritime jurisdictions, particularly beyond the 12 nautical mile territorial sea. This territorial perspective is likely to trouble Australia, which as a highly open nation dependent on seaborne trade, has traditionally supported the principle of freedom of the seas, including actively supporting efforts by the United States to ensure freedom of navigation.

Yet the second challenge is that, despite sharing these challenges, under the Coalition government that lost the election in May 2022, Australia failed to take serious domestic policy action to address its contribution to the climate crisis. Australia was also accused of being disingenuous about its claims to be meeting its Paris Agreement targets by relying on carryover credits,[87] and its reduced participation in international initiatives such as the UN's Green Climate Fund. Australia is also said to have stymied stronger commitments to address climate change within the Pacific Islands Forum.[88] At the 2019 Forum leaders' meeting, Australia is reported to have refused to support the Tuvalu Declaration made by small island Pacific states calling for the use of coal in electricity generation to end.[89] However, the Australian Prime Minister at that time, Scott Morrison, did announce a $500 million 'Stepping up Climate Resilience in the Pacific' package at the meeting.[90] But rather than representing new funding, this package drew $500 million from existing aid funds. And the Australian government's emphasis on spending, rather than domestic action, to address climate change disappointed Pacific leaders.[91]

Like the previous Coalition government, the Labor government elected in May 2022 has identified that improving Australia's relationships in the Pacific islands is a policy priority, which reflects that Australian governments have long identified that a secure Pacific islands region sits only behind a secure Australia in the hierarchy of Australia's strategic interests.[92] Defence White Papers consistently recognise that Australia has two primary strategic interests in the Pacific islands: first, to ensure 'security, stability and cohesion'; and second, to ensure that our neighbourhood does not become 'a source of threat to Australia', primarily through preventing a hostile power from establishing a strategic foothold.[93] As other powers increase their presence in the Pacific islands, the government has begun to demonstrate strategic anxiety about the 'crowded and complex' geopolitics of the region and its declining influence there.[94] Yet Australia's foot-dragging on climate change—which Forum leaders (including Australia) have identified as the 'single greatest threat' to the region[95]—risked encouraging Pacific island states to seek closer relations with powers that have interests potentially inimical to Australia, particularly China. After the 2019 Forum leaders' meeting, former Kiribati President Anote Tong commented that: 'If someone [Australia] is determined to take you down, you don't stick with them you go and look for someone else'.[96] Fijian Prime Minister Frank Bainimarama similarly commented that: 'After what we went through with Morrison, nothing can be worse than him. China never insults the Pacific. You say it as if there's a competition between Australia and China. There's no competition, except to say the Chinese don't insult us'.[97]

With the Biden administration determined to take strong action on climate change—exemplified by President Joe Biden convening a Leaders' Summit on Climate in April 2021—Australia was increasingly the 'odd one out' on climate action. This has changed with the election of the ALP government, which has made tackling climate change a key aspect of its policy platform. The ALP has committed to reduce Australia's emissions by 43 per cent by 2030, which it claims will keep Australia on track for net zero by 2050. Notably, during her initial visits to Fiji, Samoa, Tonga and Solomon Islands, the new Foreign Minister, Penny Wong, has made climate change policy a key aspect of her messaging to Pacific island partners.

Third, Australia has begun to emphasise the 'resilience' of Pacific island peoples and states when discussing the impact of climate change in the region;[98] its regional response to COVID-19 similarly emphasises the importance of resilience.[99] This could be interpreted as reflecting a recognition that Pacific peoples and states have long responded and adapted to environmental, societal, environmental, geopolitical and other shocks. Such an interpretation provides a welcome counterpoint to the concepts of 'vulnerability', 'fragility' or 'weakness' which have long dominated Australian discourse about the region, and which imply passivity, victimhood and helplessness. But Australia's emphasis on resilience could also be interpreted as an attempt to gloss over the structural factors—including Australia's role—that have rendered Pacific island states and peoples vulnerable to climate change, or have contributed to the uneven nature of economic development (including the influence of globalised neoliberalism), the underdeveloped nature of public services (including the legacy of colonialism) and frequently unequal gender relations. On this reading, the language of resilience leaves climate change as something for Pacific people and states to cope with, rather than addressing structural factors or the need for Australia and other polluters to take more active steps to prevent climate change.[100]

Fourth, this emphasis on resilience may be partly in anticipation of the fact that, as sea level rise inundates or renders uninhabitable islands and atolls in the Pacific islands, Australia will likely have to respond to calls for climate mobility. How this occurs will be challenging. If measures are implemented under international law to allow inundated Pacific island states to continue to possess sovereignty in a de-territorialised form,[101] their populations may still be regarded as citizens of that state and entitled to its protection. However, as that state would not necessarily have a defined territory (unless it is able to carve one out within another state), it is unclear where these people would have the right to move to. Alternatively, if inundated states cease to exist, then their populations may become stateless. At present the Stateless Persons Convention defines a 'stateless person' as someone 'who is not considered as a national by any State under the operation of its law'.[102] Neither the Refugee Convention nor the UN Framework Convention on Climate Change provides guidance concerning climate-induced migration.[103] In these situations it will likely fall to neighbouring states to offer refugee status to displaced Pacific island populations. New Zealand declared its intention in 2017 to create a humanitarian visa category for people displaced by climate change, but in 2018 abandoned that policy after Pacific peoples expressed their desire that New Zealand instead work towards helping them continue to live in their own countries.[104]

In the maritime domain, an important area of consideration is how de-territorialised states might cope with the challenges of monitoring, controlling and enforcing their maritime jurisdiction from afar. This may require bilateral assistance from Australia, which already provides patrol boats and support under its Pacific Maritime Security Programme. It may also involve the development and use of sophisticated surveillance technologies and regional cooperation, building on what Australia and other partners provide to the Forum Fisheries Agency and other maritime surveillance mechanisms in the region.[105] In this regard, regional states such as Australia could also play a contributing role to ensuring that de-territorialised Pacific island states will reap the benefits of fishing licences in their maritime zones. The other issue is how de-territorialised states could contribute to their conservation and sustainability responsibilities under UNCLOS when they are no longer proximal to maritime areas. Managing and protecting maritime zones generated from distant islands is not unusual, and Australia has experience in this, for example in the EEZ and continental shelves around Heard Island and McDonald Island.

Australia has remained silent on the issue of Pacific islands climate mobility, despite Australian leaders consistently referring to the importance of its 'Pacific family'.[106] This highlights the challenges of different understandings of what obligations the concept of 'family' imposes. As Pasifika academics Tarcisius Kabutaulaka and Katerina Teaiwa point out, 'kinship comes with important expectations, values and responsibilities. In the Pacific, relatives can make serious requests of each other, and it's a major cultural faux pas to say no'.[107] This raises the question of what constitutes Pacific 'family values', as well as how Australia will negotiate the obligations that family membership is generally understood to involve in the Pacific islands in the context of climate mobility. Although Australia has facilitated some Pacific labour mobility to Australia, it remains difficult for most Pacific people to obtain an Australian visa.[108] Although the new Labor government has a stated policy of offering permanent pathways of migration to Australia for Pacific people, the proposed numbers remain relatively small, and it is unclear whether there would be either political or public will to offer sanctuary to substantial numbers of Pacific climate migrants.

Finally, the challenges that climate change poses to the capacity of smaller Pacific island states to access their maritime resources under international law will exacerbate existing human security challenges, through, for example, the developmental impacts of lost revenues and increased food insecurity. The Pacific islands are already highly susceptible to illegal, unregulated and unreported (IUU) fishing.[109] Across the Pacific Ocean, the World Resources Institute estimates that 24 per cent of catch (or 15 million tonnes of fish) is unreported every year, representing an economic loss of US$4.3–8.3 billion. According to Cook Islands Prime Minister Henry Puna, the urgency behind Pacific island states' efforts to secure maritime boundaries is 'the need to secure our borders and fight against illegal fishing and illegal incursions into our waters'.[110] Beyond the EEZs of Pacific island states, fishing is coordinated by the Western and Central Pacific Fisheries Commission. In this area, distant-water fishing fleets from China, Japan, South Korea and the US are active, and in 2019, it accounted for 55 per cent of the global tuna catch. Concerns have intensified among some regional analysts and policy-makers about fishing spilling over into the EEZs of Pacific island states, with the Chinese Pacific fishing fleet expanding by more than 500 per cent since 2012.[111] If the legitimacy of EEZ boundaries becomes questionable due to climate change, this will exacerbate the risks of extra-regional actors treating the area as 'high seas' rather than within the maritime jurisdiction of Pacific island states. As the region's largest aid donor and self-identified security guarantor (particularly in the Melanesian and Polynesian sub-regions), Australia will likely bear increased costs of responding to these challenges. Australia will also likely bear much of the cost of responding to the increased occurrence of natural disasters and other climatic events caused by climate change.

Conclusion

While UNCLOS provides a valuable framework for establishing maritime order among the world's states, there remain important gaps around how to deal with the problem of rising sea levels generated by climate change. At the moment, the international community generally accepts that as territory moves, so too do baselines and the boundaries of maritime zones. Yet as the oceans threaten to engulf the low-lying land features and atolls of Pacific island states, such a view of the relationship between land and sea in international law will strip these states of their maritime resources and jurisdiction. Rising sea levels therefore pose a challenge to the maritime boundaries of climate-vulnerable states, in particular their continuing access to the maritime resources that support their economic independence.

Pacific island states are responding to these challenges through regional maritime boundary diplomacy focused on advocating for regional customary norms to fix baselines, and by emphasising the importance of maintaining their maritime zones irrespective of territorial erosion. The effects of climate change on the Pacific islands will also have implications for neighbouring states, such as Australia, which claim responsibilities to its 'Pacific family'. It raises important questions about what the loss of maritime territory means for Australia as an aid partner to the Pacific islands, the extent to which Australia will join in the calls for a customary regional norm around fixing baselines, and the role Australia can play in ensuring the maritime security of de-territorialised states. Perhaps more importantly, the challenges posed by climate change in the Pacific islands will continue to cast a light on

Australia's domestic policies and will test the new Labor government's commitment to meeting its climate obligations within the international community.

Notes

1 Pacific Islands Forum, '43rd Pacific Islands Forum Opens in the Cook Islands', Pacific Islands Forum Secretariat, 29 August 2012.

2 Pacific Islands Forum, *48th Pacific Islands Forum, Apia, Samoa, 5–8 September 2017: Forum Communiqué*, 2017.

3 United Nations Convention on the Law of the Sea encompasses three conferences, in 1958, 1960 and 1982. This paper uses UNCLOS to refer to the 1982 UNCLOS III convention, also known as LOSC (Law of the Sea Convention).

4 J Lusthaus, 'Shifting Sands: Sea Level Rise, Maritime Boundaries and Inter-state Conflict', *Politics* , vol. 30, no. 2, pp. 113–18; UNCLOS, article 19(2).

5 UNCLOS, article 33.

6 CSN Narokobi, 'The Law of the Sea and the South Pacific', *Ambio*, vol. 13, no. 5/6, 1984, 'The South Pacific', pp. 372–6.

7 UNCLOS, articles 55–8.

8 Q Hanich, C Schofield and P Cozens, 'Oceans of Opportunity?: The Limits of Maritime Claims in the South Pacific', in Q Hanich and BM Tsamenyi (eds), *Navigating Pacific Fisheries: Legal and Policy Trends in the Implementation of International Fisheries Instruments in the Western and Central Pacific Region*, Ocean Publications, Wollongong, 2009, pp. 17–46, 21.

9 Q Hanich and BM Tsamenyi, 'Managing Fisheries and Corruption in the Pacific Islands Region', *Marine Policy*, vol. 33, no. 2, 2009, pp. 386–92.

10 R Gillet, 'Pacific Island Countries Region', in *Review of the State of World Marine Resources*, FAO Fisheries Technical Paper 457, FAO, Rome, 2005, pp. 144–57.

11 D Jordy, *Pacific Possible: Climate and Disaster Resilience*, World Bank, Washington, 2016.

12 N Hilmi et al., 'Socioeconomic Significance of Fisheries in the Small Island Developing States: Natural Heritage or Commodity?', in S Pauwels and E Fache (eds), *Fisheries in the Pacific,* Pacific-credo Publications, Marseille, 2016, pp. 175–97.

13 Ibid.

14 R Gillett, *Fisheries in the Economies of Pacific Island Countries and Territories,* Pacific Community, New Caledonia, 2016, p. 2.

15 C Pala, 'How Eight Pacific Island States Are Saving the World's Tuna', *Foreign Policy,* 5 March 2021.

16 UNCLOS, article 77.

17 P D'Arcy, 'The Lawless Sea? Policy Options for Voluntary Compliance
    Regimes in Offshore Resource Zones in the Pacific', *Asia and the Pacific Policy
    Studies*, vol. 1, no. 2, 2013, pp. 297–311; MW Lodge, 'How to Mine the
    Oceans Sustainably', *Scientific American*, 11 August 2020.

18 UNCLOS, article 5.

19 International Law Association, *Baselines Under the International Law of the
    Sea*, Sofia Conference, 2012; International Law Association, *Baselines Under
    the International Law of the Sea Final Report*, 2018.

20 R Frost, et al., 'Redrawing the Map of the Pacific', *Marine Policy*, vol. 95, 2018,
    pp. 302–10, 306.

21 UNCLOS, article 6.

22 UNCLOS, article 121.

23 Ibid.

24 UNCLOS, article 13; D Freestone and C Schofield, 'Securing Ocean Spaces
    for the Future? The Initiative of the Pacific SIDS to Develop Regional Practice
    Concerning Baselines and Maritime Zone Limits', *Ocean Yearbook*, vol. 33,
    2009, pp. 58–89, 74.

25 Freestone and Schofield, 'Securing Ocean Spaces for the Future?

26 UNCLOS, article 47(7).

27 Ibid.

28 Permanent Mission of the Republic of the Marshall Islands to the United
    Nations, *Republic of the Marshall Islands: Views Regarding the Possible Security
    Implications of Climate Change*, July 2009.

29 M Gordon, 'The Impacts of Climate Change on Maritime Boundaries in
    the Western Pacific', *Seapower Soundings*, issue 28, Royal Australian Navy,
    Canberra, 2021, p. 14.

30 J Reynolds, 'A Sinking Feeling: The Effect of Sea Level Rise on Baselines and
    Statehood in the Western Pacific', *The Australian Year Book of International
    Law Online*, vol. 37, no. 1, 2020.

31 Gordon, 'The Impacts of Climate Change on Maritime Boundaries in the
    Western Pacific', p. 17.

32 Reynolds, 'A Sinking Feeling', p. 188.

33 C Schofield and D Freestone, 'Islands Awash Amidst Rising Seas: Sea Level
    Rise and Insular Status under the Law of the Sea', *The International Journal of
    Marine and Coastal Law*, vol. 34, 2019, pp. 391–414, 402.

34 M Burkett, 'The Nation Ex-Situ: On Climate Change, Deterritorialized
    Nationhood and the Post-Climate Era' *Climate Law*, 2, 2011, p. 362.

35 M Gagain, 'Climate Change, Sea Level Rise, and Artificial Islands: Saving the
    Maldives' Statehood and Maritime Claims through the "Constitution of the
    Oceans", *Columbia Journal of International Environmental Law and Policy*,
    vol. 23, no. 1, 2012, pp. 77–120.

36 VP Cogliati-Bantz, 'Sea-Level Rise and Coastal States' Maritime Entitlements', *The Journal of Territorial and Maritime Studies*, vol. 7, no. 1, 2020, pp. 86–110, 92.

37 *The South China Sea Arbitration (The Republic of Philippines v. The People's Republic of China)*, PCA Case No. 2013, Award, 12 July 2016, para. 587.

38 M Burkett, 'Behind the Veil: Climate Migration, Regime Shift, and a New Theory of Justice', *Harvard Civil Rights-Civil Liberties Law Review*, vol. 53, pp. 445–94.

39 Burkett, 'The Nation Ex-Situ', pp. 345–74.

40 C Armstrong and J Corbett, 'Climate Change, Sea Level Rise and Maritime Baselines: Responding to the Plight of Low-Lying Atoll States', *Global Environmental Politics*, vol. 21(1), pp. 89–107.

41 G Fry and S Tarte (eds), *The New Pacific Diplomacy*, ANU Press, Canberra, 2015.

42 Pacific Islands Forum, *50th Pacific Islands Forum, Funafuti, Tuvalu, 13–16 August 2019: Forum Communiqué*, 2019.

43 Freestone and Schofield, 'Securing Ocean Spaces for the Future?, pp. 58–89, 77.

44 C Pratt and H Govan, *Our Sea of Islands, Our Livelihoods, Our Oceania, A Pacific Oceanscape: A Catalyst for Implementation of Ocean Policy*, Pacific Islands Forum, Suva, 2010, p. 58.

45 Ibid., p. 58.

46 Pacific Islands Forum, Palau Declaration on 'The Ocean: Life and Future' Charting a Course to Sustainability, 4 September 2014.

47 Taputapuatea Declaration on Climate Change, Polynesian Leaders' Group, 16 July 2015.

48 Delap Commitment: Securing Our Common Wealth of Oceans, Parties to the Nauru Agreement, 2 March 2018, article 8.

49 Pacific Islands Forum, *Fiftieth Pacific Islands Forum: Forum Communiqué*.

50 M Taylor, 'Introductory Statement by the Secretary General to the Pacific Islands Forum at the Regional Conference on Securing the Limits of the Blue Pacific', 9 September 2020.

51 S Kofe, 'Closing Statement by the Hon. Simon Kofe at the Regional Conference on Securing the Limits of the Blue Pacific: Legal Options and Institutional Responses to the Impacts of Sea Level Rise on Maritime Zones, in the Context of International Law', 17 September 2020.

52 '2020 Forum Foreign Ministers Meeting Outcomes', 14 October 2020, virtual meeting.

53 S Kofe, 'Statement by the Hon. Simon Kofe at the Regional Conference on Securing the Limits of the Blue Pacific: Legal Options and Institutional Responses to the Impacts of Sea Level Rise on Maritime Zones, in the Context of International Law', 9 September 2020.

54 Ibid.

55 Resolution 5/2018, Committee on International Law and Sea Level Rise, 78th Conference of the International Law Association, Sydney, 19–24 August 2018.

56 C Trahanas, 'Recent Developments in the Maritime Boundaries and Maritime Zones of the Pacific', *Australian Year Book of International Law*, vol. 31, 2013, pp. 41–74.

57 Ibid.

58 Frost et al., 'Redrawing the Map of the Pacific', p. 306.

59 Ibid., p. 306.

60 'Pacific Maritime Boundaries: About', Pacific Community.

61 Frost, et al., 'Redrawing the Map of the Pacific', pp. 302–10; Andrew Jones, 'Why Maritime Zones Matter for the Future of Our Blue Pacific', *SPC*, 29 September 2020; 'Pacific Hailed Global Leader in Determining Shared Maritime Boundaries—Resolving 73 Percent Cases Between States', *PacNews*, 9 July 2019.

62 Frost et al., 'Redrawing the Map of the Pacific', p. 307.

63 Pacific Islands Forum, *Forty-Ninth Pacific Islands Forum, Yaren, Nauru, 3–6 September 2018, Forum Communiqué*, Pacific Islands Forum Secretariat.

64 Pacific Islands Forum, *Fiftieth Pacific Islands Forum: Forum Communiqué*.

65 D Guilfoyle, 'Canute's Kingdoms: Can Small Island States Legislate Against Their Own Disappearance?' *European Journal of International Law: Talk!*, 20 February 2020.

66 Submissions, through the Secretary-General of the United Nations, to the Commission on the Limits of the Continental Shelf, pursuant to article 76, paragraph 8, of the United Nations Convention on the Law of the Sea of 10 December 1982.

67 C Schofield, 'The Delimitation of Maritime Boundaries of the Pacific Island States', paper presented at the Proceedings of International Seminar on Islands and Oceans, Tokyo, 20–22 January 2010.

68 UNCLOS, article 77.

69 UNCLOS, article 76(9).

70 Trahanas, 'Recent Developments in the Maritime Boundaries and Maritime Zones of the Pacific', p. 72.

71 '43rd Pacific Islands Forum Opens in the Cook Islands'.

72 Kofe, 'Statement by the Hon. Simon Kofe at the Regional Conference on Securing the Limits of the Blue Pacific', 9 September 2020.

73 Pacific Islands Forum, *48th Pacific Islands Forum, Apia, Samoa, 5–8 September 2017: Forum Communiqué*.

74 Pacific Islands Forum, *The Framework for Pacific Regionalism*, Pacific Islands Forum Secretariat, Suva, 2014.

75 TS Malielegaoi, 'Address to Open the 48th Pacific Islands Forum', Vailima, Samoa, 5 September 2017.

76 TS Malielegaoi, 'Remarks by Hon. Tuil'aepa Lupesoliai Sa'ilele Malielegaoi Prime Minister of the Independent State of Samoa at the High-Level Pacific Regional Side Event by PIFS on Our Values and Identity as Stewards of the World's Largest Oceanic Continent, The Blue Pacific', UN Headquarters, New York, 5 June 2017.

77 M Taylor, 'Address by PIFS Secretary General Dame Meg Taylor—2018 State of the Pacific Conference', Australian National University, Canberra, 8 October 2018.

78 Pacific Islands Forum, 'The 2050 Strategy for the Blue Pacific Continent'.

79 Kofe, 'Statement by the Hon. Simon Kofe at the Regional Conference on Securing the Limits of the Blue Pacific', 9 September 2020. See also R Strating and J Wallis, 'Maritime Sovereignty and Territorialisation: Comparing the Pacific Islands and South China Sea', *Marine Policy*, vol. 141, 2022.

80 A Norman, 'Reclamation in Oceania: Australian Smoke Signal', *Christian Science Monitor*, 4 June 1949, p. 22.

81 Ibid.

82 'Pacific Hailed Global Leader in Determining Shared Maritime Boundaries—Resolving 73 Percent Cases Between States', Pacific Community, 10 July 2019.

83 Geoscience Australia, 'Maritime Boundary Definitions'.

84 R Strating, 'Maritime Territorialization, UNCLOS and the Timor Sea Dispute', *Contemporary Southeast Asia*, 2018, vol. 40, no. 1, pp. 101–25, 103–4; Strating and Wallis, 'Maritime Sovereignty and Territorialistion'.

85 E Roszko, 'Maritime Territorialisation as Performance of Sovereignty and Nationhood in the South China Sea', *Nations and Nationalism*, vol. 21, no. 2, pp. 230–49, 239. See also Strating and Wallis, 'Maritime Sovereignty and Territorialistion'.

86 Strating, 'Maritime Territorialization, UNCLOS and the Timor Sea Dispute', p. 102.

87 A Morton, 'Australia's Use of Accounting Loophole to Meeting Paris Deal Found to Have No Legal Basis', *The Guardian*, 12 December 2019.

88 G Fry, *Framing the Islands: Power and Diplomatic Agency in Pacific Regionalism*, ANU Press, Canberra, 2019.

89 M Clarke, 'Pacific Leaders, Australia Agree to Disagree about Action on Climate Change', ABC News, 15 August 2019.

90 S Morrison, M Payne and A Hawke, 'Stepping Up Climate Resilience in the Pacific', Joint Media Release, 13 August 2019.

91 M Clarke, 'Tuvalu's PM Says Australia's Climate Funding for Pacific "Not an Excuse" to Avoid Emissions Cuts', ABC News, 13 August 2019.

92 K Wallis, *Pacific Power? Australia's Strategy in the Pacific Islands*, Melbourne University Press, Melbourne, 2017.

93 Department of Defence, *2013 Defence White Paper,* Canberra, 2013, p. 25; Department of Defence, *2016 Defence White Paper,* Canberra, 2016, p. 69.

94 J Wallis, *Crowded and Complex: The Changing Geopolitics of the South Pacific*, Australian Strategic Policy Institute, April 2017.

95 Pacific Islands Forum, Boe Declaration on Regional Security, 2018.

96 S Hannaford, 'Australia Acting Like an "Abusive Relative" in the Pacific: Former Kiribati President', *Canberra Times*, 22 August 2019.

97 K Lyons, 'Fiji PM Accuses Scott Morrison of "Insulting" and Alienating Pacific Leaders', *The Guardian*, 17 August 2019.

98 Department of Foreign Affairs and Trade, 'Pacific Regional—Climate Change and Resilience'.

99 Department of Foreign Affairs and Trade, *Partnerships for Recovery: Australia's COVID-19 Development Response*, 2020.

100 J Wallis and H McNeil, 'The Implications of COVID-19 for Security in the Pacific Islands', *The Round Table*, vol. 110, no. 2, 2021, pp. 203–16.

101 Burkett, 'The Nation Ex-Situ', pp. 345–74.

102 UN Convention Relating to the Status of Stateless Persons, adopted 28 September 1954, UNTS 117 (entered into force 6 June 1960), article 1(1).

103 J McAdam, *Climate Change, Forced Migration and International Law*, Oxford University Press, Oxford, 2012.

104 T Manch, 'Humanitarian Visa Proposed for Climate Change Refugees Dead in the Water', *Stuff*, 29 August 2018.

105 R Rayfuse, 'International Law and Disappearing States: Utilising Maritime Entitlements to Overcome the Statehood Dilemma,' *UNSWLRS*, vol. 52, 2010.

106 S Morrison, 'Australia and the Pacific: A New Chapter', Speech at Lavarack Barracks, Townsville, 8 November 2018.

107 T Kabutaulaka and K Teaiwa, 'Climate, Coal, Kinship and Security in Australia-Pacific Relations', *Australian Outlook*, 21 August 2019.

108 T Newton Cain, J Cox and GH Presterudstuen, *Pacific Perspectives on the World*, Whitlam Institute, Sydney, 2020.

109 Pacific Islands Forum, Palau Declaration on 'The Ocean: Life and Future'.

110 Secretariat of the Pacific Regional Environment Programme, *Sea Level Rise Washing Over Maritime Boundaries in the Pacific*, 6 December 2019.

111 M Field, 'Why the World's Most Fertile Fishing Ground Is Facing a "Unique and Dire" Threat', *The Guardian*, 14 June 2021.

CLIMATE JUSTICE AND INTERNATIONAL HUMAN RIGHTS LAW

Diplomatic implications for Oceania

Susan Harris Rimmer

THIS CHAPTER GRAPPLES with two fundamental and increasingly urgent questions: what would a climate justice–centred foreign policy approach look like, and how would diplomatic practices have to change in order to achieve this? In considering this, it will review the intersections between international human rights law and climate policy in Oceania, with reference to key policies of Australia, New Zealand and the Pacific Islands Forum.

Just as all states have a duty to protect human rights, the impacts of climate change now pose a great threat to human rights around the world. It is common practice in diplomatic circles to practice 'conditionality'—where support is given to nations that protect human rights and withdrawn from nations that fail to protect human rights. And it is startling to understand that Australia may find itself on the receiving end of 'climate conditionality' unless it improves its position on climate change and places climate-based human rights at the core of its diplomatic policies when engaging in the region. The Department of Foreign Affairs and Trade's 2019 Climate Change Strategy frames climate impacts as part of Australia's development assistance program, with little emphasis on human rights, justice or more strategic foreign policy measures.[1]

Indeed, the international community's increasing recognition of the need for climate justice, as seen in the 2021 UN joint statement on the right to a healthy environment,[2] means that if Australia does not adapt quickly to this changing diplomatic landscape, we risk falling behind. In stark contrast to Australia, Pacific island nations have been leading the way in international human rights law with regards to climate justice. This is evidenced by their push for a special rapporteur in this domain, leading to the appointment of Dr Ian Fry (discussed below) and their calls for greater clarity regarding state obligations to tackle climate change through an International Court of Justice Advisory Opinion (detailed further below). This pressure from within our region and the international community more broadly presents Australia with a choice: to take the opportunity to develop smarter approaches to international human rights law and climate diplomacy in order to keep up with our regional partners and show good global citizenship, or continue with business as usual and risk a deterioration of diplomatic relationships, complicity in the denial of climate justice and potential failure to meet our international obligations. Australia can also shape the future of international law, by supporting at domestic and global levels the development of the rights of nature, the right to a healthy environment, the rights of future generations and the development of ecocide and related crimes under international law.

Climate justice and diplomacy

Australia's current approach situates climate justice only in relation to technical expertise in its aid program and to operational issues in humanitarian relief. In terms of the humanitarian sphere, Australia's approach only reaches a degree of sophistication around equity issues. Until the change of government in 2022, the nation's human rights diplomacy was also at its lowest ebb in the history of the Department of Foreign Affairs and Trade (DFAT)—although the appointment of an Ambassador for Human Rights in December 2022 and turning the Ambassador for the Environment into an Ambassador for Climate Change may mark a turning point (see Caitlin Byrne, Andrea Haefner and Johanna Nalau's chapter in this book). But despite these welcome appointments, Australia is out of step with key allies, trade partners and neighbours in the realms of human rights and climate diplomacy.

It is the duty of all to protect the human rights of people of all ages and in all their diversity from the harmful effects of the climate crisis, including displacement. States can share these efforts to ensure such human rights strategies align with each other through the practice of human rights diplomacy aimed at climate justice outcomes. Indeed, looking at an example such as Vanuatu, which successfully led a coalition of 132 nations in adopting by consensus a UN General Assembly resolution in March 2023 calling for a non-binding Advisory Opinion from the International Court of Justice to gain clarity on how existing international laws can be applied to 'strengthen action on climate change, protect people and the environment and save the Paris Agreement',[3] it is clear this collective approach should be more widely adopted and that current norms relating to diplomatic practice must change. Notably, the UN General Assembly resolution was co-sponsored by 105 states, including Australia as a late entrant, but Vanuatu thanks Antigua and Barbuda, Costa Rica, Sierra Leone, Angola, Germany, Mozambique, Liechtenstein, Samoa, Federated States of Micronesia, Bangladesh, Morocco, Singapore, Uganda, New Zealand, Vietnam, Romania and Portugal on their website.[4]

In 2020, a report from the Washington-based Woodrow Wilson International Center for Scholars states that 'foreign policy is climate policy'. The report argues that both global stability and prosperity depend on limiting the climate crisis and attenuating its impacts, and that national success in meeting this challenge will depend on unprecedented global collaboration—'the achievements of which must become the North Star of diplomacy'.[5] In light of this, it is essential that the global community work together to limit the human rights impacts of the climate crisis, and that this focus on human rights take precedence in diplomatic circles.

As part of this, I argue that Australia will need an elevated strategic approach to issues of climate justice that cuts across defence, immigration, trade, intelligence and foreign policy. This approach will require a merging of the learnings gained from the human rights diplomacy literature with contextual knowledge of how climate impacts will affect the attainment of human rights in Oceania. And unless Australia adopts this elevated strategic approach, there may be serious consequences: human rights diplomacy has often been premised on particular human rights conditions that manifest in trade, travel, official development assistance and bilateral agreements. Against this, I predict that the sudden rise of 'climate conditionality' into unrelated negotiations may negatively impact Australia. In this way, Australia's lagging climate change policies may in the future preclude Australia from getting the best outcomes during interactions including trade negotiations, bilateral agreement negotiations and other matters of international diplomacy.

This chapter sets out a vision for regional climate justice and argues for international human rights law standards to become the benchmark for the conduct of climate diplomacy in Oceania. In order to achieve this, it is not only foreign policy objectives that would have to change; diplomatic practice would have to be transformed as well. This presents an opportunity for Australia to reframe its regional and bilateral diplomacy with the Pacific and New Zealand, to show solidarity with its neighbours and become a trusted climate action partner and a partner that acknowledges ethical and historical injustice.

This chapter sets out definitions of climate justice and applies its objective to the toolkit of current human rights diplomacy as practised in bilateral and multilateral settings. I review the intersections between international human rights law and climate policy in this region, including references in key Australian policies and through recent UN human rights activism in the Pacific Islands Forum. This approach begins the work of merging the learnings gained from human rights diplomacy literature with our knowledge of how climate change will impact human rights in Oceania.

I will also review current progress in the UN system and outline three key areas in the UN human rights system which involve the

articulation of climate justice, such as the expert treaty body committees, the Human Rights Council and the UN Special Procedures.
The UN system is informed by and in turn influences the reports of
the Intergovernmental Panel on Climate Change, and these reports
in turn increasingly reference climate justice. For example, the UN's
Committee on Economic, Social and Cultural Rights' statement on climate change and the International Covenant on Economic, Social and
Cultural Rights both reference the context of a 1.5°C increase by the
IPCC report already being known and seen to impact on the potential
realisation of economic, social and cultural rights.[6] Furthermore, the
most recent IPCC report in 2022 directly references human rights in
relation to climate justice.[7]

Myriad other issues will be revealed by the climate crisis. As UN
Secretary-General António Guterres said at the Nelson Mandela
Annual Lecture in July 2020:

> Covid-19 has been likened to an X-ray, revealing fractures in the
> fragile skeleton of the societies we have built. It is exposing fal-
> lacies and falsehoods everywhere: the lie that free markets can
> deliver health care for all; the fiction that unpaid care work is
> not work; the delusion that we live in a post-racist world; the
> myth that we are all in the same boat.[8]

While regular global climate summits—the Conferences of the Parties
(COP) meetings—represent key moments for cooperation on climate,
the UN human rights system is also integrating climate into international human rights law, and this has significant implications for
Australia. In 2016, the UN's Special Rapporteur on Human Rights
and the Environment found that states have obligations not only to
implement the commitments made under the Paris Agreement, but
also 'to strengthen their obligations in the future, in order to ensure
that global temperatures do not rise to levels that would impair a vast
range of human rights'.[9] And this recognition of the links between climate change and human rights is being driven, in part, by determined

diplomacy from Australia's Pacific island neighbours, as discussed in other chapters in this collection.

Part I: Intersections of human rights diplomacy and climate diplomacy

Definitions of climate justice

Climate justice examines how climate change disproportionately impacts on the world's poorest citizens and on those least responsible for the causes of this climate disruption. But climate impacts do have implications that encompass all nations—from most to least developed; they have intergenerational implications for young people and for generations yet unborn; and they have wide geographic impacts in terms of the distribution of places that bear the brunt of climate impacts but have not contributed to emissions. Against this backdrop, the International Bar Association has noted that climate justice as a concept 'allows us to view climate change and efforts to combat it as having ethical implications, and to consider how these issues relate to wider justice concerns'.[10]

This chapter relies on the conception of climate justice offered by the Mary Robinson Foundation—that it 'links human rights and development to achieve a human-centered approach, safeguarding the rights of the most vulnerable and sharing the burdens and benefits of climate change and its resolution equitably and fairly'.[11] The Foundation has adopted a set of core 'Principles of Climate Justice', including respect for human rights, supporting the right to development, ensuring the transparency of climate change decisions and harnessing education to encourage climate stewardship.[12]

This concept also draws heavily on the history of the environmental justice movement, highlighting the ethical and human rights dimensions of climate change, the disproportionate burden of legacy pollution (such as chemicals that were used or produced by industry that remain in the environment for a long time after they were used and cause ongoing or subsequent harm), the unsustainable rise in energy costs for low-income families, and the impacts of energy extraction, refining and manufacturing on vulnerable communities.[13] Building on these earlier parameters, climate justice now adds the focus of how and why climate change affects vulnerable people.

About human rights diplomacy

Universal rights were codified into international law in 1948 with the UN Declaration of Human Rights, leading some nations to incorporate human rights into their foreign policy agendas. Just how much or how little human rights standards inform foreign policy and its implementation, or impact bilateral relations, international norms and sovereignty is still being determined at national levels and often in flux.[14] Human rights scholars such as Alison Brysk assert that 'principled states build global governance; they reshape the meaning of sovereignty to implant a slowly emerging legitimacy norm—universal human rights'.[15] And most experts consider human rights–based foreign policy agendas to be in a constant state of evolution. Examples of successful human rights–based foreign policy engagements include work in the areas of women's rights, and disability, ethnic, LGBTQI+ and religious minority rights. At a fundamental level, diplomats and government actors raising human rights in different areas of international affairs institutionalise new norms in government relations. An example of this in action may include a nation cutting foreign aid to a state that has a history of human rights abuses, such as Australia's current sanctions on Myanmar.

One trend I predict in relation to climate change will see both a blurring and an acceleration of humanitarian and human rights diplomacy. Humanitarian diplomacy is defined more as emergency policy, involving humanitarian actors negotiating access to vulnerable populations, for example, or combating a culture of impunity in armed conflicts where widespread violations of human rights and humanitarian law are occurring. By contrast, human rights diplomacy has a long-term aim to develop and change laws, policies, practices and systems to ensure the lasting implementation of human rights.[16] If we are now in the climate endgame, this long-term vision has to accelerate, even if the focus on structural injustice remains valuable.

The work of diplomats promoting human rights in foreign countries is often obscure to the general public. A great deal of the diplomatic work done behind closed doors is known as 'quiet diplomacy' and this is the hallmark of Australia's approach to human rights diplomacy.[17] At times, quiet diplomacy is a preferred method in terms of gaining results while avoiding publicly naming and shaming nations. However, at other times, this approach means that Australia looks silent on important questions—to external and internal audiences.

In contrast, some of the public techniques Australia has used to promote human rights diplomacy include a small grants scheme aimed at community programs, bilateral dialogues, special multilateral initiatives, and the nation's two-year term (2018–20) as an elected member of the UN Human Rights Council.

The Human Rights Small Grants Scheme provided small (up to A\$70 000) grants to locally based organisations in developing countries for activities that promote and protect human rights in a direct and tangible way. Priority areas for assistance were:

- educating and training human rights workers
- promoting international human rights standards including improved reporting to UN treaty bodies
- supporting national and regional human rights institutions and infrastructures
- human rights education and awareness raising
- promoting democratic principles.

That program was discontinued in 2009 and replaced with a Direct Aid Program operated by embassies with an aid mandate, and so the human rights focus of these grants has been harder to discern since then.

Another key tactic sees DFAT offer support for Pacific island nations, international non-governmental organisations and local civil society actors to amplify their voices through UN side events or other invitations or forums in New York or Geneva.

Behind the scenes, Australia may raise human rights cases in demarches; it may work to protect human rights defenders where possible, and introduce incentives and disincentives through official development assistance in the practice called conditionality. While this is often a controversial approach, this conditionality—supporting countries that promote human rights and withdrawing support for countries that fail to protect human rights—will, I predict, soon be commonly applied to issues of climate justice as well.

Towards diplomacy that promotes climate justice

As Balakrishnan Rajagopal, the current UN Special Rapporteur on the Right to Housing, reminds us, although human rights discourse is part of a hegemonic modernity/coloniality paradigm, we should not dismiss the value of human rights in our search for radical democratic alternatives—particularly given that rights help to envision what he refers to as 'counter-hegemonic cognitive frames'. Rajagopal's vision of a counter-hegemonic international law includes 'coalitions of smaller states and social movements, forming tactical alliances with larger states in particular negotiations, while increasing the prominence of sub-state actors in international law more broadly'.[18] In this respect, post-development coalitions of states complements a climate justice framework that also includes attention to issues of identity, including those relating to race, identity, gender and indigeneity. This is the direction climate diplomacy needs to move in, as evidenced by a spate of activity in the multilateral sphere at the UN.

Part II: United Nations developments on human rights and climate diplomacy

Ahead of the United Nations Secretary-General's New York Climate Summit in September 2019, five human rights treaty bodies issued a joint public statement articulating states' human rights obligations in the context of climate change. Two individual communications were also submitted to the treaty bodies asserting that states' inaction on climate change—particularly emissions reduction—is threatening the complainants' human rights, one of which concerned the Torres Strait Islands, discussed below. This decision was consequently adopted by the Human Rights Committee on the impacts of climate change and the right to life in General Comment 36.[19]

In their joint statement, the Committee on the Elimination of Discrimination Against Women, the Committee on Economic, Social and Cultural Rights, the Committee on the Protection of the Rights of All Migrant Workers and Members of their Families, the Committee on the Rights of the Child and the Committee on the Rights of Persons with Disabilities welcomed the Summit's goal to 'mobilize plans and actions to enhance the ambition of emissions reduction,' and urged all states to take into consideration their human rights obligations during any review of their climate commitments.[20]

The committees welcomed the findings of the IPCC's 2018 Special Report on Global Warming of 1.5°C (SR15), including its observation that climate change poses significant risks to the enjoyment of human rights and to the ecosystems which affect such enjoyment. The committees also noted that risks are particularly high for women, children, persons with disabilities, Indigenous peoples and persons living in rural areas.

They noted, too, that—according to the IPCC—'urgent and decisive climate action' was required to avoid the risk of 'irreversible and large-scale systemic impacts', and highlighted the importance of human rights norms to be applied at every stage of the decision-making process with regards to climate policies.[21]

In a related statement, a group of UN human rights experts— including renowned Australian international law scholar and human rights practitioner Phillip Alston—stated that states had an 'addiction to fossil fuels', making world headlines.[22] This group recognised that coal, oil and gas consumption produces the vast majority of anthropogenic greenhouse gas (GHG) emissions, leading to the 'global climate emergency that endangers human rights in every region of the planet'. It also highlighted that the share of the world's energy produced by fossil fuels has remained the same—at 81 per cent—since the adoption of the UN's Framework Convention on Climate Change in 1992. And since 1990, as these experts noted, global energy consumption had grown by 57 per cent, with coal consumption increasing by 68 per cent, and oil and gas use increasing by 36 per cent and 82 per cent, respectively.

As these experts stated, the rights to life, health, food, water and sanitation, a healthy environment, an adequate standard of living, housing, property, self-determination, development and culture were being 'threatened and violated' by climate change. Drawing attention to the already 'staggering costs' of fossil fuel use, including millions of premature deaths due to air pollution, they emphasised that immediate, urgent and effective actions were needed to reduce GHG emissions by 45 per cent by 2030, phase out fossil fuels by the middle of the century, and reverse deforestation to meet the Paris Agreement's temperature goal and limit damage to human rights.

In addition, and among other actions, these experts called for the protection of Indigenous peoples' rights; mobilisation of US$100 billion in annual adaptation funding for low-income countries; and establishment of a new fund, financed by an air-passenger travel levy, to support small island developing states and least developed countries.

General Comment on the right to life

First published in 2019, the Human Rights Committee's General Comment No. 36 (on the right to life) states that 'environmental degradation, climate change and unsustainable development constitute some of the most pressing and serious threats to the ability of present and future generations to enjoy the right to life.' Further, the General Comment notes that: 'States parties are thus under a due diligence obligation to undertake reasonable positive measures, which do not impose on them disproportionate burdens, in response to reasonably foreseeable threats to life originating from private persons and entities, whose conduct is not attributable to the State'. This may include calling out, for example, the actions of corporations' continuing pursuit of profits through extractive capitalism in that state.

Other institutions have also increasingly stepped in to address the linkages between human rights and climate change. The then High Commissioner for Human Rights has increased her advocacy on this topic, highlighting climate change in her opening remarks to each of the Human Rights Council sessions in 2019, making it the focus of her statement to the September session, and participating in the UN Climate Conference in Madrid (COP25) that year. At that COP, the Philippines Commission for Human Rights announced the key conclusions from its unprecedented investigation into the responsibility of fossil fuel corporations for climate-induced human rights harms, declaring that the world's biggest oil companies have legal and moral responsibilities to act in this space.[23]

Recognising the right to a healthy environment

On 8 October 2021 in Geneva, the UN Human Rights Council recognised the human right to a healthy environment as a binding state commitment.[24] This historic breakthrough many years after the first recognition as soft law of this right in the Stockholm Declaration in 1972 means citizens can demand that their governments consider, in policy-making, the need for clean air, water and food for humans to thrive. Because while many countries recognise the right to a healthy environment, this was the first time that right was explicitly recognised at the global level. Key elements of international human rights law—including the Universal Declaration on Human Rights; the Covenant on Civil and Political Rights; and the Covenant on Economic, Social and Cultural Rights—do not directly mention the right to a healthy environment.

Recognising this right to a healthy environment will take on especial importance as the world faces the rising impacts of climate change. The World Health Organization estimates that between 2030 and 2050, climate change will cause approximately 250 000 additional deaths per year from causes including malnutrition, malaria, diarrhoea and heat stress. Mental health issues are also expected to increase around the world.

That same October, the UN Child Rights Committee ruled that a state could be found responsible for the negative impact of its carbon

emissions on the rights of children both within and outside its territory in the case of *Saachi et al.*[25] This was the first such ruling by an
international body, which examined a petition filed by 16 children
from 12 countries against Argentina, Brazil, France, Germany and
Turkey in 2019. This ruling may be used in national climate litigation
by child litigants.

Part III: Pacific leadership on climate diplomacy
A new Special Rapporteur on climate and human rights

The UN Human Rights Council serves several functions, one of
which is to promote and monitor human rights worldwide through
the establishment of special procedures. Special procedures are individual independent human rights experts, or groups of such experts,
who report and advise on human rights issues. They are called by
many names including Special Rapporteurs, Special Representatives,
Working Groups and Independent Experts.

Special procedures have either thematic or country-specific mandates, such as the situation in Myanmar, or the right to housing. As
of October 2020, the Human Rights Council oversees 44 thematic
mandates and 11 country-specific mandates. And, throughout recent
years, the foreign ministers of the Pacific Islands Forum—including
Australia's—had indicated a willingness to be more active in reforming
or expanding the UN special procedures mandates in the context of
climate justice.

This push began at the COP25 UN climate summit in 2019 when
then Marshall Islands President Hilda Heine, speaking on behalf of 48
countries in the Climate Vulnerable Forum, called for the creation of a
dedicated rapporteur on climate change and human rights. The following year, in 2020, member states of the Forum—including Australia
and New Zealand—formally backed the call. And in October 2020,
the Republic of the Marshall Islands tabled the proposal for the
appointment of a Special Rapporteur on Human Rights and Climate
Change by the June 2021 session of the UN Human Rights Council
(HRC).

In this proposal, Pacific ministers stated that they:

(i)   Supported and endorsed the proposal for a dedicated special procedure mandate holder (Special Rapporteur) of the HRC on human rights and climate change;

(ii) supported efforts to secure the creation of the HRC special procedure on human rights and climate change through Pacific Islands Forum diplomatic missions and representation to the UN, particularly in Geneva, including through engagement in HRC sessions, side events, and other relevant activities; and

(iii) tasked the Secretariat, within existing resources, to support relevant Forum advocacy and engagement activities towards the creation of the HRC special procedure on human rights and climate change.[26]

In 2021, Fiji ambassador Nazhat Shameem Khan became president of the UN Human Rights Council and was able to use this position to support the proposal. Then, in the lead-up to the Council vote, the Marshall Islands mission based in Geneva hosted a panel on human rights and climate change. This helped garner agreement for the proposal, which was subsequently adopted with considerable global support (despite abstentions from India, China and Japan, and Russia voting no).

And so, in mid-2022, during its 49th session, the Human Rights Council appointed a new Special Rapporteur on the Promotion and Protection of Human Rights in the Context of Climate Change, Dr Ian Fry—an appointment that was the culmination of this diplomatic campaign led by Pacific Island countries. Fry is an Australian national who has worked for the Tuvalu government for more than two decades, including five years as their Ambassador for Climate Change and Environment (2015–19).[27] As Special Rapporteur, he has a mandate to study the ways that the adverse effects of climate change impact the realisation of human rights, and to make recommendations for promoting and respecting human rights in the design and implementation of climate policy. This is an important step and a prime opportunity for Australia to support this independent position and build a sense of partnership with the Pacific region. Expectations of Australia in this area may be increased. A primary way to support this new global mandate is to implement domestic legislation and policies to show best state practice and allow Dr Fry to be more influential.

Implications for Australian policy and legislation

While more than a hundred countries have already recognised the right to a healthy environment in domestic legislation, Australia has yet to follow suit. The global recognition of this right—in the 2021 UN Human Rights Council vote, and via the appointment of Dr Fry—is a unique opportunity for Australian governments to give effect to the right to a healthy environment as well. Australia also does not have a national charter of rights, and jurisdictions that do have existing human rights legislation—Victoria, Queensland and the ACT—will need to think about expanding the scope of their human rights legislation to include this new right. On 30 June 2022, the ACT government released a discussion paper to inform consideration of the introduction of a right to a healthy environment in the *Human Rights Act 2004,* and this is now under active consideration.

In the lead-up to the Glasgow climate summit in late 2021, Australia had resisted pressure from other advanced economies—and from its Pacific island neighbours—to set a more ambitious Paris Agreement target in terms of emissions reductions by 2030 and to commit more finance to help developing countries cope with the impacts of a warming world. Now, with the appointment of a Special Rapporteur on Human Rights and Climate Change, countries like Australia will be expected to take into account the human rights impacts of their climate and energy policies. Increasingly, they will be held to account if they don't.

Examples of international action for climate justice in the region

There are already powerful examples of international action for climate justice in Oceania, including examples of nations being held to account for climate inaction. These include the 'Torres Strait Eight' complaint to the UN Human Rights Committee, the *Teitiota* case from New Zealand, and the Pacific Island Forum leaders' request for an advisory opinion from the International Court of Justice regarding the obligations of nations to address climate change. All three interventions illustrate different ways in which Australia has been slower to address the human rights implications of climate change, especially in contrast with the leadership of our Pacific neighbours.

The push by the 'Torres Strait Eight' began in May 2019, when a group of eight islanders from four different Torres Strait Islands commenced a complaint to the Human Rights Committee against the Australian government (3624/2019). The claim was supported by Gur A Baradharaw Kod, the Torres Strait's leading land and sea council that represents the region's traditional owners.[28] Eight Torres Strait Islanders and six of their children made a submission to the Committee outlining the effects that climate change was having on their communities. They reported that increased temperatures have led to coral bleaching, reef death, and the decline of nutritionally and culturally important marine species. On the island of Masig, a 2019 cyclone had caused severe flooding, erosion and the destruction of buildings. Tidal surges have destroyed family grave sites and scattered human remains, and sea level rises have already meant that traditional gardening sites can no longer be used. Seagrass beds have also disappeared, leading Islanders to rely more on expensive imported food products and goods. The claimants also argued that meteorological changes mean that traditional knowledge, such as fishing practices, is more difficult to pass on to the next generation. And they claimed that Australia had failed to implement an adequate adaptation program to ensure the habitability of the islands, and failed to mitigate the impact of climate change—noting that Australia's greenhouse gas emissions per capita remain among the highest in the world.

In response, in September 2022 the UN Human Rights Committee found that Australia's failure to adequately protect indigenous Torres Strait Islanders against adverse impacts of climate change violated their rights to enjoy their culture and be free from arbitrary interferences with their private life, family and home,[29] under articles 17 and 27 of the International Covenant on Civil and Political Rights. The right to private, family and home life was found to be violated because Australia had failed to adopt adequate positive measure to address the destruction of the homes of Torres Strait Islanders, and to protect the marine resources, crops and trees Torres Strait Islanders rely upon for their subsistence and livelihoods. Australia had also violated the right conferred to minority Indigenous groups to enjoy their culture. The Committee found that Australia had not adopted adequate adaptation measure to ensure that Torres Strait Islanders could maintain their traditional ways of life, and transmit their culture and traditions and the use of land and sea resources to future generations.[30] The Committee concluded that Australia was under an obligation to provide adequate compensation and to engage in meaningful consultations with the Torres Strait Islander communities to conduct needs assessments, to continue to implement measures to secure the communities' safe existence, and to monitor and review the effectiveness of the measures implemented and take steps to prevent similar violations in the future. Australia has yet to provide a formal response to the Committee, but in the interim, two Torres Strait Islanders have launched an action in the Federal Court in *Pabai Pabai v Commonwealth of Australia* arguing the government has a legal obligation to prevent the loss of their communities to climate change.[31]

A second example of the ways in which the human rights aspect of climate change are increasingly recognised by the international community is demonstrated in the HRC's early 2020 ruling in the *Teitiota* case that governments must take into account the human rights violations caused by the climate crisis when considering deportation of asylum seekers. Even though the applicant in this case was not successful, the Committee's decision here suggests that future claims for refugee status might be successful where evidence shows 'the effects of climate change in receiving states may expose individuals to a violation of their rights'.[32]

The third example underscores the increased focus of Pacific Islands Forum members beyond their support for the appointment of a new Special Rapporteur. As the Forum has grown more active in calling for reform to UN human rights architecture, its leaders—urged by Vanuatu and a group of Pacific law students in 2019—sought an advisory opinion from the International Court of Justice on the obligations of states under international law to protect the rights of present and future generations against the adverse effects of climate change. As noted above, resolution 77/276 was tabled in the UN General Assembly in December 2022 and passed in March 2023.[33] The General Assembly has asked the Court to provide an opinion on the following questions:

> What are the obligations of States under international law to ensure the protection of the climate system and other parts of the environment from anthropogenic emissions of greenhouse gases for States and for present and future generations;
>
> (2) What are the legal consequences under these obligations for States where they, by their acts and omissions, have caused significant harm to the climate system and other parts of the environment, with respect to:
>
> (a) States, including, in particular, small island developing States, which due to their geographical circumstances and level of development, are injured or specially affected by or are particularly vulnerable to the adverse effects of climate change?
>
> (b) Peoples and individuals of the present and future generations affected by the adverse effects of climate change?

Part IV: Current Australian approaches to international human rights law and climate diplomacy

Australia has a proud diplomatic history and has often been able to pivot quickly in the past, for example, in relation to supporting the peace process in Cambodia or responding to events in Timor-Leste or the Solomon Islands. Australia has been slower to adopt a rights-based approach to climate diplomacy, and although there are some climate justice principles embedded in current diplomatic paradigms, a greater emphasis needs to be placed on human rights for Australia to keep pace with Pacific island nations and the international community more broadly.

Australian diplomacy does aim to help support Pacific priorities through a strategic focus on climate change in the development assistance program, but otherwise does not situate this assistance within a more strategic foreign policy focus on justice outcomes or acknowledging inequity as impacted by climate change. DFAT's Climate Change Action Strategy does not mention climate justice but does incorporate some equity principles, promoting social inclusion and gender equality, with a clear focus on the most vulnerable communities, especially women and girls, people with disability and Indigenous peoples.

The DFAT Strategy sets three key objectives to make the best use of our development assistance, but none of these larger justice themes are represented. Australia aims to 'support partner countries to adapt to climate change, and to plan, prepare for and respond to climate-related impacts; to promote the shift to lower-emissions development in the Indo-Pacific region, and to support innovative solutions to climate change, including those that engage private sector investment'.[34] There is no strong sense of solidarity or shared struggle here.

Similarly, Australia's Aid Investment Plan Pacific Regional, 2015–16 to 2018–19, focuses on technical support but does recognise the importance of the Pacific Islands Forum as an agenda setter:

> We will seek to maximise regional flows from the Green Climate Fund (GCF) and other relevant channels to help share the developmental burden and reduce our direct exposure to the broader relationship risks and challenges associated with enduring climate change and other environmental challenges.
>
> We will strengthen resilience through the provision of technical support to countries to help with their climate resilience and disaster preparedness, response, recovery and risk reduction. We will work with countries to implement the outcomes of the July 2015 Pacific Islands Forum Foreign Ministers' Meeting on Disaster Management and help Pacific island countries access the Green Climate Fund. We will assist the region to implement the Sendai Framework for Disaster Risk Reduction 2015–2030.

Australia needs a vision of foreign policy that puts climate change firmly at the centre and reimagines business as usual. Instead of technical and private sector solutions, Australia could invest more deeply in people-to-people links that build solidarity and rapprochement between communities. For example, Australia through the Australian NGO Cooperation Program platform in the aid program could support eligible partners to investigate ways to help communities take action to support the following actions:

- community rights to information about climate risks and to ensure the participation of citizens and non-citizens in formulating responses at the community level
- communities empowered to seek accountability for the duty of state actors to protect people within and outside their borders from climate impacts
- communities empowered to promote the rights of vulnerable people in emergencies and natural disasters
- shared community strategies to promote the right to freedom of movement and mobility justice in order to achieve a just climate transition
- community dialogues about the parameters of the right to protest and engage in climate advocacy
- support for community co-creation of an agenda for urban climate justice, and rural climate justice
- support to rethink or contextualise concepts of loss and damage, risk, insurability and intergenerational equity within communities and regions
- community attitudes to the creation of a new right to a healthy environment and create rights for nature.

This is a different foreign policy vision, and one which cedes some control from Canberra and places it more in community hands which does involve some risk. But recent activity in the UN human rights system, drawing on IPCC reports, demonstrate these key climate justice themes that could inform the future substance and style of Australian diplomacy in the region. These are a fairer distribution of the burden of loss and damage when the risks often fall more heavily on those least able to reduce or recover from them; the protection of vulnerable people during increased natural disasters in Oceania; and the need for mobility and asylum due to displacement in the region from climate impacts.

Conclusions

How can Australia reframe its regional and bilateral diplomacy with the Pacific and New Zealand to show solidarity with its neighbours and become a trusted climate action partner? This chapter has set out a vision for pursuing a climate justice approach to diplomatic practice in this region, arguing that international human rights law standards should become the benchmark for animating Australia's diplomatic practice and used in turn to create meaningful standards for the conduct of climate diplomacy in Oceania. If all states have the human rights duty to protect men and women, boys and girls in all their diversity from the harmful effects of the climate crisis, including displacement, how then can Australia show leadership domestically and support other states to protect their communities from harmful climate impacts? As a starting point, Australia can show solidarity for diplomatic efforts of the Pacific island nations and also support the rapid development of international law in the climate justice field, including the rights of nature, the right to a healthy environment and the development of ecocide and related crimes under international law.

A climate justice–centred foreign policy approach for Australia would have a clear strategy, incorporating different diplomatic practices that amplify Pacific voices, and a sense of urgency. In any case, Australian diplomatic methods will have to adjust to a role that is more supportive and amplifies the climate justice advocacy of the Pacific and other nations from the Global South based on international human rights law standards, or suffer a climate justice conditionality from these nations. Climate justice should matter to Australian diplomacy and become its guiding star.

Notes

1 Department of Foreign Affairs and Trade, 'Climate Change Action Strategy', November 2019.

2 United Nations, 'Joint Statement by UN Human Rights Experts for World Environment Day', 4 June 2021.

3 Vanuatu ICJ Initiative, 'ICJ Resolution'.

4 Ibid.

5 Wilson Center, *21st Century Diplomacy: Foreign Policy is Climate Policy*, 2020.

6 United Nations, 'Committee Releases Statement on Climate Change and the Covenant', 8 October 2028.

7 The term 'climate justice', while used in different ways in different contexts by different communities, generally includes three principles: distributive justice, which refers to the allocation of burdens and benefits among individuals, nations and generations; procedural justice, which refers to who decides and participates in decision-making; and recognition, which entails basic respect and robust engagement with and fair consideration of diverse cultures and perspectives. IPCC, Summary for Policymakers, 2022, p. 7.

8 United Nations, 'Secretary-General's Nelson Mandela Lecture: "Tackling the Inequality Pandemic: A New Social Contract for a New Era"', Speech, 18 July 2020.

9 J Knox, Report of the Special Rapporteur on the Issue of Human Rights Obligations Relating to the Enjoyment of a Safe, Clean, Healthy and Sustainable Environment: *Climate Change Report* (1 February 2016), United Nations Human Rights Council, A/HRC/31/52.

10 IBA Presidential Task Force on Climate Change Justice and Human Rights, 'Achieving Justice and Human Rights in an Era of Climate Disruption', July 2014.

11 Mary Robinson Foundation, 'Climate Justice, Principles of Climate Justice', 10 June 2014.

12 Ibid.

13 M Burkett, 'Just Solutions to Climate Change: A Climate Justice Proposal for a Domestic Clean Development Mechanism', *Buffalo Law Review*, vol. 56, no. 1, 2008, p. 169.

14 EC Rainer, *From Pariah to Priority: How LGBTI Rights Became a Pillar of American and Swedish Foreign Policy*, State University of New York Press, New York, 2021.

15 A Brysk, 'Introduction: States as Global Citizens', in A Brysk, *Global Good Samaritans: Human Rights as Foreign Policy*, Oxford Academic, Oxford, 2011, p. 14.

16 Ibid.

17 Human Rights Watch, 'Australia: Protect Human Rights in Foreign Policy', 24 June 2019.

18 B Rajagopal, 'Counter-Hegemonic International Law: Re-thinking Human Rights and Development as a Third World Strategy', *Third World Quarterly*, vol. 27, no. 5, 2006, pp. 767, 768.

19 United Nations, 'General Comment No. 36 on Article 6: Right to Life', 3 September 2019.

20 United Nations, 'Human Rights Council Resolutions on Human Rights and Climate Change'.

21 See also, Center for International Environmental Law and The Global Initiative for Economic, Social and Cultural Rights, *States' Human Rights Obligations in the Context of Climate Change: 2020 Update*, March 2020.

22 United Nations, 'United Nations Climate Action Summit', Press Release, 23 September 2019.

23 See also, I Kaminski, 'Fossil Fuel Firms "Could Be Sued" for Climate Change', *Independent*, 9 December 2019.

24 United Nations, 'Access to a Healthy Environment, Declared a Human Right by UN Rights Council', UN News, 8 October 2021.

25 United Nations, 'UN Child Rights Committee Rules that Countries Bear Cross-Border Responsibility for Harmful Impact of Climate Change', Press Release, 11 October 2021.

26 Pacific Islands Forum, '2020 Forum Foreign Ministers Meeting Outcomes', Virtual Meeting, 14 October 2021.

27 United Nations, 'Ian Fry: Special Rapporteur on Climate Change'.

28 Y Mosby, 'Here is Why We Are Taking the Australian Government to the UN Over its Inaction on Climate Change', *The Guardian*, 14 August 2020.

29 UN Human Rights Committee, 'Views Adopted by the Committee Under Article 5 (4) of the Optional Protocol, Concerning Communication No. 3624/2019', 22 September 2022.

30 ClientEarth, 'Torres Strait Islanders Win Historic Human Rights Legal Fight Against Australia', Press Release, 23 September 2022.

31 Federal Court of Australia, *Pabai Pabai v Commonwealth of Australia*, Online File, 25 July 2023.

32 UN Human Rights Committee, *Teitiota v. New Zealand*, UN Doc. CCPR/C/127/D/2728/2016, 24 October 2019. See also, Climate Change Litigation Databases, *Ioane Teitiota v. The Chief Executive of the Ministry of Business, Innovation and Employment*, Supreme Court of New Zealand, Judgment, 20 July 2015.

33 United Nations, Resolution Adopted by the General Assembly on 29 March 2023, 7/276: 'Request for an Advisory Opinion of the International Court of Justice on the Obligations of States in Respect of Climate Change'.

34 Department of Foreign Affairs and Trade, 'Climate Change Action Strategy'.

INDEX